NICK BARLAY is the author of four acclaimed novels and was named as one of Granta's 20 best young British novelists in 2003, until it was discovered he was too old to be young. Born in London to Hungarian Jewish refugee parents, he has also written award-winning radio plays, short stories and wide-ranging journalism. www.nickbarlay.com.

Praise for Nick Barlay's Fiction

'Nick Barlay is a fine chronicler of London's grittier sub-cultures.'   *Time Out*

'Rarely does one read writing so inventive, yet so tensed against habituation… brilliantly literary.'   Alex Clark, *The Guardian*

'Funny and melancholy… ultimately thought-provoking… This writer has thought about the country we live in and how it got to be the way it is.'

Hilary Mantel

'Barlay's controlled and energetic demotic fixes you to the page… superbly bitter-sweet… a fine literary novel.'   *Daily Telegraph*

Praise for *Scattered Ghosts*

'Between fact and fiction, archival research and genealogy, Nick Barlay re-enacts the torments of Hungarian Jewish history from the Holocaust to 1956 and to exile in London, where he was born to refugee parents. He takes us to the margins and the cracks, the streets, the houses and the cellars. His tale is an astonishing *tour de force*, it is a memorial to the unsung heroes through the prism of his family: compelling and informative, deeply moving and scrupulously understated.'

Irène Heidelberger-Leonard, author of
The Philosopher of Auschwitz

'An intriguing and moving narrative. Barlay writes calmly, but with feeling. The fortunes of a Jewish family during the Holocaust and the Communist rule in Hungary come across powerfully and ultimately with a dash of optimism.'

Ladislaus Löb, Emeritus Professor of German, University
of Sussex, and author of *Dealing with Satan: Rezső Kasztner's
Daring Rescue Mission*

'Is it family history? It is. Is it poetry? It is that, too – charming poetry. But clouds soon darken the scene. There's the smell of blood and the tumult of Arrow Cross pogroms. What binds these family fates together is fine writing – and Hungarian cherry strudel.'

Peter Fraenkel, translator, broadcaster and author of
No Fixed Abode: A Jewish Odyssey to Africa

Scattered Ghosts

ONE FAMILY'S SURVIVAL THROUGH
WAR, HOLOCAUST AND REVOLUTION

Nick Barlay

Published in 2013 by I.B.Tauris & Co Ltd
6 Salem Road, London W2 4BU
175 Fifth Avenue, New York NY 10010
www.ibtauris.com

Distributed in the United States and Canada Exclusively
by Palgrave Macmillan
175 Fifth Avenue, New York NY 10010

MIX
Paper from
responsible sources
FSC
www.fsc.org   FSC® C007584

ISBN: 978 1 78076 662 1

A full CIP record for this book is available from the British Library
A full CIP record is available from the Library of Congress

Library of Congress Catalog Card Number: available

Text design, typesetting and eBook by Tetragon, London
Printed and bound in Sweden by ScandBook AB

Contents

Knock upon yourself as if upon a door and walk upon yourself as if upon a straight road.

Silvanus

'I was there too that night,' said my brother. 'You've airbrushed me out.'

Robin Barlay

'Ne piszkáld ezt a dolgot. Reménytelen.' ('Leave this thing alone. It's hopeless.')

Bandi Gömöri, second cousin

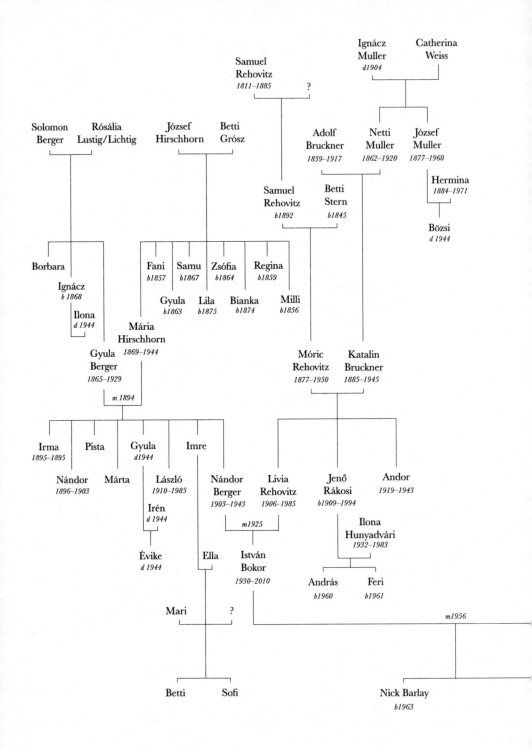

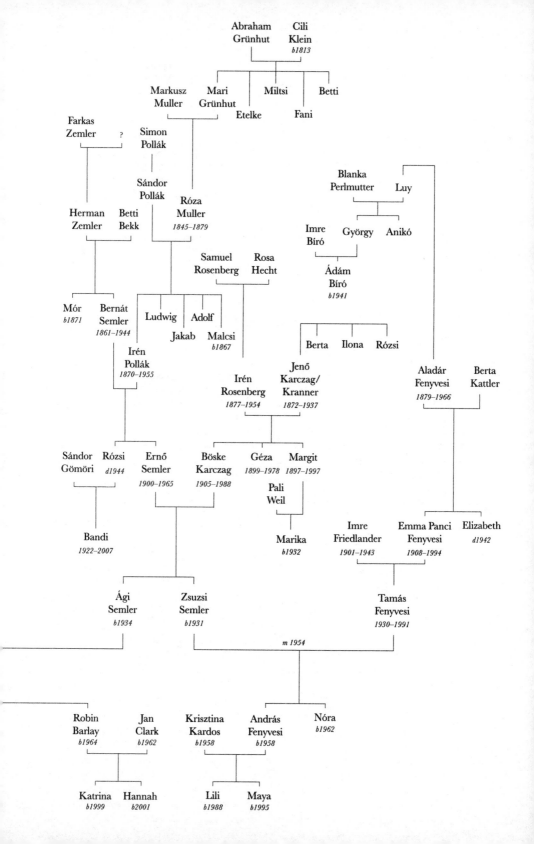

Ghosts

The Knock

IT'S A RECURRENT DREAM, them turning up.

One dark and stormy night, goes this dream, when I am snug under a duvet, protected from wind and from rain, there is a knock at the door. I ignore this knock, attributing it to the dream, to a dream within a dream, or an imagined knock, or a melodrama brought on by years of conditioning, a cultural assault of dark and stormy nights and knocks on doors.

But, of course, the first knock is followed by a second, the second by a third, and on until, so goes this dream, I am awake. Conscious, partly, I connect the knuckle at the door to some midnight hoaxer or some giggling bingers crabbing their way home. But, of course, the knocks continue, more insistent still, louder still, even threatening, as if more than a jest, more like a solitary madman sent by some malign occult force to mess with my slumber. So a battle of wills begins: to respond or not, to do something or not. And eventually, in this dream, unable to ignore the knocking, unable to sleep, I find myself going to the door.

I open it a crack, just to catch a warning glimpse of a face. Instead of one face or even two, there are twenty or thirty, a proper crowd, a silent crowd. It's difficult to count the heads, in the dark, during a storm. The crowd could be forty-strong, to say nothing of all the bits, all the stuff, all the luggage that they seem to have brought with them, their unwieldy bags, their weather-aged suitcases, their last-minute bundles, their unleavable heirlooms, their wayfarers' essentials stuffed into pockets. There they patiently stand, their stout shoes mud-encrusted, their coat-tails spattered, their hat brims dripping rain. It's obvious this isn't a lynch mob or a pack of debt collectors. There is no anger in them, no menace. They do not loom. There is only hope in their faces – the hope, perhaps, that they can get out of the wind and the rain. But why here? Why me?

As I squint, the answers to these questions come into focus. I begin to recognize them, at least one or two or three or half a dozen among them. There is the one who was kissed by an emperor. There is the one who interviewed statesmen, and over there the one who almost died rich, another whose assets were dust. There's the religious one, the one who went mad, and the one who committed suicide. There are the two who had strange accidents. And the one who went missing but came back, another who disappeared, never to be seen again. Then there's the one who danced, the one who played the piano, the one who wrote. Then there are the ones who were taken away and killed.

I recognize them because I have met them, some in life at close quarters, a few at a distance when the moon was blue. The rest I have met in albums, in yellowed photographs and faded snaps or in brown envelopes containing special portraits that were lost and found and lost again. Now, they have turned up at my door en masse, together, as if someone had planned it, wearing the very clothes that they wore in the pictures, that they have always worn or seemed to wear.

As I pull the door further open, they're waving papers at me – flaking documents, delicate and rarely unfolded certificates, stamped passes, special authorizations, counter-signed exemptions, official permits – as if to prove that we're connected, that they have a peculiar right of entry granted by some long-dead functionary on behalf of a long-gone administration. And in this dream, in accordance with some obscure small print, they have arranged themselves alphabetically. There are the Bergers, the Bírós, the Bokors and the Bruckners, then Diamantborn, Fenyvesi, Finkelstein and Friedlander, Gömöri, Hirschhorn and Karczag, followed by Kranner, Müller and Pollák, with Perlmutter and Rehovitz just ahead of Rosenberg, Semler and Stern, and finally Weil and Zemler at the rear.

I know then that I can't shut the door. You can't, not on this lot. Not on this crowd. Not on my family, for that's what this crowd is. You can't shut the door on a gathering of familiar ghosts, not on a dark and stormy night like this. You can't shut the door on a list of relatives. You can't shut the door on a disappeared world. What to do? Of course I let them in.

And in they come, my spectral ancestors, the people who recognize me because I resemble them. They are the people I might have been. Some shuffle. Some stride. Some are loud, some quiet. They are relieved or resigned, argumentative or grateful, complaining or conciliatory. One by one, I recognize these ghosts. I match names to faces, the faces of the ones I have met, the faces of the ones I have seen, to the names I have heard. There's a great-grandmother, Mária Hirschhorn, with her generous chin, her six sons and a daughter. There's my cousins' father, Tamás Fenyvesi, the psychiatrist who suffered a tragic accident. There's a four-year-old girl called Évi, who never saw her fifth birthday. There's another great-grandmother, Irén Rosenberg, renowned for her enormous bust and her cuisine, able to conjure nourishing meals in the hardest of times. There's a great-grandfather, Bernát Semler, pebble-spectacled, moustachioed, religious. There's a great-great-grandmother, Netti Müller, twig-boned and hollow-cheeked as if born ancient. Then there are the ghosts of ghosts, such as Rózsi Gömöri, a great-aunt who vanished without trace, or my paternal grandfather, Nándor Berger, who died on a distant path far from home, whose final resting place can only be guessed, who was taken away forever, last seen at a railway station.

At least now they're sheltered from the weather. I go to close the door, and see instantly that this stormy night is not a stormy night at all. What I have taken to be flashes of lightning, ripples of thunder, have a different cause altogether. Far off, simultaneously, there are two world wars going on, and two revolutions flaring up in between, and two totalitarian regimes competing with each other to make the rules. There are bombs and bullets and tank shells. There are conscriptions, deportations and round-ups. It seems that four generations have fled together, the ghosts of a disappeared world, the ghosts of ghosts, the survivors of the wars and the revolutions, the bombs and the bullets.

Here they are, finally, with their long-road mud and fugitive bags, with their tales to tell, their revelations to share, their mysteries to solve. Here they are, finally, arriving at a small hour that was the favourite of their former persecutors – the secret police of one denomination or another. Here we are, my dead relatives and me, about to close the door on all of that noise, all of that chaos. And, on the table, as if by magic, a pie has appeared, still oven-warm, still settling. It's a cherry pie, a *meggyes pite*. One of them must have requested it, another must have made it, another must have carried it; a well-travelled pie born of a well-travelled recipe, its ingredients weighed by the eyes and the hands of mothers and grandmothers.

The pie, it goes without saying, will be divided. All of us will get a piece, because if anything connects these people, the paternal and maternal lines, the generations, the genders, the diverse livelihoods, the beliefs, the fates and final outcomes of these people, it's their willingness to sit at a table, coffee percolating on the stove, and eat. So goes the dream.

But, dream aside, it would not be the first time a Hungarian had journeyed to my door bearing cherry pie. They have come before, from the shadow of the Carpathian Mountains, across the Great Hungarian Plain, and from the coffee houses of Budapest and Vienna. In turn, it would not be the first time I journeyed to Hungary in search of the same. I have eaten cherry pie at the famed Gerbeaud coffee house to the sounds of an Austro-Hungarian string quartet, on Budapest street corners from fast-food outlets, in the homes of relatives in the old Jewish quarter. I know full well the difference between the sweet and the sour cherry, the *cseresznye* and the *meggy*, and between pastry and pie, *rétes* and *pite*, and if I could have stepped into pre-war photographs of family gatherings in which oven-warm pie was settling on a dinner table, I would have.

To trace the stories of my Hungarian Jewish family is to trace the story of cherry pie. So, in the words of an old folk song that my mother once sang: '*Gyere... szedjük a meggyet...*'

Come, let's pick the cherries...

The Night

ONE DECEMBER NIGHT, we found ourselves at the Vár, the medieval castle that stands high on the west bank of the river. On a summer's day, the view is a tourist attraction, full of strollers and sightseers, clicking cameras and posing families, who soon picture themselves set against the historic bridges of the lively Danube or against the splendid parliament building on the opposite bank. But on a freezing winter's night, ice wind chewing earlobes, the place is almost deserted. The tourists think there is little to see, and the river, far below the ramparts, is obsidian black, secretive, deathly.

Yet we went up there, my father and I, him ill with flu, 50 years after the Revolution of 1956, half a century after my parents' escape, and over 60 years since the Second World War had passed through their lives and through the city. We went up there because there is one place that makes the effort worthwhile. Somehow, despite being battered during the siege of 1849 and almost destroyed along with the rest of the castle district during the siege of 1944–5, the small Ruszwurm confectionery and coffee house survived. Its Biedermeier furniture, its ornamental glass cabinets, its cream pastry, its grand cakes, such as the *Szamos*, the *Eszterházy*, the *Mátyás* and the *Dobos*, have stood the test of time. Its Linzer biscuit practically fought for freedom, according to one story. But its cherry-wood counter speaks of something else.

Buda might long ago have given way to Pest as the important half of the city, yet the hills of Buda look down, more than anywhere else, into the streets where so much of this story begins. So it's possible for someone who has been through all that, who has survived all that – a war, a siege, a revolution, not to mention some of the big cakes of the Old World – to climb up Castle Hill, then to look down and say, 'I'm still here.'

And Buda is still here; and the Ruszwurm is still here; and the cherry pies, pastries and strudels are still here. Even the ghosts of the tourists, my father joked, are still here. He was referring to the Germans, who came and went, and the Russians, who came and went.

But what about the others? Did he see them? They, too, were there that night, collars up, stout shoes stiff with cold, peering down across the river, waiting to be counted, waiting to give their opinions, if only I'd asked. Sure, if every ghost had to give his or her version, his or her interpretation, tell his or her story, things would soon get confused. Issues of factual accuracy would arise, issues of memory, issues of collective memory. Two Jews, three opinions, goes the old joke. To say the least at the best of times.

That night was not the best of times, ice wind chewing, my father ill, ghosts haunting. If I had looked over my shoulder, I would have seen them. I would have heard them complaining of bad dreams. I would have heard them telling their story or telling somebody else's story that they took to be their own. Issues of accuracy. Issues of memory. Somewhere there must exist a record of what each of them said and what each of them did. Somewhere there must exist a photograph of all the ghosts who were present on Castle Hill that night. I can look back – anyone could – as if at a collective photograph cut and pasted together by imagination. It's easy to see it. It's easy to see them.

In this photograph there is Móric Rehovitz, paternal great-grandfather. His brassy buttons catch available light. He stares back, caught in a military pose, just like in his official photograph. Conscripted, uniformed for 'K and K', for Kaiser and King, he did his bit for the Empire, whether he liked it or not. 'So you want to tell this story?' he would ask, tunic stretching uncomfortably on his round, belted belly. 'Then you must know the territory.' And, still staring, still in uniform, he would insist on taking me back up one of Buda's hills

in broad daylight. He would point east towards the *puszta*, the Great
Hungarian Plain, or north-east to Hungary's restless borders, or to some
front or other where war went on and where he was made to serve.

Others would interrupt him. Erzsébet Fenyvesi, a great-aunt without a face, without features, would point south to Novi Sad, where
she began, then north to Poland, to that place she ended up in whose
name she cannot bring herself to say. One grandmother, Lili, would
point west to Vienna, to where she packed her first bag, the first of
many. Another, Bözsi, would point south-east to Arad, to the town of
her birth that was once in Hungary and is now in Romania. Others
would point deep into the Ukraine, to the far-off places they were sent
to and where their remains still lie.

All of them, surely, would point down, across the river, into the
streets of Pest. That's where they would point the most and say the
least. 'Don't let's talk about those things,' someone would say. 'What
else is there to talk about?' another would respond. Like all survivors,
they would divide into those that do and those that don't talk. Whether
one chooses to talk or to remain silent, both the talking and the silence,
like the ghosts, last forever. A ghetto or two, an address or two: that's
what their pointing fingers would point out down there, across the
river. Or perhaps a shooting or a beating or a little pogrom.

'Et cetera,' someone would breathe into the freezing air, 'et cetera.'

Which of them died happy, with the taste of cherry pie or strudel
in their mouth? Some of them didn't, that much is certain. But in this
photograph, and in the freezing air on Castle Hill, there is evidence
of opposing fates. One brother lived. Another didn't. There are two
sons who married two sisters. Two fathers who disappeared. Two
great-grandmothers who brought the cherry pie or strudel. Two fig-
ures shod in stout shoes who came to a junction and chose different
directions. And so on.

The ghosts had to wait outside that night. The Ruszwurm was
never big enough for a coach party, for a whole family, just my father
and me, two coffees, two slices. My father, who for reasons best known
to himself had taken to wearing a felt fedora around that time, like
he'd found religion, might have answered a question or two, sat in the
Ruszwurm with his hat off, his earlobes thawing, flu steaming. He,
too, complained of a bad dream. In this dream, he said, there was

the smell of blood. It was the smell of blood, he said, that took him to a certain street across the river, to a certain address on a certain night. It took him through the gate of a high block, into the hallway between the gate and the stairwell. It took him precisely to where blood once covered stone.

My father was never short on detail. He remembers the streets across the river, his childhood haunts, a poem, an incident, a trip, the crate that hid him from fascists, the shells from Soviet tanks. But his dreams were rare and slight, only the vaguest of clues that there was more detail still, detail that mattered, bits of the big picture, the sweep of it – the loss, for instance, of his father. He might have filled in such details that night, if I'd asked, which I didn't.

The wind rattled the glass doors. It was getting late. The ghosts were loitering, shuffling. Sure, you can go up Castle Hill on a freezing night and look across the dark river spume to the streets on the other side. You can tell yourself you're not a tourist, that you didn't come up here to take pictures. You can listen to the wind rattle the glass doors. You can hear voices. You can believe in ghosts. You can realize that it falls to you, accidentally, out of a black sky, to put it all together, all the clues and stories, the letters and postcards, the scraps recording a life and a time, the crumbs left on plates at closing time. You can put these crumbs together and reconstruct the pie.

Maybe, without knowing it, that's why we came up here: to remind me that, in the streets across the river, I have appointments to keep with ghosts.

The Road

WHO KNOWS NOW what goes on inside his head? His glasses are flecked, spotted, spattered, as if he'd raced a motorcycle up some dream highway, oil, insects, dirt flying at him. Who knows where he's been inside his head? Who knows where he's been in his dreams? My father won't say, not in so many words. But ever since his stroke in 2007 he has travelled. First, he went to a darker, more distant place than he'd ever been. A hospital bed. A drip. Breath that barely registered.

Then he returned, almost, to a place he knew, a place almost within familiar reach, to points he recognized, people he knew. He almost returned to where he'd been. But he stopped somewhere en route. Mid-step, mid-thought, his attention is caught by something, a light, a primary colour, a big number, and he stops to peer, to stare. Then he looks past the obvious into the spaces between things, where logic is just a feeling. As his maternal grandmother, Katalin Bruckner, once told him, 'The first to get to sleep should shout "Hurrah!" with his feet.'

Somewhere between places, half here, half there, he is elusive. He shouts 'Hurrah!' with his now swollen feet. He puns. He jests. He grins. He forgets. He forgets, in particular, where he has placed his feet, where he has been. Every day or night or both, he travels between mental addresses, the good ones, the bad ones, the well-appointed ones, the dilapidated ones. Every day or night or both, he is present at some address or other, absent from some address or other.

Maybe listing addresses, the places he has inhabited through a lifetime, would help to pin down where he goes. But of course it's not just these addresses. It's also the addresses of people he knew, his mother's addresses and all the places he's ever been with his now swollen feet.

The familiar addresses, the ones he'd recognize, I practically know by heart; not in the order lived, more in order of the importance attached, the importance I have attached. The Budapest ones come thick and fast, a cascade of street names and numbers: 59 Népszínház Street, 77 Baross Street, 22 Pannónia Street, 10 Csokonai Street, 27 Eötvös Street, 69 Izabella Street, 102 Király Street, 26 Katona József Street...

A family history should have some sense of the addresses inhabited, a chronology of its front doors. Yet my father seems to be in several places at once. Only genealogy has chronology. Family history happens in moments, in blinks, all people reflecting all other people, all events reflecting all others. Pick a moment apart, look into the space inside, and you will find forty ghosts. They will stand at the same front door at the same time, as if front doors had been rationed and everyone had to share.

It wasn't just the cherry pies that were shared over three generations. The doors were shared, too. Once, twice, several times, people were forcibly herded together. One front door served twenty, fifty, a hundred people. 'The moving together', the so-called *összeköltöztetés*: a great Hungarian compound noun for a great compounding of people behind one front door.

Then, in another era, there came 'bell fright', the so-called *csengő-frász*, when people feared the pre-dawn ringing of their doorbell, the attendant black car, the impossibility of resistance. Either way, it all rests on moving addresses, moving together, moving apart, the fear of staying, the fear of leaving, the understanding that fates could be decided at thresholds, the knowledge that some fates were decided exactly there, between warmth and cold, between family and the outside world, between the smell of home and the smell of a leather seat in a black car. This is the tyranny of front doors. Not even half of it, as the Hungarian saying goes, is funny. Somewhere there must exist a student thesis entitled 'The role of the front door in Hungarian history with reference to the social significance of the Hungarian doorbell'. Perhaps, then, it's no surprise that my father moves so easily between mental addresses, instinctively staying a step ahead. The rest of the time he moves less easily.

Ablutions have been impossible since the stroke clawed his left hand, locked his fingers, disturbed his balance, fuzzed his concentration, divided his attention into twenty equal slices, and threw his voice, his smoker's voice, his deep-accented voice, his old-world voice, into the far distance. A woman comes in the morning to help him wash. He calls her the corpse-washer. 'What would you like to wear?' she asks him. 'A white sheet,' he replies. It takes her a while to acclimatize to the humour. They couldn't acclimatize in Accident and Emergency either. One night, he was admitted after a fall. A nurse asked him how he would like his tea. 'With arsenic,' he replied. They put him on suicide watch. It was difficult to explain that it was just his sense of humour.

He might spend two hours staring into the middle of a page of a book on Hungarian history, lost somewhere between the 1456 Siege of Nándorfehérvár and the disastrous 1526 Battle of Mohács. Who knows where he goes inside his head?

'*Avanti o papele*,' I tell him, a play on the Italian communist song '*Avanti popolo*', 'Go on, people', and *papele*, Yiddish for father.

'*Avanti, lópopó*,' he replies. 'Go on, horse's ass.'

'That's what we used to say,' he whispers from the far distance. Or, more like: 'Zet's vut ve used to say.'

Yet he does go on, horse's ass and all, puns and jests and grins and all. He goes on and up the dream highway, visiting his mental addresses, his flecked glasses the only clue as to where he's been, how far he's travelled. 'The insects are wearing glasses,' he once said in the middle of the night. Who knows?

Maybe it's not the places he has been that count, but the souvenirs from those places. Maybe these are the real clues. One of his addresses is also the last, the closest. His desk, deserted since the stroke, is more than an address. It's a territory. Deserted yet intact, preserved like furniture in a heritage home, it's the territory on which he wrote a dozen books, on which he enacted his versions of the 1456 Siege of Nándorfehérvár and the 1526 Battle of Mohács. It was here that his personal victories and defeats were played out.

Fire, air crashes, industrial espionage and human trafficking drama-
tized the desk-scape. Writing a book takes over a desk. I know this
because, unwittingly, years later, before I knew what I was doing, I
recreated his desk to write my own books. It's surely what the desk is for.
A book itself is transient. It comes and goes, blows in like tumbleweed,
snags for a while, then detaches and recedes in memory. But the perma-
nent citizens of the territory stay on for the next book. Objects, unique
as DNA, are the real survivors. Silently, on my father's desk, they wait:
leather luggage tags with old addresses handwritten in their windows;
yellowed newspaper cuttings relating to projects yet to be undertaken;
ancient bulldog clips; odd stones and exotic coins; bits of antique
watches – a spring, a strap, a winder; dated yet timeless postcards from
specific yet universal places; a printer's rule; an initialled lighter; some
type from an old block; a tram ticket; a cigar box; a copyright stamp.

These objects can be read, perhaps not from left to right, perhaps
only blindly, by touch. But implicit in their chance configurations is the
story of a moment or a series of moments, an accident, an address,
59 Népszínház Street, a front door, a smell of blood. Implicit in them
is the story of a refugee who found a new territory, a new address,
an oak desk that became a home. As a child, I could not see past the
steep ascent of the typewriter's keys. I used to imagine that the desk
stretched to the horizon, and beyond.

But there is a ghost there, too. It sits at the apparently vacated desk.
It's his ghost, of course, still attacking the typewriter with index fingers,
still chain-smoking Woodbines, still sliding a heavily indented sheet
of carbon between fresh paper. He sits nearby, unaware of his own
ghost. His clawed left hand, which he has named Margit, perhaps
in recognition of its female struggle for equality and independence,
perhaps after an island in the Danube, pinches a random page of
The Times. His eyes seem to have settled on an advertisement in the
'Encounters' section. It's from a 'Hermès-scarf-wearing Sloane', 58,
who likes Scottish dancing and is looking for 'a real gentleman'. Maybe
her name is 'Margit', and maybe he secretly likes Scottish dancing.
Who knows what goes on inside his head?

His ghost continues to type, trying to make sense of notes or cuttings
or some research or other, all the while depositing layer after layer of
grease and dirt on the keys. Layer after layer; book after book; object

At my father's typewriter: me, the author, taken by my mother in 1966.

after object: the assemblage of a life; the trace of what remains of it; its final signature. Take a picture of this desk, and you have history without chronology, a snapshot through time rather than of time, an odd stone rippling out, an exotic coin flipped, a moment in which all places are simultaneously inhabited and deserted.

Margit inches a biscuit mouthward. A crumb detaches and falls. And another. Crumbs at closing time. Crumbs the traces of memory. As his paternal grandmother, Mária Hirschhorn, once wrote in a letter: 'We'll cook together if there is anything to cook.' Crumbs are signs of family life, their absence the opposite. Mária Hirschhorn's letter is her crumb. It's the only crumb she left.

But if my father or his grandmother had looked, they would have seen another trace, the faintest of traces, a little way off, on the side of the refrigerator. It's the trace of a transparent and brittle tape. The tape once stuck a sheet that, in turn, had yellowed, its feint-ruled lines kitchen-stained and fingerprinted. On the sheet was a recipe, copied by hand by my mother from an older version that, in turn, had once been stuck to another refrigerator in another home in another land, written in an earlier maternal hand. And so on backwards. A regression of yellowed sheets and brittle tape. A regression of refrigerators. But the same recipe for cherry pie. 'We'll cook together if there is anything to cook.' A cherry pie would bring men back from the front, and make men in labour camps long for home. Maybe it will bring my father back, too.

Men

The Disappearance of a Father

THERE ARE MANY WAYS a father can disappear. He can disappear from view, from the range of one's hearing, even from memory. He can disappear so that he leaves no trace in the living, no sign, no clue, no picture of how he was or what he was. Or he can disappear and leave a trail, a hundred points of reference, each sign, clue and memory a struggle against his disappearance. That's the way it feels with Nándor Bokor, my grandfather, my father's father, who did disappear. 'I think about him getting weaker,' my father once said after his stroke, not that he ever said much about him, even before.

Nándor Bokor did get weaker. He struggled against it. Then he disappeared: *eltűnt*. That's what the only remotely official version says. One word terminates the record. There is even a date to go with it, as if disappearing were that specific: 17 January 1943. But there is no suggestion of where this non-event took place nor what led to it.

In fact, there is more than one date for it, for this non-event. There are several dates, several possible last moments, one after the other, each slighter, less substantial, greyer, weaker than the one before. There is, for instance, the photograph. 'It's the last one of my father,' so my father has always said, so the story went, so this single fact has been handed down. A single fact, a final photograph: the beginning, middle and end of a life.

This last photograph was the first thing I knew about Nándor. I've always been aware of it, at least the fact of it. The fact of it being the last photograph was always bigger than the photograph itself because the photograph itself is faded, has always been faded, as if taken faded in the first place. Nándor stands against a nondescript outdoor background of light grey and dark grey: a cracked pale wall, a hint of a dark window frame, him in faded clothes, worn down to a greyscale. His eyes stare out at the photographer but without expression, distant, between thoughts, between places, in a grey and time-free somewhere.

He has, in fact, stood like this, hands in pockets, between thoughts, under a sun, in his heavy faded jacket, grey trousers bulging at the knees because tucked into boot-tops, for 65 years. For many of them, his photograph has stood on a shelf, between books, not at eye level, not displayed, as such, not noticed easily if at all. When, at some point, I became aware of this photograph, the last of him, I knew that I wanted to see beyond the edges of the frame. If this is the last photograph, where was it taken? What was he doing there? When was he last seen? Who last saw him? Who took the photograph?

A memory. A snapshot. My father last saw his father at the railway station. It was Keleti Station, Budapest's eastern railway terminus. They lived not far, at the poorer end of the eighth district, at 59 Népszínház Street, barely a tram ride, half a walk. So Nándor was on a train, in the last carriage, leaning out. My father was ten or so, give or take, depending on a date, depending on a moment. He was leaning out of the train, maybe not a carriage but an open wagon. He was waving, singing. '*Ez a harc lesz a végső,*' is what my father heard. 'This fight will be the last.' The last-seen Nándor had last words. From the last wagon he sang about the last fight. Light through the vaulted glass of the station roof. Smoke. Special effects. Train receding. Train a speck. Train gone.

It wasn't of course a military song that Nándor sang but 'The International', a song associated with the Union of Ironworkers, whose rallies Nándor regularly attended. He was SocDem, left-wing, a socialist: a cause of worry for his wife – my grandmother Lili – and a spark for equally regular arguments. She was afraid when he came home with *Népszava*, a left-wing newspaper. In the prevailing atmosphere, with all that was going on, this might have drawn the wrong attention, marked him out. It was a bit late, by then, that thinking. Because it wasn't only his views that would have marked him out. There was race, too.

There are several dates for Nándor's disappearance, several final moments, but one thing is certain: the war Nándor went off to asked for him by name. He wasn't really going to war. He was being taken to a war. And of course he had no intention to fight, merely to return. He would have got a notification, a summons. It might have come with an 'S-A-S': '*Siess, Azonnal, Sürgős.*' Hurry. Immediately. Urgent. He would have had a week to report, to present himself somewhere. In Nándor's case, he had to present himself to '1 Bev. Kozp.' A *bevonulási központ*. A draft centre. Draft Centre 1. Labour Flag 1. Unit 101/5. However personal the notification, however singular the last time he was seen, Nándor was not alone. Thousands of men like him, other male Jews like him, would have received the same notification, whether they came home with left-wing newspapers or not.

Munkaszolgálat, the Hungarian Labour Service system, really began in 1939 with the principal purpose of conscripting Jews. In a previous war, Jews in the Hungarian Army had had guns, ranks, uniforms. They had been soldiers. Now, they were conscripted into an armless army, deprived of rank, status or a means of self-defence. Their 'weapons' were shovels, picks, sledgehammers. By mid 1940 there were already 60 such battalions in existence, and recruitment, like the war, had barely got underway. Scanning history doesn't help to pinpoint a date. Did the history books record the thousands of wives who carved out the insides of thousands of green peppers to fill them with *kőrözött*, a spiced home-made cream cheese, different in every home, to be spread on bread? Or the thousands of husbands who would have packed their rucksacks leaving space for the precious cargo? Nándor was not alone. He was one of them.

And my maternal grandfather, Ernő Semler, him too. He was a conscript for this labour army, and went off with a rucksack like the rest, but at another time, one summer later in the war, leaving footprints in the asphalt. That's what Zsuzsi, my mother's older sister, remembers. They were there for days, mud-crust on a melted road. Ernő, born in 1900, had been just old enough to serve in the First World War as a soldier, too young for rank but old enough for a rifle. A war later, the same Jew was a forced labourer. One of Lili's younger brothers, Andor Rehovitz, had to serve, too, at another time in another unit. And my cousins' grandfather, Imre Fenyvesi, him too. They all went.

Why choose one of these four over another? Why Nándor? Maybe it's because of the last photograph, because he's always been there. Maybe there was no choice. Or maybe the four of them, Nándor, Ernő, Imre and Andor, are all in some way the same person, the same male ancestor of the same period and the same circumstances. They all went off looking the same, more like they were going on an outing. Jackets, hiking boots or stout shoes, trousers tucked into boot-tops, personal possessions, a special knife, a pen, letter paper, envelopes, a camera. Civilians going off for a weekend with their friends. A crowd of men. Families, women and children, wives and mothers, waving them off. Them, the men, waving back. Keleti station – built in the age of steam, of locomotion, of fine dining, its restaurant marbled, pillared, wood-panelled, gaudy, gold – was crowded with people and jackets and bags and carefully wrapped green peppers. A crowd. A herd. Emotions transmitting from one to another, rippling through families, families that were familiar to each other. The men were chosen by name yet each was like the others. Each disappeared in his own way, in his own time.

Nándor was not alone at Keleti station, nor did he sing alone. But was this the last time he was seen? Which year was this? Were those his final words? The more you know, the more you can know. The same photographs, looked at again and again, change. Their greyed meanings brighten. There are photographs of Nándor walking up a country road, a rural road, with a bunch of other men. In one, the bunch of men poses, some sitting, some standing, taller ones, including Nándor, at the back, like a team. They've been hiking, surely, sleeves rolled up, patched with mud and dust, sun-browned, a bit sweaty, the day behind them rather than ahead. A bunch of men, in their twenties and thirties and forties, in a dreary rural landscape, on a stony path, framed by a conifer, a slope, a hill and a white house, just never captured a childhood imagination. They weren't interesting. These weren't even 'the last' photographs.

But look closer and Nándor is wearing the clothes he wears in his last photograph. The photographs are dated 1940. Have the photographs faded or have the clothes? A place name has been written at the top: Gödemesterháza. It's one of those tortuous Hungarian village names that one looks at once and spends a lifetime trying to remember. Once looked at again, once remembered, the name disappears from view. It disappears from the map, the names of villages shifting with shifting borders. Gödemesterháza is now Stânceni, once Hungarian, now Romanian. What belonged to one and ended up belonging to the other was the principal reason for Hungary throwing in with the Germans. Territory lost in the First World War would be regained in the Second, so the thinking went, and Northern Romania was nothing if not bitterly contested. A bunch of men were rounded up, supervised, guarded by soldiers with real weapons, sent into a forest to chop wood, sent up a half-built road to build the rest.

Nándor would have been fine. He was an accountant who did Greco-Roman wrestling, a wrestler who could add up. Thicker set, he would have been fine, at first, with some physical labour, gripping a pickaxe, counting the hours. Unlike others. There would have been many others who were Jews, lefties and generally unreliable but, from the beginning, could not break stones or dig ditches to save their lives, which was a good reason to do both. Nándor would have found a way. He was pragmatic, a keen bridge player who was used to finding the best way to play the hand he was dealt. And there had been one or two disappearances before, minor ones, natural ones.

It was among the reeds and ducks and golden sunsets of Szigetszentmiklós that the almost six-foot, bespectacled Nándor first appeared, in 1924, to my five-foot-nothing, moon-faced grandmother. Lili, eighteen at the time, was on holiday with her parents, Móric Rehovitz and Katalin, and her younger brothers, the fifteen-year-old Jenő, and Andor, who was then just five. They would have rented a bungalow, one in a row along the branch of the Danube that creates Szigetszentmiklós, St Nicholas Island, on Csepel Island just south of Budapest. Nándor, too, would have been on holiday with some of his numerous family. Perhaps not all six siblings would have come up from the provincial town of Székesfehérvár, not in the heat of summer. But the glassy waters of this branch of the Danube are attractive enough for a break, for rowing without effort. The shade is cool enough for a rest, a piece of bread, a green pepper and *kőrözött*. Beyond the reeds, there are quieter spots to fish in by day, and the sunsets are golden enough for romance.

They married in 1925. Nándor left Székesfehérvár behind to live in the capital. He became an accountant for a coffee importer. By this time, he had also left a name behind. Born a Berger, he Magyarized his once Germanized name. Many Jews had done the same, were increasingly finding ways of doing the same, in a changing climate, with a sense, perhaps, of what lay ahead – and, if not, a sense of what lay behind. Others in his family remained Bergers. Nándor played the hand he was dealt but whatever he called himself made no difference. In 1940 he was labouring in the countryside, loading gravel into wagons. Wherever he finally disappeared, it was not in Gödemesterháza. This was where he lived, breaking stones and chopping wood by the banks of the River Mures, not where he disappeared. There's more evidence of that in the box.

Whether the documents were eventually collected in a spare box or whether the old box was always there and documents filled it one by one, as they turned up, is difficult to know. After a certain time, it's impossible to separate the two, old box and old documents. Their usual place is in a corner of the living room. Which living room doesn't matter: the parental living room or that of one of their parents before them or one of theirs before that, and possibly a box before that one, too, emptier or fuller, emptying or filling, and on back. Either way, Nándor's two postcards survive in the plastic covers my grandmother found for them, in the box of undifferentiated documents in the living room.

They are addressed to my father, István Bokor. They use grand terms that the ten-year-old István liked very much, such as *tek*, short for *tekintélyes*, 'honourable', or *nagyságos*, 'esteemed', or *Drága Kisapám*, my 'dear little-father'. They are written barely a month apart, the first from Szatmár, now the Romanian Satu Mare, dated 30 September 1940, and the other from Gödemesterháza, dated 23 October 1940. The dates and places are themselves evidence of certain conditions: forced labourers were allowed to write home at this stage or in this unit. The postmarks aren't military secrets. One postcard has a picture of the Hungarian Army marching into Romania, 'to commemorate the liberation of Erdély' – Transylvania. The other has a picture of Admiral Horthy, the Hungarian leader and ally of the Nazis, in military uniform surrounded by his staff and officers during another commemoration of the same recent event. 'Dear little-father,' writes Nándor, 'I'm sending you a very nice picture…'

The leftie Jew could still make his views known, irony ghosting past the military censor, to transmit to the adults taking care of his son back home. But if the irony escaped the censor, then the overall sentiment did not, could not. The cards read like any cards would from any distant father to any distant son: he offers greetings and hugs; he wishes he could send himself instead of the card; he hopes his son will still be happy to see him; he offers hugs and kisses and more hugs. Nándor and the bunch of men who went for a hike could only write what was allowed, to the edges of permitted emotion, using a range of phrases that persecutor and persecuted each had in his head. The rest could be read into by relatives, imagined by loved ones. But did they imagine the rest? At least then, in 1940, the forced labourers were allowed to write, and maybe Nándor was allowed to choose a nice picture from a range of nice pictures.

When Lili received this, she would have worried more. There's too much hoping, wishing, too much sending from a distance, and too much irony in too short a space. She would have worried that someone might have noticed. But Gödemesterháza was not where her husband disappeared. Thirty years later, in another country, Lili wrote a three-page life history, a list, more or less, of dates, and words to go with the dates. Twenty years after she died, I first read it among the documents in the box. One of the things she noted was that she married in 1925 and that, after 16 happy years together, on 27 April 1942, 'my happiness ended'. The ending of happiness, and the beginning of 'the hell of hells'.

They'd moved to 59 Népszínház Street in 1930, the year my father was born. It was from here, according to Lili, that on 27 April 1942 Nándor was 'taken away'. Maybe she didn't mean that phrase literally. Maybe she meant that he was called up from here. But it means that he returned from forced labour, that the photographs and postcards were reunited with the person in them, with the person who wrote them. It means that he was called up again, sent away again, 'taken away'. *Innen vitték el...* 'They took him from here.'

One searing hot August afternoon, my older cousin Andris and I find ourselves at the deserted railway station in the village of Dabas, 20 miles south-east of Budapest. 'Why the fuck are we here?' Andris asks, quite reasonably. As a doctor, he's used to asking quite reasonable questions and even getting quite reasonable answers. There was a kind of an answer to this question, but it snakes away like the rusty Dabas rails into the distant woods. This name, the name of this village, is something that came out of a book. Given that the vast majority of records relating to the forced labour battalions were destroyed in the final months of the war, anything specific is rare.

Published in 1962, the book is entitled *Fegyvertelen álltak az aknamezőkön.* 'Weaponless, They Stood in the Minefields' conveys the melodramatic title of a book containing a range of documentation about the labour battalions between 1942 and 1945, from ministerial and governmental directives about what Jews could or could not have, could or could not do, to a few survivors' accounts. Unit 101/5 is mentioned, barely rather than specifically, in connection with Alsódabas, Lower Dabas. Lower and presumably Upper and Middle Dabas are now just Dabas, an amalgam of villages creeping out into the fields, teenagers on mopeds in the town square and an international company or two prefabricating the outskirts. It seems that Unit 101/5, with its 200 or so men, passed through here. It might have been a staging post where the men were organized, lined up, trained, about-faced, marched around, exercised relentlessly to kill time, made to await further orders, and where they sat around wondering what those orders would be. Home still close. Budapest up the road. Guards between. The railway-station building was renewed postwar, but not the cast iron water pump, the rotten wooden bench, the rusty rails curving into the distant trees. Barely rather than specifically, it feels a step closer to where Nándor disappeared.

There is a second answer to the question of why we are here. It's in the 'we'. My cousin's grandfather was Imre Fenyvesi. He and Nándor were friends. Imre's wife, Panci, was Lili's best friend. The lives of their sons – István, my father, and Tomi, Andris's father – were already entwined and would continue to be for many years in many ways, through school and beyond, each of them marrying one of two sisters. Imre and Nándor, our grandfathers, were both in Unit 101/5. Look closer at the photographs, know more, and there is Imre walking up the country road, sun-browned, sweaty, sleeves rolled. There is Imre posing for the camera with a bunch of urban men in civilian clothes, Gödemesterháza, 1940.

But there is another photograph of Nándor, the wrestling accountant, and Imre, who worked for his father-in-law's gentlemen's outfitters. It drops out of an album. It doesn't matter which album, an old one, with stiff pages, in a musty cupboard, lost and found, forgotten and remembered, rediscovered, looked at again through the lens of a fresh fact. The photograph is distinctly different from the others. It shows the two of them together, Imre Fenyvesi, once Friedlander, and Nándor Bokor, once Berger. It's nearer, sharper, more intimate than any of the others, taken inside as opposed to out, in a tight, claustrophobic space. It is black and white, not greyscaled, lit as if with a single bare bulb between them and the photographer. The men's jackets hang behind them, and there are other garments too, the jackets of other men. It is a shared, communal space with clothing bundled into the corners. Imre is seated, his chest sunken, wearing two shirts, one on top of the other, both open to the navel and tucked into his trousers. His hands are clasped together in front of him, his nails dirt-edged, greasy. An empty, smokeless pipe juts from his closed mouth. Wide-eyed, weary, almost nonchalant, he stares at something beyond the frame. Nándor, standing by his side, crumpled shirt hanging from beneath a far-too-short sleeveless pullover, stares at the camera, a heavy smoker without a cigarette, his eyes and mouth tensed with what could once, years before, have been the birth of a smile. They look like miners from deep down, like they have worn out the clothes they had, the lives they had, and now make do with what they find. They look like they are between stretches of labour.

It's what you might call a grim portrait, without either of the men or the photographer thinking of it as such. It is dated 1942. It is a photograph taken after Nándor was taken. In other words, this is the second time. He went. He came back. He went again. By the time this picture reached anyone it was meant to reach, it was historical, a sign of the

The last photograph: my grandfather, Nándor (right), with my cousins'
grandfather, Imre, on forced labour, Ukraine, late 1942. The picture was
probably taken by a bribed guard. Both men would be dead within weeks.

past, not of the present. In the stark light, everything seems a deception: Imre's smokeless pipe, tobaccoless, too; Nándor's short pullover
and ambiguous expression that follows you. It's as if the picture itself
is a deception, taken to deceive the living into believing in the dead.

It is this photograph that must be the last photograph. When I suggest
this to my father, he says, yes, it must be. He says it is more than likely
that a guard took it, was paid something or given something to take
it on his own camera. The guard was paid to take a snap that would
be the last snap, and then paid to send it home. Look closer. Know
more. This would account for the expressions, the weary nonchalance
on the face of one, the ambiguous glimmer of a smile on the other.
Each is posing in his own way, half for a loved one back home, half
for an unloved one taking his picture.

So here we are, my cousin and me, under the hot Dabas sun,
knowing that the story of Nándor's disappearance is inseparable
from Imre's, that one is nothing without the other, that the fate of
one was bound up with the other. Imre's wife, Panci, she too wrote a
life history, a list of a dozen dates with words attached. Years before

Lili, she inked the facts onto the inside cover of a black, hard-cover prayer book, an Israelite prayer book for women. One of the dates is that of Imre's departure: 27 April 1942. The only thing, according to Andris, that separates them, our grandfathers, is the date of each one's disappearance. In the list of names, the *nevek*, of Jewish victims of Hungarian labour battalions compiled from a range of sources by the Beate Klarsfeld Foundation, these dates are distinctly different: Imre, 11 January 1943; Nándor, 17 January 1943.

Historically, both dates point to the direction of the journey they were forced to make this second time, on this second round of forced labour: east. They went in the direction of the Eastern Front, towards the events of the Eastern Front, towards what would happen there, events that would consume hundreds of thousands of men, big numbers in a big picture.

At the military history museum on Castle Hill, there is nothing but the big picture, the primary colours of a big war showing how Hungarian troops 'accomplished hopeless and heroic combats', how the Second Hungarian Army suffered a hundred thousand casualties in a single month. The dead, the injured, the frozen, the captured. January 1943. Collectively, it is often referred to as 'the Don bend catastrophe'.

Of course, it wasn't a catastrophe for the Russians. It was a hugely important victory, one that changed the war, turned the tide against the Germans. It began when the Russians broke through the Hungarian lines at the Uriv bridgehead near Voronezh, a few miles from the Don River. In a corner of the museum, away from the heroic combats and catastrophes, there is a life-sized dummy of a man in the 'ancillary labour service'. He has a shovel and a uniform. He has no face. Presumably, in his facelessness, he is meant to represent one of those Hungarian citizens who was 'unfit for military service owing to reasons of origins, political convictions, morale or health status'. These were the ones who 'disappeared'. Hungarian soldiers, non-Jews, did not disappear with a word. They always died with a phrase: '*hősi halált halt*', 'he died a hero's death'. There is still a debate, apparently, over whether forced labourers were soldiers or slaves.

A museum attendant, middle-aged, rounded by years of sitting on her museum chair, sees me staring at the dummy and asks me what I'm looking for. I say I'm not sure. But with my Anglo-Hungarian accent, we soon get to talking about family, family history, first and second generations, and on. She says she has been here long enough to see those who went and came back. She uses an odd, unfamiliar, word, an old country word, '*gyütment*', literally a 'came-and-went', someone who leaves and comes back and who is therefore a nobody because from nowhere, a stranger everywhere, like the Hungarians, she says, who left in '45 or '56 and came back half a life later, one even returning with the specks of Hungarian soil he had taken away with him so many years before, as if to bring them home, as if to come home.

Nándor and Imre went but did not come back. They became, and remained, strangers in a strange land. Nándor had once dreamed of this, of going but not returning. He had even planned for it. It was just before the war, around the time between the first Anti-Jewish Law, passed in Hungary in May 1938, and the second, in May 1939. The first was aimed at removing Jews from economic or professional activity; the second defined Jews racially as opposed to religiously. Nándor dreamed of America, and a dream of elsewhere is only a shade of grey from an escape plan. The accountant knew he had to learn something new. So he learned how to make uppers for shoes, a choice perhaps influenced by his father, Gyula Berger, who had died in 1929 but had been a shoemaker. Nándor also figured that playing bridge would be a useful skill on the long voyage, a skill that would help him to make friends and contacts. My father, aged eight and a half, reacted very badly to his father's dream of America, and sang the Hungarian national anthem. It is a song that, to the best of my knowledge, my father never sang again.

But what did Nándor sing, far from home, when the last photograph was taken? What did he dream of in 1942? Maybe he remembered family gatherings or the pictures taken of gatherings, pre-war celebrations where the women made hats out of napkins, and a few of his siblings would come up from Székesfehérvár, and they drank and smoked and ate cherry pie and apricot dumplings. Maybe Imre dreamed of going to work in the morning at the small, elegant, Baross Street gentlemen's outfitter, dreamed of entering, counter to the left, umbrella stand to the right, racks of ties ahead, shirts behind glass all around. In the end, whatever they dreamed, they dreamed too late.

*Between wars: my recently born father, held in my grandmother Lili's
arms, at a family gathering in Székesfehérvár in 1930.*

The same survivor of Unit 101/5 – a survivor being someone who
went and who came back – writes that on 2 July 1942 the men of the
unit set off from Alsódabas. They headed towards Russia.

So here we are, my cousin and me, miles from the Eastern Front,
staring down the Dabas branch line into the distant, heat-hazed trees,
trying to put faces and voices to those long gone, wondering about last
carriages and last words and last photographs, about grandfathers and
sons and grandsons, and about how the living might still believe in
the dead. Miles from the Eastern Front, there is still space to be filled.
There is so much less than the big picture. There is micro-history.
There are the little steps of faceless people.

It occurs to Andris and me that if Nándor was able to write postcards, at least in 1940, then how come Imre didn't? Or, if he did, how
come none survive? It's inconceivable that he would have missed an
opportunity to write a card or that, if he did, it wasn't kept somewhere,
in a box, in a living room.

A day or two later, I ask my aunt Zsuzsi if she knows of anything
like that, of a postcard Imre would have sent to his son, Tomi, her

husband and Andris's father, who died in 1988. She can't remember but moves her glasses to the edge of her nose and back, momentarily focusing on the past, on what she knows but has forgotten. Behind her, through the broad windows of her flat, the Danube flows, carrying either an American summer cruise boat or a freezing winter rower, having swept away the falsifications and clarifications of Hungarian history, as well as many of its bodies. Zsuzsi says she will root around. Her flat is still, calm. It's so still you can hear the ghosts rereading their way through the books that line the shelves. And through the *lichthof*, a vertical hole running through the middle of the building from top to bottom for light and ventilation, you can hear voices from elsewhere, from beyond, ghosts coughing or wheezing or muttering.

A day or two later, Zsuzsi finds – refinds, rediscovers – not in a box but in a drawer, a flaking, faded postcard among flaking, faded papers. It is a pencilled postcard from Imre, the only one, addressed to his wife, Panci. Unlike Nándor's postmarked picture cards from 1940, this is a plain white, officially distributed, military card with a 'camp post' stamp, omitting any mention of place. It is dated 16 December 1942 and written under the supervision of a Lieutenant Doby.

My dear Panci, again I'm writing only briefly, and don't take it badly if I write bluntly. Next time I'll write more. I'm well. It's pointless to worry. I'm very proud of Tomi. I wish Mum every happiness on her birthday. I received Miki's camp number. Numberless kisses, Imre.

Imre's words are as deceptive as his last photograph. More, perhaps. He means to deceive and is meant to deceive. Deception was all that he was allowed and all that he allowed himself. It proves, at least, that he wrote before but that previous cards have disappeared, disappeared from sight and from memory. He'd written before and so he hoped to write again. Next time, he said. But this was 16 December 1942. There would be no next time. A few weeks later he was gone.

In the meantime, he was deep inside Russia. The conditions were worse. Marching on a piece of bread and half a litre of water. No winter clothing. Digging earthworks. Marching. Building fortifications. Marching. Misevo, Pukhovo, Kovalevo. Villages. Places in combat zones. By mid July 1942, the Second Hungarian Army had reached the Don, south of Voronezh. Over 100,000 would not return. By then, forced labourers in the area numbered around 50,000. Of those, only a few thousand would return. They came up from Alsódabas into the Ukraine, then to Gomel, Tim, Stary Oskol, Misevo, Pukhovo and on. They came 1,000 miles to stand 'weaponless in the minefields', weaponless and unexaggerated.

The circumstantial truths are well known: Jews were made to walk into minefields in order to clear them. They were starved, shot, tied outside in the snow until iced. Not all the Hungarian guards were uniformly sadistic, but what they lacked was supplemented by the presence of SS or other military units. In Unit 101/5, in late 1942, 14 are recorded as dying of starvation, weakness and constant beatings. The Eastern Front allowed anti-Semites and Semites to be together.

Of course Imre was not well. He sold gentlemen's accessories. And the Greco-Roman wrestler was not getting fat either, not on a piece of bread, half a litre of water. Imre was proud of his son. He wished Mum a happy birthday. He thought of Miki, Panci's sister's husband. He sent numberless kisses. But he was not well.

Miklós Radnóti, the poet, Hungarian, Jew, forced labourer, on whose disinterred, bullet-holed body a notebook of poems was found, wrote on 15 September 1944 that 'foolish is he who, collapsed, rises and walks again...' Nándor and Imre were not fools. They might have taken the advice from a poem entitled 'Forced March'. They did not walk again, and their deaths could have come in any one of a number of ways. That is, if shooting, beating or starvation didn't kill them, then exhaustion, freezing temperatures or typhus probably did. Andor, Lili's brother, in Unit IX KMSZ, died in Dimitrievka, aged 24, in the same general area of operations at the same time, 7 January 1943. Circumstantially, Andor, Nándor and Imre died of what all other forced labourers died of. But what is a circumstantial death?

Over the years, my father has mentioned different possibilities. Nándor, seeing a chance to escape, went over to the Russians who took him prisoner and he died in a Russian prisoner-of-war camp. Many did. Nándor, a heavy smoker, traded his last piece of bread for a cigarette. Many did. Nándor, Lili claimed to have 'proved', died on German soil. Many tried to prove the same, possibly to gain some postwar compensation, at least something for someone.

But another document, refound by Zsuzsi along with the postcard, is a notification from the Budapest Red Cross office. Dated 26 January 1944, it informs the recipient that Imre Fenyvesi disappeared on Russian territory. If Imre, then Nándor, too. And the date of this disappearance: 17 January 1943. The same day as Nándor. If Nándor, then Imre, too. In a final twist, these notifications state that they died 'in the anti-Soviet war', as if either had entertained the slightest motivation.

One day, while I am reading a yellow-paged book in a Budapest archive, the old men come, three of them, one at a time. They have thin faces and thinner bags, and inside the thinner bags are pieces of paper so thin as to be translucent. They hold them with their trembling and brittle fingertips. They apologize for the disturbance. They just came to tell something, a story, their story. After all this time, after sixty years or more, they would like to have their stories heard. Before I can call the archivist for whom they have mistaken me, they are telling their stories. They mention the names of places, distant and strange, such as the Silesian hills or Nagykáta or Stary Oskol or Gunskirchen. They mention uncles and aunts and mothers and fathers and children and childhoods. They appear, thin and translucent, as if to prove that ghosts exist, that ghosts return, that going and coming back is possible.

The windows of 59 Népszínház Street are open here and there on all three floors. A muttering head leans out of one, senses the sharpness of the sun, and withdraws again into shadow. A light breeze shifts thin papers down the street in the direction of the railway station. Lili and my father continued to live in the flat during the war, and beyond. Panci would move in with her son, Tomi, in 1944. Of course, Nándor and Imre never knew of the events that unfolded in Népszínház Street the following year. Similarly, their wives and sons barely knew of their fates.

They would die very close together. Nándor was not a poet. Nor Imre. Notebooks of poems would not have been found on their disinterred corpses. But they struggled against disappearance nevertheless. They chose the last carriage or wagon. Perhaps they struggled to get into it because the last carriage or wagon would afford the longest last moment, the longest last moment to commit to memory. Then the train became a speck like a speck of soil. Train disappeared. Fathers disappeared.

The Coming of
Uncle Józsi

I F IT HADN'T BEEN for Great-Great-Uncle Józsi, I might have
been a retailer of ladies' underwear.

'Don't knock it till you've tried it,' said my mother.

Despite this ancient wisdom, I still can't help feeling grateful that
Uncle Józsi survived a war and then, with a timely appearance,
removed my grandmother, Lili, from Vienna to Budapest just as
Vienna's population was suffering greatly. Lili's mother, Katalin, née
Bruckner, stayed on for a while to keep the clothes business afloat,
while her father, Móric Rehovitz, was still soldiering on a distant front.
Had my grandmother stayed, the Bruckner and Rehovitz Modelhaus,
a clothes workshop and retailer at 51 Mariahilferstrasse, today a
Viennese Oxford Street, might still be in family hands and I could
be its fragrant proprietor. But Uncle Józsi survived mountain winters
and battles to come to Vienna in December 1917 on one final mission: to save Lili, aged 11, from weakness, rationing, illness and the
impending collapse of the Austro-Hungarian Empire. This is the one
fact that Lili recorded about him, that he returned from war for this.
It is how he exists and the sole reason he comes into my existence. If
I owe him anything, then it is, at least, to shed light on his directions.

Uncle Józsi travelled from one edge of the creaking, war-torn, multi-lingual administration to the other, from its high, lonely peaks to its demoralized capital. But who was he? It's difficult to spot a single man, one soldier, in among the crowd of nine million men that Austria–Hungary put into uniform during the First World War.

Detail by detail his identity has emerged over the years, but it is still as fragmented as the jagged limestone shards that once rained on his head up a freezing mountain. His last name was Müller, and he ended the war a *százados*, a captain. Captain Müller. As someone who attained this rank, he must have performed his military duties with more than average commitment. As an uncle, he was the son of Great-Great-Great-Grandfather Ignác Müller, a generation before Great-Grandfather Móric Rehovitz, yet of similar age, both having been born in the mid 1870s.

But in the flux between uncle and captain, Józsi's story twists through mountain paths, always shadowed by the ambiguities of a great war. Perhaps it's much easier to say who Uncle Józsi/Captain Müller wasn't.

He wasn't Uncle Zolti. Every family needs a war hero with a tall story and Zolti's story is tall enough to set the standard. It's the only thing that remains of him. No pictures. No last name. No specific kith or kin. Just the story. In early December 1914, Zolti participated in the legendary Battle of Limanowa. The name of this Polish village south-east of Krakow on the edge of the Carpathian Mountains is inscribed in Hungarian history. It was here that far greater Russian forces were repelled by weaker Hungarian ones, thus preventing a Russian invasion of Hungary. Zolti not only did his bit, he returned home. The most significant aspect of his return was what he returned without. Somewhere along the way, Zolti lost one of his little fingers. Whether it was on his right or left hand is not known. What is known?

'He vuz a razzer small fellow,' my father once said of him.

'Relative to whom?' I asked.

'Relative to the Russian lancer who bit off his finger,' he replied.

For that was Zolti's story. The story of Zolti's little finger is precious, just as the little finger itself was surely precious to Zolti. It's a symbol of what was sacrificed by a soldier for his country or by a Jew who, a war later, would never have been accepted into the proper army. Zolti arguably altered the course of Hungarian history. His little finger was the indigestible morsel needed to put the Russians off their prey, thereby saving the country. This has yet to be acknowledged by historians. At least the little finger has provided the family ever since with a unit of measure, a 'Zolti', as in the response to the question, 'How much espresso would you like?'

Zolti, with his small frame and tall story, whoever he was and however he was related, was not Uncle Józsi. Neither was Móric Rehovitz, my great-grandfather. His was a funny little war, and his contribution to the Austro-Hungarian Empire was somewhat more mundane, his worldly concerns outweighing his desire to perform heroic feats. What remains of his soldiering between 1914 and 1917 are two postcards and one photograph.

Capable of looking fabulously distinguished in suit and tie, Móric, once in uniform, had the demeanour of a friendly, slightly damp sandbag best used for sitting on. Beregszász, now Beregovo in the sub-Carpathian Ukraine, spring 1916: Móric and company pose for their first pay-day parade outside a barracks veiled by leafy trees. The soldiers of the Austro-Hungarian Common Army, in the presence of

A funny little war: Ukraine, spring 1916, my great-grandfather, Pay Sergeant Móric Rehovitz, stands behind the pay table at a safe distance from the front line.

a seated, older-than-usual Austrian officer, stand in a wide and deep arc, first the non-commissioned officers, then the privates, around a single wooden trestle table where the plump, amorphous, smiling Pay Sergeant, slouching in riding boots and breeches, is doling out their wages. The Pay Sergeant is Móric.

The soldiers, without service medals, campaign badges or decorations, have either yet to go to war or, more likely, form a reserve battalion behind front lines. Either way, it's obvious that Móric was never the martial type. He didn't altogether lack a hunter's instincts, but they emerged only later in life, after the death of his wife in 1945, when he would take walks in the park to befriend women. Later still, before his own death in 1950, he would lean out of a window to lure the neighbourhood cats to within striking range of his walking stick. Those activities required a certain instinct. But, throughout his deployment in the First World War, he never picked up a Steyr-Mannlicher Repetier Gewehr M95 straight-pull, bolt-action, standard-issue rifle to shoot so much as a pigeon, and no enemy ever bit off any part of him.

His nice handwriting, inherited by my grandmother, was his greatest asset, as evidenced by his postcards home. Those postcards also reveal his wartime preoccupations. On 16 January 1915, he writes via the military post from Esztergom, a pretty northern town of strategic value that a great Hungarian poet once dubbed the 'Hungarian Rome' for its imposing basilica overlooking the wintry Danube. The postcard was addressed to his wife at 51 Mariahilferstrasse in Vienna.

My dear wife, could you send me my service booklet by registered post and with it or separately six rubber hooks made for trousers...

At this point, he draws an example of a rubber hook made for trousers... ◡ ... before continuing:

... like the ones I bought at Reisz's. With these could you send three 'Gillette' razor blades but only this brand, how are you, well I hope!'

Maybe this peculiarly punctuated stream of consciousness shows how anxious the plump Pay Sergeant really was about the military implications of his falling trousers. His war depended on it. The drawing suggests that his dear wife, Katalin, had to get this right. No mistakes. It was an issue of national importance, this and the correct brand of razor blades to work around his nationally important moustache. Among other issues he raises, such as inoculating the children, ensuring they used 'the emulsion' and mentioning that he'd sent a new year's postcard but to the wrong address, Móric vacantly adds 'just that there are great battles' taking place on the territory between the military zones of Esztergom and Kassa. 'The rest,' he writes, 'you can imagine.'

Maybe this, too, reveals the secret of the Pay Sergeant's war, a war that he asked his wife, as an afterthought, to imagine. Why? Because he also had to imagine it. He was close, in other words, but not that close. As he held up his trousers wondering what the morning post would bring, Móric heard the rumble of artillery, the stamping and snorting of horses. He watched the hauling, piece by great piece, of killing machines as big as houses with their wrenches as big as men. Over the hills they went, and through the woods to the front, while Móric used his little fingers as hooks.

After rubber trouser hooks, close shaving, the kids' emulsion and the imagining of war were out of his system, poetry got the better of him. He signs off with 'hugs and kisses as numberless as the stars, to the grave, your loving Móric'.

The tale of Great-Grandfather Móric's war is as slow and banal as Zolti's is sudden and tall. Neither of them, however, was Uncle Józsi. His was a different war, brought to life with the magical word 'Isonzo', a word rarely seen in British history books, and rarely unseen in Hungarian ones. I first saw it written by my grandmother, an abracadabra revealing a forgotten place, a password to a land beyond the horizon. Isonzo was a front that lasted two and a half years, shifting uneasily up and down and around a valley without getting anywhere. There were 12 battles in 11 languages, not counting Italian, the principal language of the Austro-Hungarian enemy. It left a million Italians and 700,000 polyglot Austro-Hungarians dead or wounded.

Growing up in Britain made the First World War so much simpler. There were us. There were them. There was right and there was wrong. There was mud. There were trenches. Between the trenches, there were corpses. The whole terrible business killed almost 900,000 British soldiers and wounded almost twice that number. A lot of poetry came out of it, not the 'numberless as the stars' type of poetry but poetry of a quality that somehow justified the whole terrible business, poetry that could not have been written without the whole terrible business. But for whom or for what were my ancestors fighting?

While Móric was finding ways to uphold his honour, Józsi was on a train. Trains took soldiers to the war. No doubt it seemed a good idea at the beginning. By the end of the war, two thirds of the Empire's rail network was clogged up by the military and its weighty equipment. Unlike *The Good Soldier Švejk*, Hašek's great literary creation who was caught marching away from the front while claiming to be in search of it, Uncle Józsi's deployment was as difficult to avoid as conscription: the vast majority of men between the ages of 18 and 53 were called up. By then, he was 40 years old, an engineer, a constructor, suddenly a non-commissioned officer in the artillery, the *tüzérség*. He was trained in horsemanship, as well as the theory and practice of artillery fire control. Then he was on a train with killing machines as big as houses, whose great pieces were built on great new assembly lines.

After the train, there was the chaos of the roads. After the road, there were the mountains. In early June 1915, Józsi found himself humping his large frame up one of the range of peaks overlooking the meandering Isonzo valley, somewhere between the river's source, high in the Julian Alps, and where it flows out into the Adriatic. Krn, the highest peak at almost 7,600 feet, would be a key military vantage point for the next three years. Its now tree-covered slopes were bare and craggy a century ago, with little cover on the way up or down.

Hemingway called it 'the picturesque front'. Climb high above the green and foaming river, past waterfalls with luminescent lizards, past wispy snakes and black-red butterflies between sun-sprinkled leaves, and it's difficult to disagree. The white water attracts a kayak or two, the shaded paths a hiker or two. But notice the steps beneath your feet, each planked, timbered, held in place by a billion nails. Walk the trenches cut into solid rock, zigzagged to prevent shockwaves and shrapnel. Run a hand along splintered subterranean bunks overlaid with corrugated iron and turf. Peer into the dry-stone-walled observation posts. Step in. Peer out. The picturesque disappears. The Italians, having attacked in May 1915, only really crossed the 50-mile

Austro-Hungarian line of defence in 1918, once the Empire was half dead. But it was not for want of trying. Soldiers, whole armies, dug holes for themselves to avoid the picturesque.

High up above the ground was never a natural place for Hungarians whose main geographical reference point was the Great Hungarian Plain. They were armed, for the first month at least, with Napoleonic maps. New villages and roads must have seemed magical to them, too. They were also armed, of course, with a *feldwörterbuch*, literally a 'field word book', that facilitated communication:

'*Wie geht es Ihnen? Gut oder schlecht?*'

'*Hogy van? Jól vagy rosszul?*'

'*Kako je, dobre, zlo?*'

'*Jak se vam vede? Dobře nebo špatně?*'

'How are you?' they would ask in German, Hungarian, Croat, Bohemian and so on. 'Good or bad?'

For the Slovenes, Croats and Serbs, resisting the Italians represented a people's struggle against a foreign invader. For Lieutenant Erwin Rommel, the Isonzo's Mount Matajur was the place to make his name, to earn a 'Blue Max', so that he could become what he became a war later. Mussolini, too, conscripted into and invalided out of the army, would have fought for Italy, for Italian land. Later, he would make propaganda visits to the area, dedicate a charnel house, and build his fascism on the ruins of the Italian army. But what was Uncle Józsi doing up there, a soldier of the K.u.K. Armee? Which 'k' was he fighting for? For kaiser? Or for king? For God? Or for honour? Did he have a big idea about it?

It made no difference to the mountains. Some say that the Italians' only success throughout was Krn. They had specialist mountain troops called Alpini who climbed Krn in the middle of the night and swept away the surprised Hungarian defenders on 16 June 1915. The Italians called it Monte Rosso, 'Red Mountain', in memory of the blood. The victory would be illusory. Illusory victories are the currency of war. They keep them going while the human cost mounts. Already the losses were heavy on both sides. The first four serious battles would take place before Christmas. The guns kept arriving. They had to blow holes in mountains. Death by explosion. Death by limestone shower. Death by rock. The good helmets, the steel ones with ear protection, came only later. By then the snow had arrived, around 20 feet of it. With it came death by avalanche, shells dislodging snow and mass-burying hundreds at a time. Grenades were more inventive, more diverse: canisters, sticks, bowls with wicks. But closer-quarter weapons did just as well in the hand-to-hand fighting during the Second Battle of the Isonzo: trench clubs, maces, daggers, knuckledusters. When the guns were silent, the sound of drilling and hammering filled the air. A hundred field lights for illumination. A branch. A bunk. A trench. A new path cut into rock. Earthworks. Fortifications. Workshops. Brothels. Cemeteries. The military's sense of society.

At some point between December 1915 and spring 1916, Uncle József became a discernible soldier. He attained both rank and medals. In peacetime, a non-commissioned officer would not have been promoted. In war, promotion was attained through bravery. The only photograph of him was taken just after he became a lieutenant, or *oberleutnant* or *főhadnagy*. It's a typical military black-and-white three-quarter profile produced in a photographic studio, with Lieutenant Müller wearing his walking-out dress, an M1915 greenish-grey officers' peaked field cap, stiffer and higher than that of other ranks, and his regimental collar patches with their gold or silver wire stars. On his left breast are his distinctive Austro-Hungarian medals with their triangular ribbons. Given that it's his right profile that is closest to the camera, the medals are modestly blurred. They are more than service or campaign medals yet what he got them for is uncertain. His upper body is commanding, stout as the wooden chair he sits on, squeezed by his brown leather belt. His weasel-black eyes and arched eyebrows, hands curled almost to fists in his lap, give him the impact of a trench club. You wouldn't want Lieutenant Müller leaping at your throat on a moonless night in the mountains. Or on any other night.

Between winter 1915 and spring 1916, Uncle József saw what cavernous holes the 420 mm Howitzer could create. He shot Italians as they charged uphill. He did not go to war to avoid such things. He saw hillsides of corpses. He watched his comrades-in-arms freeze in their little holes, sodden to the bone, blained, chancred, then iced, feet bitten black with frost but de-iced in an instant by the nitroglycerine that exploded their faces and their tunnels. For the rest, it was about the supplies that failed to get high enough. Some would dehydrate

Great-Great-Uncle Józsi, 1915, posing in his lieutenant's uniform while serving in the Austro-Hungarian Army on the Isonzo Front during the First World War.

on the waterless terrain, starve, die while waiting. Uncle Józsi would have seen them, dried out, weather-burned, broken-headed, reaching for a *feldwörterbuch* to cry for idiomatic help.

Lieutenant Müller's face is stone, the colour of a limestone crag in winter. It wasn't necessarily the strong who survived, nor the fortunate. It was the rock-like, those who could out-stare a rock. On the Isonzo front, everyone had a worst battle. Doberdo, Caporetto, Monte San Gabriele: each has a major stakeholder. The Doberdo plateau, some 13 miles north of Trieste, saw one of the bloodiest of battles. Gas was used for the first time on 29 June 1916, killing over 6,000 Italians.

Phosgene. Diphenylchlorarsine. The gas shells were fired by artillery.
Lieutenant Müller was an artillery man. What do these things mean?

My father remembers the Doberdo joke, handed down, one that
Uncle József would have known:

Two soldiers are standing by the Isonzo, urinating. The first urinates
into the river. The second urinates onto the first.

'Doberdo?' the first asks the second.

'No,' the second answers. 'I just can't piss straight.'

Everyone had a worst battle. Lieutenant Müller's was still to come.
Within the following months, he would again be promoted. This
time he would become a captain. He would become a part of the
arcane history of Jewish captains, legendary in Habsburg times yet
constantly battling not only an external enemy but the anti-Semitic
internal one, too, one that prevented their promotion. Fighting for
national, military and personal honour was a way of gaining acceptance. Honour, at least in principle, could not be denied to anyone in
the Austro-Hungarian army on the grounds of nationality or religion.
Around 300,000 Jews served in this army, and Jews had contributed
financially to the war effort.

The 1940 Jewish memorial book to the Jewish soldiers of the First
World War expresses the accompanying view: '*Magyarok vagyunk, és nem
zsidók...*', 'We are Hungarians, not Jews...' By 1940, of course, there
were no Jews in the Hungarian army, their former ranks and deeds
and personal honour having been progressively nullified. Captain
Müller certainly lived long enough to see his rank, his deeds and his
honour nullified. How did he feel about these things? Rock-like, what
did he outstare?

The clues come later, long after, like accidental rocks tumbling onto
the path you happen to tread. The first comes in a place called Telki,
a placid, upscale, residential satellite six miles west of Budapest. It is
here that I meet, after 30 years, my second cousin, Feri, and his family.
He's one of the two sons of my grandmother's younger brother, Jenő.
They always seemed much older, Feri a soft-voiced lawyer with musical
talent, and his brother, András, a concert pianist and piano teacher
in Germany. The musical line can be traced to a distant musician,
Great-Great-Grandfather Sámuel Rehovitz, married to a certain
Borbála. Actually, only a few years separate them from my brother

and me, yet the absence of a generation gives them the gravitas and the distance of older family members.

We're sitting in Feri's study, drinking *szilva pálinka*, plum brandy, surrounded by double-stacked books on literature, politics, history, Judaica. A boxful of fragile documents and photographs is spread on the table. Many relate to his father, who died 20 years ago and was at various times a skilful hockey player, a military tractor driver and a musician who could, like his son, András, play directly from what he heard. I happen to ask Feri if he has ever heard of or knows anything about a certain Uncle Józsi. He replies with a question: 'The painter?'

Uncle Józsi, it seems, painted landscapes. These paintings once hung in Feri's childhood home in the village of Dunaharaszti, where we first met 30 years ago. 'They were pleasing scenes,' Feri remembers, 'panoramas, mountains and so on, but I'm not sure of where exactly.' Uncle Józsi, Lieutenant Müller, with his dark-eyed stare and weasel brows, clearly painted what he observed – possibly the places he visited or, much more likely, the places he was sent. The Gulf of Trieste and Dalmatia and Caporetto. Yet what he observed, what he recorded, was not the violence he surely experienced. The images seem to have been untroubled by military struggle, the places undisturbed by troops and artillery, as if the painter did not think of himself as a soldier. Perhaps he succeeded in willing the noise of war into silent contemplation. Uncle Józsi must have known that the whole terrible business made no difference to the mountains. So he painted the picturesque.

The paintings no longer exist. Feri's father disposed of them as life moved on. A shedding of documents. A shedding of places. A shedding of memories, and the memories of memories. Nullification. Trieste. Dalmatia. Caporetto.

The last of these places, near today's Italian border, was where Lieutenant Müller headed in mid 1917. Caporetto, the Italian name for the Austro-Hungarian Karfreit, now the Slovenian Kobarid, sits on the western bank of the Isonzo. In *A Farewell to Arms*, Hemingway briefly described it as 'a little white town with a campanile in the valley' and 'a fine fountain in the square'. The latter has gone but the defining campanile is still there and Caporetto remains a little white town, little beside the surrounding sharp-edged peaks, and little beneath the hillside charnel house built by Mussolini for the Italian troops who fell near the river. A war later, it would be a sympathetic Italian *tenente*, a Lieutenant Raphael Barbiero, who would fake the papers that allowed Feri's father to 'Catholicize', hiding his racial origins, and thus surviving.

In 1917, the depleted and demoralized Italian soldiers, having taken Caporetto early in the campaign, crumbled. They ran, retreated by all means necessary, leaving behind masses of dead and wounded, 295,000 prisoners, equipment of every dimension, and their national, military and personal honour. Caporetto would become an Italian synonym for disaster. 'It was a Caporetto,' they would say a generation later. This, the twelfth and final Battle of the Isonzo, began on 24 October 1917 with a massive gas attack. At dawn, the First Austro-Hungarian Corps attacked down the valley. With substantial German help, they pushed the Italians back from one river to the next, from the Isonzo to the Piave almost 60 miles away.

Lieutenant Müller led 150 men and a big gun. With his painter's eye and his artillery man's instinct, he could pick targets from a distance and close in on the detail. On the Isonzo, the artillery tactics were new. Generalized bombardments followed by soldiers over trench-tops gave way to information gathered by reconnaissance. Every gun, observation or communication post would be individually targeted. Lower-ranking officers were meant to take the tactical initiative. This is how lieutenants became captains.

Later, much later, long after this war and the next, after a revolution, cities, towns, countries and the rest of the twentieth century have flashed past, on a cool autumn day in London, I mention Uncle Józsi's lost paintings to my father. His voice is thin, distant. But the name has dislodged another little memory-rock, and it tumbles into view. He points somewhere behind him, to a wall or a thing, some object or other associated with this name, a memory of a memory forming, connecting.

I guess straight away what he means with this gesture unaccompanied by words. On a connecting wall, between large paintings that are garish and decorative, is a small, framed, soft-pencilled sketch that I have been aware of all my life. I have also been aware that it was linked to a nameless entity in turn linked to family. The sketch depicts two old men, one seated, eyes downcast in concentration as he hunches over the stringed instrument that he strums with a gnarl-fingered right hand. His companion stands beside him, profiled in a bobble hat, glint-eyed, chin folding around a toothless smile, staring off somewhere behind the player. They are two old men, two old musicians, of Caporetto, Karfreit, Kobarid.

The 'story' of this drawing is the story of 'somewhere behind', a pointing behind, a looking behind, a gesture of time and memory. That is what Uncle Józsi, Captain Müller, did, too. He looked behind the ephemeral to the enduring. He looked past the war to the panorama, and recorded landscape not warscape. He saw the silent mountains just as this drawing, a detailed, lifelike portrait, records the people behind the music. He saw them and he heard them. He was close enough to look behind.

Caporetto, Karfreit, Kobarid was a place where languages came and went, where the front stopped and moved on or else fled for its life, leaving little people behind. To know the little white town is to know its silence. My father says he's always liked the composition of the drawing, the feel of it. He's liked it for 70 years. It was framed in Budapest, and passed hand to hand, living-room wall to living-room wall, nail to nail, its silent music awaiting the name of artist. Uncle Józsi.

So what was Uncle Józsi's worst battle? The answer rushed ahead to Caporetto, from one river to the next, but is no longer obvious. After all, Uncle Józsi lived several decades beyond what should have been his worst battle. He lived to experience the creeping anti-Semitism of the 1920s, the beatings of Jewish students in the streets and the debate as to whether Jews were Hungarian Jews or Jewish Hungarians. He also lived to experience what might have been his worst defeat: the loss of his daughter, Bözsi, her husband and their child, who were deported from the Hungarian town of Miskolc to Auschwitz in 1944.

Unlike Uncle Zolti, Uncle Józsi was, according to my father, 'a razzer large fellow' who lived, in the late 1930s, with his wife, Hermina, at 59 Népszínház Street. In other words, he saw my grandmother as a child, then my father as a child. A second memory surfaces: Uncle Józsi discouraged my eight-year-old father from reading that pioneer of science fiction, Jules Verne. Instead, he encouraged him to read Karl May. *Winnetou*, which would become May's most popular novel, translated into more languages than the Austro-Hungarian Empire could imagine, was first published in 1893. What distinguishes this tome covering the life of a young Apache chief, as told by his white blood-brother Old Shatterhand, is not that May wrote it from experience or research. He didn't. His visits to the America of great mountains and rivers came after his works were written, and he never actually ventured out to the Old West territory of his fiction. Yet what shines through, or at least imposes itself, is May's portrayal of an oppressed and dying people, of friendships based on mutual understanding set against the great forces of racism and lust for power: 'If all Indians were as Winnetou was,' remarks one character, 'if all palefaces followed the example of Old Shatterhand, the Indian and the white people would live side by side like brothers, love, and help each other, and find room enough on this earth for all their children.' The panorama of Uncle Józsi's life comes into view: he was a romantic and an ideal-ist, someone who pictured the future. He was also someone who met great mountains and rivers.

By mid November 1917, having chased the Italians deep into Italy from the Isonzo to the Piave, Captain Müller was as exhausted as the rest of the army. By now, they were too stretched, too thin, too eroded by nature. It was the high point of the Austro-Hungarian tide, the final froth of white water in the Isonzo campaign, after which began the great recession, the great shrinking as an empire was sucked back in on itself. The British and French would soon arrive to bolster the Italians but, really, everyone just wanted to go home.

'*Andiamo alla casa!*' said the Italians.

'*Menjünk haza!*' said the Hungarians.

'*Dovolit us běh domov!*' said the Czechs.

'*Gehen wir nach Hause!*' said the Austrians and the Germans.

'*Gremo Domov!*' the Slovenians would have said, but they were already at home.

Uncle Józsi, finally relieved of duty, would also have headed home to Budapest. But of course he didn't. He went, at the behest of Pay

Sergeant Móric, to Vienna, to the home of rubber trouser hooks, now the capital of disintegration. What he found there, as he stepped off the crowded train at the Westbahnhof, would have shocked even a decorated captain.

'There was little food, everyone lacked iron, and there was general weakness.' That is what my grandmother remembered, and what she wrote half a life later. In truth, there were huge grain shortages, meatless days imposed by law, inflation, a thriving black market, price riots in the previous year, strikes to come, simmering civil unrest. Before the war, the Austro-Hungarian Empire had been self-sufficient in food. Only three years later, in 1917, the Empire could no longer feed itself. And by now the population had met a few of the war's victims in the form of maimed soldiers reduced to begging on the streets or selling flowers.

Captain Müller walked out of the station in civvies. He was Uncle Józsi once more. He walked down Mariahilferstrasse, which runs alongside the station then all the way down the gentle slope to the Burggarten, the famous landscaped garden with its famous monuments and famous butterfly house. Number 51 is not that far down. It's a grand five-storey commercial block, two reliefs of smiling faces overlooking its ground floor, which is now occupied by retail outlets reflecting myriad similar glassy shops, gleaming boutiques and gaudy clothing stores that dominate the street. Back then, the whole building was an *Industrie-Hof*, a commercial court, that title still inscribed on the building's facade. Uncle Józsi would have gone through the interconnecting workshops that opened onto internal courtyards.

The Bruckner and Rehovitz Modelhaus, a mixture of workshops and retail, had been started by my Great-Great-Grandfather Adolf Bruckner, Uncle Józsi's brother-in-law. There were a few employees, including a tailor, a cutter and a saleswoman, producing and selling blouses, dressing gowns and *konfekció*, confection, which included everything from brassieres and knickers to gloves and scarves. Adolf had died that year, aged 78, in Kassa, now Košice in Slovakia, and his body had been taken back to Budapest for burial. In the absence of the men – Adolf and his son-in-law Móric – it was Katalin who ran the business and the family. Broad and capable, with a generous face, her hair waved by iron tongs and parted in the middle just like her mother Netti's, and just like her daughter's would be one day, she was a skilled seamstress and tailor. A fragment of her output survives in the form of a silk memorial sash embroidered with intricate pictorial clues to the words: 'Be good and forget me not.'

Vienna had been hot through to September but illness, such as the intestinal infections reported by Sigmund Freud in one of his letters, was rife. Winter was closing in, food was in short supply and Katalin, a diabetic, couldn't cope on her own with all this and two children. Lili, eleven, and her eight-year-old brother, Jenő, Feri's father, didn't have enough to eat. At least they could still enjoy the space of the interconnecting workshops, opening onto internal courtyards, that allowed them to race their bicycles after one another.

Uncle Józsi, now 43, would have heard news of Móric and his trousers, perhaps of Zolti and his finger, too, and he would have gained a clear sense of the way things were heading. He looked behind the front and saw how his distant war was unravelling, how the things he thought he'd fought for day by day were losing their value. Vienna in 1917 was not a place for idling. Within days, a decision was made. Uncle Józsi and Lili would take the Budapest train. They would head to the station, the little girl's hand clasped by the artillery captain's.

Deployment takes place away from home; so does escape. The great locomotive would have pulled a crowded train, the sediment of so many families shifting with fortune and circumstance. Once on board, the little girl was more excited than frightened. Maybe she spoke of bicycling through the workshops, and of the fire that engulfed blouses, gowns and *konfekció* before being put out. She would definitely have recounted, as she was to recount many times in her life, the time she was taken to the Burggarten, and old Emperor Franz Josef was there, too. Ruddy-faced with cotton-wool whiskers, he had no doubt been taken for an airing before his eventual death at the Schönbrunn Palace in Vienna in 1916. That was when Lili's great moment happened, the moment when, on a winding path, perhaps near where his statue now stands, the Emperor kissed her. 'I was kissed by Franz Josef,' she would say, or 'Franz Josef kissed me,' and she would have told the story to Uncle Józsi.

And Uncle Józsi, blinking away death-bitten places, would have told her of high peaks and green rivers and picturesque little towns and the music of the mountains. And all the while, as the train went east and German gave way to Hungarian, Uncle Józsi would have felt the captain in him receding. All the while, without yet fully knowing it, he headed towards his worst battle, the one he could not fight, the 20-year, day-by-day, hour-by-hour, battle against extinction, against nullification.

He could only sense that fighting for honour, for country, for acceptance, was no longer a possibility. There was only a fight for family. Several of them – Adolf and Netti, Móric and Katalin, Józsi and Hermina – would eventually be reunited in the now dusty, overgrown, half-sunken graves of a Budapest cemetery.

Then they were quiet, the little girl who'd been kissed by an emperor and the uncle who'd saved her. They no longer looked back or pointed behind. They stared out of the train window in their own ways, at their own dreams. They sped towards their futures, towards a new life in a new place.

The Anatomy of a
Massacre

H E KNOWS OF A MASSACRE never told. He remembers the smell of blood. He remembers the darkness of a hiding place. He dreamed only recently of both the smell and the darkness of a certain event on a certain night. He wrote plenty of lines about plenty of things but never a line about this. The history books, too, however detailed, however thorough, never mention it.

The memories are muddied, sunken into the earth like a grave in a Budapest cemetery. Or they are heavily dusted, unopened and forgotten like a diary in the archive of the Budapest ambulance service. Yet the events can only be pieced together from these memories, and from the documents in front of me: a handwritten paragraph from my grandmother who died in 1985; a broken Israelite prayer book for women; a strange passport. Why disturb them? Why not leave them be?

Possibly because there are certain memories, like certain objects, that come to stand for a life. The memory, for example, of a disappearance. Nándor. Or the memory of an arrival. Uncle Józsi. There are other memories that stand for part of a life, like a childhood, or for part of a childhood, like a day. This memory, of blood, of darkness, stands for a day in the childhood of my father.

Some of my father's childhood memories are as follows:

> Running along the 'gang', the corridor outside the flats on every floor of the block, while avoiding the glass jars of pickles and preserves fermenting in sunlight;
>
> playing football against a neighbourhood wall with a kid called Sándor Kocsis who would one day head goals for Hungary against England;
>
> picking up discarded siphons outside the soda factory for a special use;
>
> racing his best friend, Tomi, through the square, a snap catching them mid-step;
>
> waving goodbye, Tomi and him, to their fathers at the railway station;
>
> punching holes in family photographs for amusement;
>
> having a family servant, a country girl called Rebus;
>
> being the only one made to wear long woollen socks to a children's party.

And then there is the smell of blood in the courtyard, the darkness of a cellar in which he and his best friend, Tomi, hid.

Memories have weight. Some are heavier than others. Their gravity pulls lighter things towards them. Their gravity even bends light. We are made to see things their way.

In 1978, my father returned to the courtyard where, over 30 years before, the blood had been, to where the smell had been. I was there, too, as old as he was 30 years before. I remember a long, wide street, its pavement shadowed by its tall, silhouetted apartment blocks, the height of the front doors. I remember my father talking to a woman. I remember my brother was there, too, and he remembers a building. We were in Budapest to visit family, but the point of this trip to visit someone in a building on a hot day was opaque. She was not family. Perhaps that is why the memory of it, mine and my brother's, is also opaque. There was a woman in a building, that's all, and neither obviously belonged to a holiday.

István Bokor, my father, aged seven in 1937, on the 'gang' outside the top floor flat, 59 Népszínház Street. The courtyard below would be the site of a massacre.

It wasn't that we looked away. It was the light, that day, bending around something heavy.

I now know the name of the woman and, 30 years later, as old as my father was when he returned to the building, I have returned. I'm standing outside the street door, separated from the courtyard where the blood was, where its smell was, near where the hiding place was. The woman's name was Mrs Farkas. She was the widow of Rezső Farkas, who was the concierge of 59 Népszínház Street. Mr and Mrs Farkas lived, as did all concierges, on the ground floor near the stairwell.

The event that led to a smell of blood, which led to a memory of a smell, which led a father who was a boy to return, which led a son who remembered his father's memory to return, occurred over 60 years ago. It occurred after certain ghosts had been and gone. Uncle József had lived here in the late 1930s, and Nándor had been taken from here in 1942. The event that brings me to 59 Népszínház Street occurred two years later, on a particular day in October 1944. Why disturb it? Why not leave it be?

Possibly because it has never been told. In the hot summer after the war was over, when my father looked out over the broken-bridged Danube, he looked forwards, upriver. Like many of his generation he did not look back. What would looking back have been good for? Like many of his generation, he did not think back, either. Many of his generation, despite knowing each other a long time, never discussed what happened to them and their families during the war. These were shared gestures, a collective gesture of forgetting. The rubble of a rubbled city, through which the Germans and Russians had passed, was slowly cleared, mostly cleared. Along with it, the stories of lives were swept away. Many citizens were involved in clearing up after the war was over. They took brooms and swept up their own memories. Some claim to remember nothing, nothing at all.

Should this story be told simply because it has never been told? It's too late because I have a memory of a woman in a building. I have a memory of my father's memory of a smell. The story has already begun. It began without me. By the time I come to write it, I know more than anyone else about it, about what happened. More and not enough. My father's memories occur randomly in my head.

I'm standing outside the street door. Behind me, the wheels of the number 28 tram jog the pavement, drowning out sounds of the past and of the present as they roll towards their terminus, the Kozma Street cemetery. There's nothing to be done except to push open the door.

Lili steps into the dark hallway for the first time. She's carrying her new-born baby, István. Behind her is Nándor. He's carrying suit-cases. It's early 1930 – he's 27 and she's 24 – and they're moving in along the tiled hallway, climbing the dank and stained staircase with its wrought-iron handrail, its pocked and powdery walls, its wooden spittoons layered with sawdust in the corner at each turn of the staircase. Theirs is a three-roomed corner flat on the top floor. It has a small balcony. Flat 4 is not of the less desirable *udvari* type whose windows look inwards to the courtyard. Its windows are at the apex of the triangular building and look out onto the bottom end of the street, to where it becomes Teleki Square.

Number 59 was meant to be grand. The last building before you reach the square was constructed to order in 1898 in an era of archi-tectural pretension, and was meant for the upper classes, for nobility. It dominates a corner near the bottom end of the wide and busy street. By 1930 its tiled roof and halls, stucco mouldings and fancy facade are dilapidated ironies. Népszínház Street, with its tram terminus at the top end, its prostitutes in subtle gradations of sidestreets, from the quality brothel at 12 Víg Street known as 'the dozen' to the well-heeled streetwalkers of Conti Street and on to the budget ones of Kender Street, is part of a poorer district, the eighth *kerület* on the east side of Pest. Its down-at-heel population comprises many Jews and Gypsies. There are small prayer houses dotted around and a cheap cinema called Eldorado.

The open space of Teleki Square has become a shambling, perpetual market of shanty stalls, home to beggars and peddlers, rats, money-lenders and close-knit merchants, some with their own Yiddish, others with the street slang of Budapest. They come with old clothes, with a goose or a chicken, with crates of vegetables from the countryside, with boxes of trinkets, junk, coat buttons and heirlooms to pawn and to barter. It's a place where István will see a Gypsy woman giving birth while leaning against a lamp post, her baby conjured from beneath a voluminous skirt.

Today, drunks keep pigeons company on patchy grass. The genealogy is clear. There are pigeons with ancestral faces. There is something in the air that has held the place back, kept it where it was like a perfectly remembered moment. Lili said she had the happiest marriage of all her friends, a long 16 years before her husband was taken. They argued about his left-wing views, his activities, his socializing at the Union of Ironworkers, his attitude to political developments. István overheard these arguments. He wasn't supposed to. '*Zsindely van a háztetőn*,' Lili would say. 'There's a tile on the roof,' meaning 'be quiet, someone is listening,' someone like a child. But these arguments over politics were the only ones they had. The rest of the time, as if it were a long and perfectly remembered moment, they were happy.

Isn't that the way of it, the way of such stories? These stories often say, 'they were happy until…' or 'their happiness came to an end when…' as if the happiness and the suddenness were absolute, as if an out-of-the-blue and very sudden suddenness changed everything. But pick up some history book or other and the story is not quite as sudden. Instead, it is often written that 'the storm clouds were gathering…' or that people began to 'sense something in the air…' People were happy but, all the while, storm clouds were gathering. Can storm clouds gather suddenly? How sudden is sudden? Who knows what storm clouds really are?

As they climb the stairs for the first time, do they know, Lili and Nándor? Whether they suspect the future or not, whether they sense something in the air or not, they never have a second child. Maybe it was a lack of money. Or the lack of prospects in the eighth *kerület*. Or the fact that it had been a difficult first birth. 'I was tearing the sheets,' Lili once told my mother a lifetime later. So maybe it was this that put her off. Or maybe she really did notice a storm cloud.

In the early 1930s, the whole *mishpocheh*, the whole clan, gathers in the countryside in Székesfehérvár, where Nándor's mother, Mária, and numerous siblings come from. The men are in jackets and shirts, the shirts open-necked and folded over the jackets' collars. The women are in hats and short-sleeved blouses. They hold children. As the day ages, the men are in shirts, talking over newspapers, then in deckchairs, dozing, while the women, hatless, lie in the shade of a tree. Among them is one much older woman, Great-Great-Grandmother Rozália, around 90 years old, face set and wrinkled like dry *shtetl* mud. When the sun begins to sink, they all sit around a big wooden outdoor table to eat and drink, a family at home in their land.

By the end of the decade, István expends considerable energy drilling holes in family photographs. Ventilated in this way, another great-great-grandmother, Netti, has survived a long time, air passing through her heavy layered dress to her angular bones beneath. A single child looks through a hole in a photograph and sees the past of a family, where it has come from. Then he flips the photograph and looks through the hole again to see where it is going. He senses the branches of the tree around him.

Some late-summer afternoons, Lili takes her son on a short walk from Népszínház Street to Mária Terézia Square, a shaded interruption on busy Baross Street. She dreams of moving up to Baross Street, the classier central thoroughfare of the eighth *kerület*. But the reason for Lili taking these walks is not so much to dream but to enrol her son at a fashionable *Svéd torna*, a Swedish gym class that takes place in an elementary school. You never know who you might meet, who might help you to get from Népszínház Street to Baross Street. The children are equal in their white gym outfits, although a small difference can make all the difference. One gymnast, a four-year-old girl, wears a distinctive white hairband. Every time Lili takes her son, this same girl stands at the front because of course she's the best in the class. Her name is Ági. One day, István will marry her.

Then it's time for school. István Bokor, as he was then – or more accurately, since Hungarian family names come first, Bokor István – stands, aged seven and three quarters, on the *gang* outside flat 4. He's in uniform, an immaculate pale grey wool jacket with embroidered lapels, arms rigid by his sides just like he's been told, shorts, white socks and lace-up boots. The boots, made by a local cobbler, were originally ski boots with metal tips and edges that are 'good for kicking doors'. István's black hair has been slicked by his mother's saliva-moistened hand, a hand that will one day slick her grandchildren's hair, too. He might be smiling at the camera but there is impishness and chutzpah in his face.

The smoke from his father's cigarettes, their blend of two types of Turkish tobacco, fills the flat, especially on card nights. Bridge is the game that István watches the men play, one that he will grow up to play, while his mother stands behind them, ever the *kibbitzer*, a commentator, an 'adviser' who provides a commentary on their hands. The only time István gets a hiding is when he disturbs the game, demanding cake. At this age, he resembles one of the kids from Ferenc Molnár's much loved novel *The Paul Street Boys*, the 1906 Budapest-set story of a group of boys who have to fight for their territory, their *grund*. István and his friends go past the soda factory on the way to school. They collect discarded siphons or barter cigarettes for them with the workers. The siphons have inner glass tubes that they can repurpose as deadly blowpipes. But who are their enemies?

István goes to the Madách Imre school in nearby Barcsay Street, running up the steep steps to the entrance with 800 other kids, each a 'Paul Street boy' to one degree or another. They play football with a ball of compacted paper bound by string. They reenact scenes from *The Mark of Zorro*, the masked champion of the people. They barter cigarettes. They aim their blowpipes. But in 1939 a change takes place. The world is reorganized. The pupils are divided into Jewish and non-Jewish classes, 'A' and 'B' classes. Some don't really know they are Jews until they are told. Others don't know they're not for the same reason. The new world contains a 'B' class with 40 Jews. In his class, Bokor leads the alphabet, followed by Bolgár, Fenyvesi, Freund, Gadó, Gara, Gerlei, Grósz, Grünfeld, Gyenes, Hedvig, Heksch, Herzog, Hirsch, Ivanovszki, Kelemen, Kelen, Kertész, Klein, Klein W, Kovács, Lazarovics, Lóránt, Mandl, Pártos, Reichman, Reiner, Schönfeld, Schwartz F., Schwartz G., Seregi, Solt, Steiner, Strausz, Szegő, Taubner, Tehel, Tormási, Wárman, Winternitz.

Some of the school's teachers try to resist this change. The headmaster even writes to the government in late 1940. His long letter argues against segregation for the most complex and contorted of reasons: because at this particular school there are trainee teachers taking classes, and if they see that Jewish classes are better than non-Jewish classes, it would have a negative effect on the trainees. Some teachers, such as the one who accompanies the 'B' class on a trip up to Kisinóc in the mountains north of Budapest, see no difference between 'A' and 'B' classes or between 'A' and 'B' mountains. Lower down, things are less abstract. A new verb has entered the schoolboy lexicon: *zsidózni*, 'to Jew'. It's a verb whose meaning is free-range, beginning with an abusive name shouted in a corridor, an act of singling out in a classroom, before roaming further afield, before becoming a physical education teacher with a discriminatory length of rope. The Jewish boys have to do a form of community service while the non-Jewish ones go into the Levente. Taking its name from the old Hungarian word for 'knight', the Levente is a paramilitary youth organization.

All the while, Farkas, the concierge, maintains 59 Népszínház Street. He exchanges pleasantries, coordinates the cycles of carpet-beating in the courtyard, fixes little problems, takes care of Mrs Farkas and the children, his flat constantly exuding an odour of cabbage, onions, paprika. But the job of block concierge is one that hides a potentially limitless range of tasks, including the locking of the gate at 10 p.m. People coming in after that have to ring the bell, and either the concierge or his wife has to get out of bed to open up. A tip is in order. Duties and favours grow organically, depending on the character of the concierge and the character of the tenants. Farkas is also the '*hat. eng. vil.*' – the abbreviation for 'officially authorized electrician' that is signed on the door of his flat. It gives him power over light and dark.

Bokor sees his best friend, Fenyvesi, all the time. Their fathers, Nándor and Imre, are already ghosts, away on the first round of forced labour, then back, then gone, gone for good. Their mothers, Lili – rounder, shorter, darker – and Panci – blonder, taller, slimmer – are best friends, Panci living nearby, on the more desirable Baross Street. They are single children with single mothers, all bound together by the disappearance of the men. Maybe both mothers had difficult births, tearing at the sheets.

Aged 13, the boys become 'sons of the commandment'. This is not because their mothers are religious. A bar mitzvah is just the thing to do. Through this special ceremony, on 18 January 1943, István comes of age. He becomes a man. 'Mine vuz a cheap vun,' my father grins in another century, referring to his last religious act. Even the memory of it, bubbling to the surface for the first time in the present, is surprising and strange in a godless family. When did religion leave the family? Or when did the family leave religion?

And when did István really leave the country of his childhood to become an adult?

These are merely everyday questions, as ordinary as the everyday questions that creep into the curriculum. By 1943, two to three times a week at noon on the first-floor mezzanine, with the boys grouped on the steps and in the mouths of corridors, a teacher gives a short talk about the Hungarian nation, its former lands, the lands recently reclaimed with Germany's help, the territory it should have and should have had; the ancient gripes of the Hungarian nation. These 'everyday questions' are developed in a class that is distinctly different from the others: it's fascist propaganda.

The boys dream of slipping out of school to play ping-pong. Back at home, István spies on the washerwoman who lives and works in the attic. He plays with the red-haired Sperber brothers from two floors below. He notices one of his uncles, László, going regularly into the flat next door, and later learns he's having 'an affair' with a female neighbour. István also visits the Dávid family across the *gang*. They have a loom in their flat and use it to make rugs and carpets. He and Lili learn to operate it. What Lili produces, she sells. It's the only income there is.

Around this time, on one gloomy Sunday or other, Rebus commits suicide. Gloomy Sundays are all the rage, inspired by the haunting 1933 Hungarian song of that name, '*Szomorú vasárnap*', which already has a reputation as the suicide anthem. Rebus, like many country girls, had come to Budapest to look for work and to escape poverty. Like many, she'd found a place with a Jewish family who had no money to pay wages but offered food and a bed in exchange for domestic help. There are no pictures of Rebus, no sense of what she was like, except that she was like other country girls, stick-thin, hard-knuckled and hard-working. There is one other fact. When she died, she smelled of gas, the oven gas that killed her, slowly, eventually, in the draughty kitchen of 59 Népszínház Street. The cause of her gloom was most likely her accidental pregnancy, with the most likely father being a policeman. Maybe on Rebus's afternoon off they went to the Eldorado cinema on Népszínház Street, where a box with its own door was the cheapest way for amorous couples to get intimate and a bell would warn them that the lights were about to come on. Then they had a *szilva*

Two boys, two destinies: my father (left) and my cousins' father, Tomi,
in Budapest, 1940. They would marry two sisters.

pálinka. Or two. And then it was too late. She feared the unavoidable gossip. One perceived shame compounds another. A difficult birth. A difficult death. Everyday questions.

István still goes to school. His name leads the alphabet, and his academic results aren't far behind. By now, he has grown out of deadly blowpipes and punching holes in pictures. Instead, on Fridays, he passes by the synagogue in Nagyfuvaros Street with its concealed entrance, not out of religious fervour but to spy on the girls. He also develops a keen interest in football, playing for a youth team but mostly in the street.

Then, one other Sunday, some of the boys are at the big game between Elektromos and Vasas, the electrical and iron workers. The former is a team of fascist character whose opponents are often helpfully depleted by arrests; the latter has its roots in the left-wing Union of Ironworkers, headquartered near Népszínház Street, where István's father regularly attended meetings. The Sunday is 19 March 1944. As the game progresses, with the boys cheering the red and blue players of Vasas, word goes around the crowd that something major has happened in the world outside the stadium: the Germans have invaded.

The 14-year-olds know little of the Hungarian leader, Admiral Miklós Horthy, except perhaps from the picture postcards sent by their fathers on forced labour. Horthy isn't even in Hungary. He's at Schloss Klessheim, near Salzburg in Austria, having been 'invited' by Hitler because of his overtures to the Allies about getting Hungary out of the war. The springtime invasion, with its springtime name, Operation Margarethe, takes place in his absence. There's no mistaking the seasonal storm cloud.

It brings with it SS Lieutenant Colonel Adolf Eichmann, who installs himself close to the clouds up at the top of a winding, pitted road called Sváb Hill. One of the hills of Buda, Sváb Hill is home to a discreet group of tree-shrouded pensions, its cool air making it an attractive summer retreat from the heat of Pest across the river. The Majestic and Little Majestic become Eichmann's headquarters but he also takes over other pensions, including the Mirabelle on Karthauzi Street, one of a pair of hotels that once belonged to a woman called Ibolya. Ibolya was a cousin of my maternal grandmother. From leafy Sváb Hill, from a place where my mother went to play ping-pong a couple of years before, Eichmann's 200-strong Sonderkommando can direct a nation of Hungarian officials, police, gendarmes and clerks below.

From early April, these officials begin to record Jews, a precursor to the so-called *összeköltöztetés*, the 'moving together' of people behind designated front doors. Yellow star houses, 2,600 of them, become homes for 170,000 yellow star people, each house marked with a canary yellow star of precise dimensions, 30cm on a black background of 51cm x 36cm, to be kept in a clean condition. From early April, each Jew is similarly identified with a personal star of 10cm x 10cm to be sewn on the left breast of all outer garments. The skills of a few generations of tailors and ladies outfitters are put to new use.

Three weeks after the invasion, school is over. As the members of the blowpipe gang go home, their enemies are materializing every-where. On Népszínház Street there are several designated yellow star houses. One of them is number 59. The familiarity of the street is erased, its people divided unevenly. Lili struggles with the unfamiliar. She finds it difficult to get used to things generally. She doesn't need to imagine things to fear them. She simply needs to look through the window. Now, like everyone, she fears stepping outside. The shops she knows proclaim that 'Jews are not served here'. Some display the *turul*, the mythological bird that guided ancient tribes to the land of Hungary. The entrances to certain flats state that 'no Jews live here.' When she's not looking out of the third-floor window into the sky above Teleki Square and imagining the worst about her husband, Lili fears for her son. She hears stories from the streets more fright-ening than clouds.

From one day to the next in June, the population of number 59 triples, quadruples. Where there lived 70–80, there are now 200–300. There is a constant scuffing and shuffling and grating and scraping up the dirty steps, the sound echoing around the *gang* on each floor. People bringing their belongings. People with their *batyu*, their bundles. People with their salvaged wealth – a ring concealed in a mouth, a bracelet in an undergarment – heirlooms travelling through time.

One room is allowed per family. Flat 4 now has 11 people, including Lili's parents, Móric with his walking stick to chase cats, and Katalin who, with her diabetes and swollen legs, has to be carried up to the top floor by Móric and his grandson on a specially adapted wooden chair. It also includes the Pogány family, friends of Lili's, and one or two ghosts from the neighbourhood. These have all been moved out of their homes by Hungarian officials to make way for non-Jewish families whose own homes have been bomb-damaged.

Since early April the bombs have been falling. The first bombs are American, dropped in daylight. Then come British bombs, dropped at night. The bombing has an effect on policy, on whether Jews should be ghettoized or not and whether this might adversely influence Allied bombing patterns. In June, the decision is taken to leave the yellow star houses spread across town to avoid giving the bombers easier non-Jewish targets.

Later that month, on the 24th, Panci and her son Tomi move in. Panci's sister and her children, who lived in Novi Sad, were deported as early as 1942. The verb Panci uses, and records in her flaking prayer book, is one rarely heard or written: *vagonírozták*, 'they were wagonized'. She tells Lili, but neither has any idea where the wagons were going, just as they have no idea of their husbands' fates. They cannot look behind them in case they see all that has been left there.

The scores of newcomers are allowed to bring what they can carry, their personal baggage and whatever furniture fits. Farkas, the concierge and officially authorized electrician at the hub of life in the block, is suddenly out of his depth on the ground floor. He's overshadowed by someone else higher up.

One of the few other non-Jews left in the block is a tall and gaunt man named Molnár. He lives on the third floor, two doors away from Lili's flat. Until now, he has barely been noticeable except for the death of his son a couple of years before. It sticks in István's mind because the cause of death is difficult to forget: a twisted bowel. It makes an impression on everyone. But it is not the tragedy of his son's death, nor his height, nor his gaunt demeanour, that is Molnár's defining characteristic.

In this new atmosphere, with Jews having to live in yellow star houses, Molnár volunteers as, and is appointed, the officially author- ized *házparancsnok*, 'house commander'. Every such house has one. Number 59's is a keen if opportunistic sympathizer of the Hungarian fascist Arrow Cross – Nyilas – party. Formed in 1939 from a range of ultra-right 'Hungarist' groups, the party is on the up, and so is Molnár. He doesn't wear the green party uniform or barbed cross armband, but he dresses for the part, donning his old Hungarian army uniform, complete with holster and service pistol. An opportunity presents itself, an opportunity to exert power over the 'B' class, and Molnár transforms into or emerges as or simply becomes something other than he was. Whatever the verb, his new position defines his actions.

As house commander, his main duty is to 'supervise' the resident Jews and to inform them of new regulations. Given that the young men are mostly gone, taken on forced labour, the remaining residents are old men and mothers and children, whose names are listed on the locked gate, whose movements are controlled by specified hours.

One of Molnár's other duties, which he carries out with religious zeal, is to bang the length of iron rail that now hangs in the courtyard to warn of the bombing raids. The sound echoes around the stone walls before funnelling up towards the sky. In the blackout, everyone grabs their panicky little bags or prepared parcels and descends to the cellar, its steps cut into one corner of the courtyard, Katalin carried down on her chair, Móric with his stick, packed in among the coal sacks and wood piles and crates.

The bombs might be aimed at Nazis and fascists, at the weapons plant in Csepel or the main Keleti railway station, but they fall blindly, and especially heavily, on the eighth *kerület*, the explosions too frequent to remember. Some say that the bombing is a warning to the Germans about making the Jews wear yellow stars. Others read the leaflets distributed on the streets which warn that every dead Christian will be avenged by the killing of 100 Jews.

The banging of the iron rail might as well be a general warning. István can't go out on his own. Lili has to venture out for food despite the many dangers. There are stories of Jews being thrown off moving trams or being arrested or simply disappearing from the street. The help of a non-Jew is essential. But such people are rare. The non-Jewish concierge and his wife find ways of passing on potatoes or peas or cabbage or bread or flour or butter. The cucumbers fermenting on the *gang* diminish to rations, to single bites at a time.

Around the armed and uniformed Molnár, people tread carefully. He tells them to watch their step. Lili and István see more of him than most as he stands on the *gang* outside his door looking down at the rows of windows to the courtyard, to Farkas's flat. If Farkas has power over light and dark, Molnár has power over him. If anyone sees what's coming, Molnár does. But nobody at number 59 has any real idea about what's going on in the countryside, from the middle of May and into June, in places like Székesfehérvár, to people like István's grandmother Mária.

In early July, someone arrives in the capital who knows more about what is facing Budapest's Jews than they know themselves. Raoul Wallenberg, the Swedish diplomat who would disappear into Russian hands after the war and whose whereabouts and likely death would inspire endless speculation, comes to Budapest with only one purpose: to save as many Jews as possible by placing them under the protection of the Swedish state. There are others, too, working through the Vatican or the Red Cross. Everyone soon knows what is happening, that new documents, the right documents, could ensure survival. One of Nándor's four brothers, László, queues for hours outside 29 Vadász Street, known as the 'glasshouse' because of its facade and former purpose, where the Swiss legation is doing similar work to Wallenberg.

That name, Wallenberg, I first heard as a child. It was only half heard, muttered by my grandmother, but I liked the sound of the syllables, and the way she pronounced it with a 'V', Vallenberg, and the way she rolled the 'r'. It was like a codeword, a shibboleth, as if she were momentarily closer to an otherwise distant faith.

On Tuesday 10 October, Panci shows Lili a type of passport, a hard-backed booklet, black, with a gold-encircled red cross, bearing three words in three languages, Swedish, Hungarian and German: '*SKYDDSBREV*'; '*OLTALOMLEVÉL*'; '*SCHUTZBRIEF*'.

It's one of the documents given out by the Swedish Red Cross to as many Jews as possible, providing the protection of the Swedish state. Among Hungarian Jews, Yiddish speakers, it is referred to by its German name. Panci's *Schutzbrief* is valid from 10 October 1944 to 10 January 1945, made out to her mother, Berta, also living at number 59, with Panci and her father, Aladár, named on it. The feel of this document in Lili's hands, its impressive gold and red and black, makes her all the more anxious. To be without one. To lack one. To fail to save yourself. To fail to save your son. A document that saves also divides.

Lili stands by the window, as she stood so often later in life, looking out at the things she does not know and cannot imagine, at the politics she does not understand. Her home is a prison. She fears simply what she sees. And what she hears, too, such as a catchy Arrow Cross ditty that her son will remember all his life, all the way to a spring afternoon in north London:

> *Egy rabbi,*
> *Két rabbi,*
> *Megdöglött a főrabbi!*
> *Bátorság!*
> *Éljen Szálasi!*
> *Éljen a Szálasi!*
> *Meg a Hitler!*
> *Innen a zsidóknak*
> *Pusztulni kel!*

> One rabbi,
> Two rabbis,
> Dropped dead, he did, the chief rabbi!
> Courage!
> Long live Szálasi! [The Arrow Cross leader]
> Long live Szálasi!
> And Hitler!
> From here the Jews
> Must be eradicated!

The following Sunday, the 15th, is more than gloomy. It's when everyone's worst fear is realized. At noon the Hungarian head of state, Horthy, announces that he has requested a ceasefire from the Soviet army, but his attempt fails. Around 9.30 that evening, a proclamation of the Arrow Cross party is broadcast. Ferenc Szálasi, the party leader, is now effectively *nemzetvezető*, 'leader of the nation', Hungary's own Führer.

The name of the Arrow Cross newspaper is *Harc*, 'Combat', and the party's enemies in this combat aren't difficult to find in their starred clothes and starred houses. Already that evening there were incidents, shootings, Arrow Cross gangs on the prowl, suicides. Months before, there had been older Jews who had committed suicide rather than leaving their homes. Now a new spate of suicides begins: self-poisonings, hangings and the desperate attempts of those who jump from first-floor balconies.

Molnár only needs to look out of his window to see his enemies, not the street window because Jews are few and far between on the street but around the *gang*, down the stairs, to the home that is their overcrowded prison. He has had an opportunity to do something about his cohabitants once already. Shortly after the German invasion, there were rewards offered for denouncing Jews. The national response had been tens of thousands of denunciations. But there is nothing to suggest that Molnár took advantage of this. He waited. He has waited.

On 15 October, like the rest of Hungary, he hears the broadcasts. The deportation of Budapest Jews had been stopped at the end of June; the condition of Jews had improved in the summer; in September the curfew had been lifted. In mid October, deportation is in the cold air again. It's in the clouds. But for Molnár, Sunday evening is not so gloomy. His uniform is off. His feet are up. His service pistol is around, in a drawer or hanging in its holster or on the table in front of him. It's most likely a Frommer Stop, a remnant of a previous era but still in use by the army and police to the end of the war. A gun takes a certain maintenance. A certain amount of time must be spent on it to keep it in working order. When was the last time he oiled it? When was the last time he used it? He has waited years to put on his army uniform again, and he's been waiting years to use his gun.

On the afternoon of the 16th the doors of all yellow star houses are closed by police order. Nobody is allowed to enter or to leave, not even doctors. The Arrow Cross have plans for the eighth *kerület*. A trial deportation – or a prelude to them – is scheduled for Tuesday, the 17th. At some time, late at night on the 16th or in the early hours of the 17th, under cover of dark and the general blackout, Molnár loads his pistol, opens the window, not the internal window looking onto the *gang* but the street window, and he fires a shot.

Where the bullet goes nobody knows for sure. According to one resident, the shot kills someone. Péter Kutas had just turned seven on

15 October. His family had moved in two months earlier and were living in an aunt's flat. Molnár, according to him, shoots and kills an Arrow Cross man deliberately. But it's more likely that Molnár fires into the sky or over the rooftops or towards the street. That's what István is later told. Either way, Molnár's objective is the same: to attract the Arrow Cross to the building by reporting that a Jew was responsible for firing. Killing an Arrow Cross man is much the riskier option, and Molnár does not need to go that far. He simply needs a gunshot, the sound of a gunshot from a certain quarter on a night when the whole city is simmering and there are shots from other quarters. Even a general denunciation or a hint about an armed Jew or a suggestion that a Jew had fired would easily have been enough.

Late on the 16th or in the early hours of the 17th, Panci and Lili take their sons down. In the October darkness they descend three floors, turn right out of the patterned-tile stairwell, cross the puddled courtyard and, with the concierge's help, sneak the two boys down the low steps in the corner of the courtyard. The cellar extends beneath the flats opposite Farkas's flat. It is divided into padlocked sections with planks of wood, each section belonging to a flat and accessible along a narrow corridor. According to Panci's note in her prayer book, the two boys are hidden in the cellar, in one of its sections, from the 16th. According to Lili, Farkas helps to hide them there. Also according to her, Molnár knows of this. In fact, he allows it. He allows it because, in Lili's words, 'We were his acceptable and chosen Jews.' '*Mi voltunk a kiválasztott és megkülönbőztetett zsidai.*'

Of course, she writes these words afterwards, later, beyond the event, once it's all over. But it means that late on the 16th or early on the 17th, Molnár makes it known to some people, his certain Jews, his chosen Jews who live on the same floor, with whom he must have exchanged a thousand greetings and benign pleasantries before the day he donned his uniform, that something is about to happen. He must also have told Farkas. In other words, on this October night, the concierge and his wife and the two mothers are forced to make a decision. They can hide certain people but not others, and the two mothers must hide their children without hiding themselves, accepting the possibility that they will not see each other again.

With so many living in the building, it's difficult for a few chosen residents to hide or to be hidden without being noticed by others. So, on the night of the 16th or in the early hours of the 17th, Lili and Panci sneak their sons to the cellar. The boys are told to get into a large crate. Final words, a word about food, a word more about noise and silence and staying put, another final word, a hug, a hand, a pointless slicking of István's hair. They are then covered with sacks and pieces of wood. Is Molnár looking down from the third floor? Do they – the mothers, the concierge and his wife, the two boys – look back up at him? The boys have already said goodbye to their fathers. Now they say goodbye to their mothers. Then the cellar door is closed.

The two mothers return upstairs. What can they say? What can they do? They know something is about to happen. How much did Molnár tell them? Lili has a word for him, a very specific word, but that comes later, much later. The two mothers return upstairs with the burden of what they know. The rest of the night is sleepless.

Just before dawn on the 17th, the Arrow Cross arrive in force in the eighth *kerület*. They seal the neighbourhood and squads begin to enter the yellow star houses, some in uniform, others in civilian clothes with Arrow Cross armbands. All along the mile and a half of Népszínház Street, from the tram terminus to Teleki Square, there is huge commotion as Jews are roused.

Number 19 is a house designed by the Jewish architect Béla Lajta before the First World War, its intricate doorway with floral reliefs pointing to a previous era of Jewish life. From here, the residents are ordered out and told to line up on the opposite side of the street. Anni Frankl, eight years old in 1944, a family friend in 2008, remembers that back in the summer a strange thing had happened at number 19: a Catholic priest turned up offering to convert the resident Jews as a way of helping to save them. But this makes no difference as everyone is ordered out onto the street, where they will stand until, as Anni Frankl remembers, she loses track of time.

Further down, at number 29, a 65-year-old man hangs himself. At number 32, from where residents are also forced into the street, Gyuri Badacsonyi, a friend of Anni Frankl and ten at the time, remembers Arrow Cross 'thugs' shooting into the roof of a building for several minutes. The justification is that someone is shooting at them, but

Gyuri doesn't recall seeing any return fire. At number 42, someone wounded by gunfire, most likely Arrow Cross gunfire, is taken to hospital in South Pest by ambulance. In neighbouring sidestreets, such as Bérkocsis Street, other shootings occur.

At number 59, most residents are unaware of Molnár's actions the previous night. Ibi Temes, another friend of a family friend, was 11 years old at the time. She lived with her mother on the same floor as István, and remembers a single bullet coming through the window of the flat. It passed over her head before ending up in the ceiling. Who fired this is unclear, but she remembers Molnár with a single word: *dög*. It means, literally, 'corpse', and is usually preceded by the adjective 'rotten': the rotten corpse.

When the Arrow Cross enter the building, yelling, with Molnár banging the rail in support, residents immediately assume they are to be taken somewhere. They're being ordered out, all of them, from every overcrowded flat. They dress in a hurry, never forgetting their starred outer garment. Reflexively, they grab their air-raid bundles, and emerge onto the *gang*. All the front doors are open or opening, people more or less queuing to get to the stairs to go down, the Sperber brothers, the Dávid family, Lili's parents, Móric with his stick, Katalin on her chair.

From the cellar the boys can hear footfall on the stairs and on the courtyard stone. They can hear shouts and the echoes of shouts. *Gyerünk!* 'Come on!' *Büdös zsidó!* 'Stinking Jew'. Or *rohadt*, 'rotten'. Then the boys hear the cellar door opening, Arrow Cross men shouting then moving down the narrow corridor. They hold their breath under the coal sacks. The Arrow Cross order anyone hiding to come out. Give yourselves up and we won't shoot you, they say. If you don't, and we catch you, you're dead. But the boys are well hidden, good at keeping quiet. The Arrow Cross leave. The cellar is deserted once more, pitch black once more.

Marshalling so many people takes several minutes, a procession of the elderly, children and their mothers. At the bottom of the stairs, the Arrow Cross are waiting with their weapons, a machine gun, a pistol or a rifle. One of them, according to Lili, is a postman wearing his postman's uniform. They order everyone to throw their bundles into the yard. At the same time, men are being separated from women and children. The latter are led outside and lined up along the next-door building. People in non-Jewish houses, woken like everyone else by the noise, look out of their windows. Inside, from the group of males, some are picked out. A selection is made.

According to Jutka Goodman, born at 19 Népszínház Street but whose grandfather lived at number 59, the selection takes place on the basis of the *minyan*. The noun is collective. It represents a group of ten men, 'sons of the commandment' over the age of 13, necessary for a religious service. If this is the basis of the selection, it's the Arrow Cross's sense of humour shining through. However the selection is made, it comprises 22 men. According to what Jutka learns as a child from her mother, Frici, who was a friend of Lili, her grandfather, the 68-year-old Artur Frankl, is among the selected men. So, too, is 19-year-old László Ádler, a student of the rabbinical seminary and the oldest cousin of Péter Kutas. The ages are typical: old and young.

From the cellar, Tomi and István hear the shouted commands: 'Get over there!' or 'Stand here!' or 'Move!' Is there a mention of a reason? Is Molnár present? Each of the 22 men is then taken, one at a time, along the tiled hall to the high-arched doorway, the *kapualj*. Each is then shot in the head.

From the cellar, Tomi and István hear the shots. The stairwell is an echo chamber. The hall and doorway are drenched in blood. The corpses will shortly disappear. But where? Who takes them? It's possible one or more residents are shot on the street just outside the door. The bloodstains will remain for some time, the bullet holes for many years.

Everyone has heard the shots, and their echoes. The women and the children, together with most of the men, are not allowed back inside. Instead, they – Lili, her parents, Panci and the rest – are marched halfway up the street, hands raised, to the adjoining Tisza Kálmán Square. The square will host historical events in another generation under another name, but on 17 October 1944 the Arrow Cross have commandeered its main building, the Városi Theatre, and are using it as a centre to register names and documents.

There are some German soldiers present, standing on the steps between the now derelict theatre's grey columns. A *Wehrmacht* photographer takes pictures, some of which survive. One shows a crowd of people standing and watching, some laughing. One shows a uniformed

Arrow Cross man on the steps, peaked hat pushed back. In another, an SS officer is shouting at a cringing, pale-haired, yellow-starred old man who has his hands raised above his head.

The raising of hands is a gesture I cannot associate with my grandmother. She gripped her bags. She sewed and embroidered. She fried paprika and boiled dumplings. She smoothed her son's hair, her grandchildren's hair. If she had to reach for something, there was always someone taller to do it for her. Yet she walked down Népszínház Street with her hands raised above her head, holding nothing, reaching towards nothing. She is walked into the square and up the broad steps like the old man.

A woman walks her dog across the patchy grass in front of the derelict theatre. When I ask her about the building, she points to a nearby wall. The graffiti on it complains that the square is becoming a desert. To me it seems to be full of people, walking, being walked.

Around midday, during the registration process, Lili and Panci are separated. Panci's *Schutzbrief*, not necessarily respected by the Arrow Cross, is the likely reason why this happens. She and others with certain papers or documents are taken to Budapest's main synagogue in Dohány Street, where thousands are soon concentrated. Lili and her parents, with everyone else, are taken elsewhere.

Opposite the Keleti railway station, on the main Kerepesi Road that comes into Pest from the east, is the Tattersaal horse-racing track, an alternative spelling from Richard Tattersall's London horse market. The racing is traditionally between single-rider, one-horse buggies or chariots. All that remains of the Tattersaal is the single-tiered main stand, now a canary-yellow curiosity, an obstacle in front of the commemoratively named Arena Plaza shopping centre. On the 17th, through the morning and well into the afternoon, Jews from the eighth *kerület* are brought here.

'Are brought here'? 'Are walked to'? 'Are taken to'? 'Are marched to'? The language of history books is vague, general, passive. Lili, too, puts it passively. In her passive words, 'We are driven like sheep with lots of beatings.'

Herded, driven, pushed, shoved, struck, hit, and on along the Kerepesi Road to the racing enclosure, Móric without his stick, Katalin without her chair. Lili might have been one of Molnár's chosen Jews on the 16th, but on the 17th, on the way to the Tattersaal, there is no such thing. She must suspect by now Molnár's real intention. He clearly doesn't expect any of number 59's Jews to return.

The courtyard is silent. The two boys hear nothing. Tomi, the more fearful, wants to get out of the crate. István persuades him that they have to stay put. The tension between going and staying, running away or hanging on, will return to their lives a decade later. Sometime that afternoon, Mrs Farkas, 'a small woman with a sweet smile', manages to bring the boys some soup, which she will bring again several times. She tells them it's not safe to come out. The boys stay put. They can hear occasional activity outside. Perhaps it's the sound of corpses being removed.

According to the diaries of the Budapest ambulance service, ambulances are frequently called to the area between the 17th and the 19th. No ambulances are called in direct connection to the killings at number 59, although there are many individual, numbered, 'events' noted in and around the street, and at that address. The Arrow Cross didn't want to register Jewish deaths for obvious reasons, and also for a less obvious one: the concern that the deaths could elicit the sympathy of non-Jews. The ambulance diaries nevertheless record call-outs to number 59 on the 18th, albeit for ambiguous reasons. The term used is *ismeretlen kapcsán*, 'unknown connection'.

Since the Arrow Cross control the street, and generally prevent burial, it's possible that they arrange for the removal of bodies or that they commandeer ambulances. It's possible that some bodies are taken to the Jewish ghetto hospital in Wesselényi Street. What happens to most of them is not immediately clear.

The other residents, those taken or marched or driven like sheep or beaten along the Kerepesi Road to the Tattersaal, are made to sit on the grass at the centre of the racetrack. There are Arrow Cross guards, some German soldiers, some Hungarian soldiers and some policemen. These groups are sometimes united by anti-Semitism, and sometimes the majority of them unite in their contempt for the Arrow Cross.

Gyuri Badacsonyi remembers his mother, and others from 32 Népszínház Street, worrying about deportation because Keleti railway station is close to the Tattersaal, and the branch-line train station of Jozsefváros is not far. His mother has brought a tin of sardines. 'We'd better eat it before they take it,' she tells him. Another mother also worries. Lili doesn't know if she has left her son behind forever. There's no food as their air-raid bags had to be left behind. The longer they're kept, the worse it looks. The rest of the day, the freezing night and the next day are spent in the open, Katalin with her diabetes, Móric wondering what he fought for a generation before. There are no horse-drawn chariots to watch, just the sounds of odd shootings and woundings and beatings. Móric is hit on the head with a stick. László Solymár, a school friend of István's, remembers seeing him days later with a head wound that he learns was sustained at the Tattersaal.

After dark on the 18th, the cellar of number 59 is unlocked. Mrs Farkas has come to let the boys out. Apparently, it's safe. It's just that Mrs Farkas doesn't know what's happened to their mothers. István and Tomi emerge into the courtyard. The human mess, the smell, the bullet holes are still there. István thinks he sees bodies still lying in the hallway. He asks Mrs Farkas about the shooting. She tells them people have been killed, residents, men, and mentions in particular a young man in a prayer shawl. The one she's referring to is László Ádler, Péter Kutas's cousin. The boys are glad to be out of the cellar but of course can't leave the building. In any case, where would they go? So they return upstairs to the empty flat, hoping their mothers will return, too. All they have that night are memories playing tricks, photographs with holes in them, slivers of light in the dark courtyard.

At the Tattersaal, the situation is described in different ways, according to where people sit, according to the influence of the moon on the racecourse, according to the mood of individual guards. There's a story of a German officer preventing an execution of Jews, a story of Jews shouting or being made to shout 'Long live Szálasi!' on being allowed out of the Tattersaal, and Gyuri Badacsonyi's story of being allowed to return home in a group of 50 to 60 bedraggled people, escorted by policemen, only to be fired at by Arrow Cross militiamen around Tisza Kálmán Square. The policemen, according to Gyuri Badacsonyi, return fire 'to their credit'.

Only on the 19th is Panci able to return to number 59 from the Dohány Street Synagogue. Later that day, the gate of the Tattersaal is opened by Hungarian soldiers. Lili and her parents, the residents of number 59 and the Jews of the eighth *kerület* generally, are allowed home, home being a blood-soaked courtyard soon filled with the sound of crying women and children. Two mothers at least have their sons back.

But the blood, the smell of blood, the bullet holes, and Molnár: Lili has a word for him that she holds inside her, that only comes out later. The word is *gyilkos*, meaning 'murderous' or, if used as a noun, 'murderer'. Lili uses it in a phrase: '*a gyilkos házparancsnok*', 'the murderous house commander'.

The murderous house commander isn't going anywhere. He doesn't have to leave. For Lili, it's impossible to stay. On the following day the Tattersaal becomes a deportation hub, a centre for the gathering of forced labourers, for which the events of 17–19 October have been a prelude. Protective passes are no safeguard as the Arrow Cross are known simply to tear up or confiscate them. But one of the other residents of flat 4, Lili's friend Babi Pogány, manages to get a Swiss protection letter to a so-called 'protected house' near the Danube. After 14 years at 59 Népszínház Street, a decision is made in a moment. The family escapes.

But the war isn't over. Nor is number 59. It's just that there's a compression of memories, a flash of events that concertina towards the end. Some of my father's memories between October 1944 and January 1945 are as follows:

> Two weeks hiding with false papers, two nights spent with Catholic friends of Lili, followed by a brief spell at the Swiss protected house at 26 Katona József Street, forty people in a three-room flat;

> an Arrow Cross 'search for weapons' during which he hears a *suhogás*, a 'whoosh', the sound of a woman with a rucksack jumping from the fifth floor, falling, air rushing, no sound of landing;

> being led out with others, including his grandfather, to Szent István Park beside the river, slipping on an Arrow Cross armband procured from somewhere, his grandfather telling him he's mad, then leading people out of the park;

being marched at gunpoint to the main Budapest ghetto;

being in one of the crowded ghetto cellars at 4 Wesselényi Street;

the baker and her husband who smuggled bread to them;

seeing his mother naked for the first and only time during an Arrow Cross raid when there is a so-called *vetkőztetés*, an 'undressing';

being selected by the Arrow Cross as one of three men, him first, and feeling not scared of imminent death but proud of being selected as a man;

pushing his watch up his arm to hide it, then having to push a cart piled high with all the clothes to an Arrow Cross head-quarters on a Budapest ring road, as Russian planes strafed the street and pigeons dropped from windowsills.

He also remembers saying to his mother, while in the boarded ghetto where 70,000 people – mostly women, children and elderly men – were concentrated, 'We'll be out of here by my birthday.' The night before his birthday, on 17 January 1945, Soviet forces liberated the ghetto. Soon after he turned 15, he smoked his first cigarette, not a Levente, a brand that reminded him of a fascist youth organization, but a Szimfónia, a 'symphony'.

Somewhere in these memories, a child became an adult, a boy became a man. And sometime after the war in Hungary was over, in April 1945, his mother went to the police headquarters to report on the events at Népszínház Street, to tell about Molnár and the ones who did what they did. There were thousands indicted in people's courts after the war, but I have no idea whether these included Molnár. Jenő Levai, in his postwar *Black Book on the Martyrdom of Hungarian Jewry*, collected many examples of atrocities, but even now the events at Népszínház Street are shrouded in mystery.

I manage to find the location of around ten graves directly associ-ated with number 59 at the Kozma Street Jewish Cemetery. Highly unusually, they are connected by the street name. The graves include Artur Frankl, grandfather of Jutka Goodman, and Márton Steinkohl, uncle of Péter Kutas, and some ten others. It's just that the *parcella*, the plot, that the graves are in is overgrown and almost impenetrable. It's no coincidence that several of the graves are consecutive, nor that the burials apparently took place on the same day. It's just that the registered date of these burials cannot be correct: 1 October 1944. It is as if the victims were put into the earth 16 days before they were killed, as if the Arrow Cross had nothing to do with them. There is no way of knowing whether the date of burial is a mistake or a falsification.

The events of October 1944, like general memories, were swept away along with the rubble of the war. But experience is a thing, a noun, that rubs off, that shapes character, that is carried forward, that is transmitted. Tomi once told me, when I was in my teens and he was chief psychiatrist at the central Budapest hospital in the 1970s, that history could easily be falsified, especially our own. Yet traces do survive, and they are transmitted.

In the archive of the Kresz Géza Ambulance Museum, one of the archivists asks if I am related to Stephen Barlay. He asks because he has read documentary books by him. Stephen Barlay, once István Bokor, translated from English to Hungarian, returns in many ways. He returned 30 years after the events in Népszínház Street as Stephen, and his son returned 30 after that, and in the flat once inhabited by the Bokors another family now lives, and in the silence of the inner space of the building present and past are fused into a single tense. On the staircase, the handrails, the *gang*, the windows, the stairwell, the cellar, the courtyard and the doorway, traces remain of the unfalsified residents, the concierge, the house commander, the victims.

Number 59 still guards its impenetrable truth. And it still stands on its corner plot overlooking Teleki Square. And the light on Népszínház Street, especially on October dawns, still seems to bend as if around something heavy.

Women

The Memory of Paper

B Y 17 OCTOBER 1944, she was dead. Great-Grandmother Mária, née Hirschhorn, who married a Berger, one of whose sons was Nándor, whose grandson, István, barely knew her, ended up in Auschwitz. She was one of the 1.1 million of whom it is said that he/she/they 'ended up' there. She was one of the estimated 437,000 Hungarian Jews deported there from the provinces between 15 May and 9 July 1944 in the fastest and most efficient extermination carried out by the Nazis. Beneath this slab of facts lie the stories of the vanishing Bergers and the disappearing Hirschhorns, many of whom ended up on the same train, from and to the same place, at the same time. Only genealogical stragglers and geographical wanderers survived. With one of the stragglers came a unique letter.

The last of that generation was one of Mária's sons. László survived the war in Budapest with luck and a Swiss protection pass. My father's uncle was, by various accounts, very tall and *buta szemű*, 'stupid-eyed'. Photographs go some distance towards confirming these observations. László's voice comes from a memory: my father, aged seven, was reprimanded by his uncle for addressing him with the informal 'you'. *Tegezni*: to use the informal 'you', as opposed to *magázni*. 'I'll tell you,' said László informally, 'when you can *tegezni* me. Until then, call me Uncle Laci.' The diminutive of László, as long as it was linked to formality and a title, was apparently acceptable.

Immediately after the war, in August 1945, László became a member of the Hungarian Communist Party where, no doubt, his egalitarian outlook found a home. At around the same time, he was employed as an accountant by a pen company. Some misdemeanour or theft or fraud landed him in prison, after which he moved to the working-class Budapest district of Csepel, and carried on working despite his advancing years. In fact, he died on the way to work in 1985, aged 75. In a flat where, my mother remembers, mould had developed between his death and the slow completion of legalities, László left behind the morning toast, his Communist Party membership card, a few photographs and a few pieces of paper. My father divided his stupid-eyed uncle's photographs and papers with his only cousin, Marika. The rest of his uncle's possessions, utensils, furniture, clothes, went to the concierge of László's block, who had kindly offered to 'help' circumvent the complex by-laws concerning dustbins. Cousin Marika's half of the photos and papers went with her to Sweden, where she had two daughters, a Betti and a Sofi, whom I once met in Leicester Square in 1978, and with whom contact was lost after Marika died and they got married.

So who are the genealogical stragglers? Where does a line end?

One of László's pieces of paper seems to pose the same questions. It is more of a crackling sheet that has been folded, and folded again, to fit a missing envelope. It is a pencilled letter from a mother to a son, from Mária to László, from the provincial town of Székesfehérvár to the capital. It is dated 25 May 1944. It begins, *Édes drága Lacikám!* 'My sweet dear Laci!'

The slab of facts might be familiar but the life beneath is unknown. Without the letter I might never have known anything of this great-grandmother's existence. Yet the existence she describes is somewhere between what her life had been and her imminent death. It describes a life in death, in the shadow of its historical inevitability, and it begins after the beginning of the end, without the writer knowing, with the writer still hoping. Within weeks, the writer was dead. In the box where such things are kept, there is nothing else like this letter.

Is it possible to know a great-grandmother by reading her only words and forgetting the rest? Or is it better to stand on the straight railtrack in between a crematorium and the main entrance of Auschwitz–Birkenau?

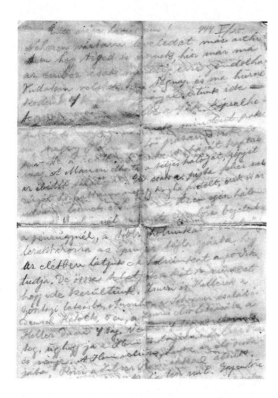

The memory of paper: Great-Grandmother Mária's almost indecipherable letter, written on 25 May 1944, 23 days before her death in Auschwitz. It lay unread for 65 years.

Or should I walk down the tree-lined street she lived in, Gyümölcs Street, 'Fruit' Street, in the provincial town of Székesfehérvár?

Some Auschwitz survivors have found metaphors that evoke truths greater than facts. For Primo Levi, there was the 'Auschwitz caesura'; for another former prisoner, Imre Kertész, the Nobel Prize-winning Hungarian writer, schoolfriend of my father, former Budapest neighbour of my mother, there is the 'Auschwitz horizon'. For another generation – the second, mine – the truth of metaphors is beyond reach. We have fact to fall back on, and feeling, the fact and the feeling of what remains. One survivor, Éva Barabás, a friend of my aunt in Budapest, told me on a stifling summer day in 2008 that, on her arrival in Auschwitz in May 1944, as she got out of the wagon, there was 'beautiful sunshine'. Auschwitz sunshine.

There was sunshine when I went, too. It made me squint down the straight railtrack to a vanishing point. Sunshine helps when it comes to reading my great-grandmother's letter, finger-smudged, its lead now eroded, some words illegible. The light seems to separate the writing on one side of the paper from the other. Otherwise the letter's instinct is to retreat from the light, to close up along its fold lines. Paper has a memory. It returns to where it was, to how it was. This paper seems to want only shadow. To open it up and to keep it open feels like an act of will against the will of the writer.

My sweet dear Laci!

It has been difficult waiting for your letter. I thought they might already have taken you. That's all you can think of these days. I'm letting you know that today and yesterday we moved four vanloads here. Ilona and the house commander helped. Manczi brought all his bedding, sewing machine and dining-room furniture. I could only bring the white cupboard and a kitchen table. These will fit into the yard. My bedding [...] Everything else has been registered with the finance office, stored with the community or at the Epinger brick factory. Whether we will ever see any of it again God knows. But we can put our hands together that we got here. Zsuzsi and the Kellers went to Gosztonyi's flat [...] and the Schwarcz family and Kató Deutsch's family of five went to Zsuzsi's first flat [...] and the four Kellers [...] Ilona is with us, Lenke in her front room, Rózsi with Rózsi Z——.

We'll cook together if there is anything to cook. We still have something but no meat. We hope it won't get even worse. Our flat was requisitioned by our lodger. It hurts my heart but what can we do? Maybe fate will allow us to be together again.

I got a letter from Pista yesterday, asking if I could send cigarettes from here to Ági but he gave no instructions about money, Sanyi went to see Pista and no doubt they talked about money because I gave it to him [...] Sanyi is very afraid of having any contact with us. I haven't been there for three weeks and it hurts because Márta is seriously ill and the doctor went yesterday. Pista writes that there's a severe curfew. Even to go out for one or two hours to Pest is very dangerous. The courtyard here is like Teleki Square but we've got a roof over our heads.

I send my blessing for your wedding and it really hurts that I can only think of you from a distance. Be happy and may God grant you all the best and happiness.

Don't take it badly if I'm writing in pencil as I don't have pen and ink to hand. I can hardly write down in my great sorrow how happy I am that Imre is out. If I get back to normal I will write to Imre and family but for weeks now we've been in such a state because every sign points to the G.

What a movement of people there is. Many are without a roof and have nowhere to go. Who is at Lili Bokor's flat? I can't begin to write down how much it all cost, this moving, 500 pengő if we add it all up, and what we had to carry ourselves. But it would be all right if only they'd leave us in peace. It's just that we're scared of being raided again. I'll write of Pista's things next time.

With love to the whole family, especially Lili, your loving mother.

Food, money, home, bedding, wardrobe, friends, concern for relatives, her sons, her daughter, her daughter-in-law, what has happened, what is happening, what she fears will happen: nothing is omitted. Yet the most striking detail is the occasion on which the letter is written: Laci's wedding. In the middle of all this, in Budapest, Laci's affair with an unnamed woman from 59 Népszínház Street has blossomed.

Tacked on to the end of the letter are two messages from aunts, one from Lenke, the other from Ilona, mentioned twice in Mária's letter. Both messages are in celebratory ink:

My dear Laci,

I take this opportunity to write a few lines to congratulate you from the bottom of my heart on your engagement and wedding. We hope to meet your bride very soon. To you both we send our love, your loving auntie, Lenke

Pista is concerned about Lili. He's fine and thank God he's in a good place.

Dear Laci,

We wish you happiness together with your fiancée. I hope that God will allow us all to be together happily and in good health and we send our love to our new relative.

Ilona

I'm writing this during the hurcolkodás [the great moving around], *but […] we will be together with God.*

In the middle of all this, there is a wedding to celebrate. But what is the middle of all this? Each detail implies a million others. Who are all the people mentioned? What exactly happened? The chronological point of the letter sends ripples backwards and forwards in time.

I know now that the Bergers and the Hirschhorns were present in Székesfehérvár long before the train that took the last of them. They were there even before the station was built. I also know how Great-Grandmother Mária, née Hirschhorn, who married a Berger, whose son kept her celebratory letter, spent her last days. If paper has a memory, then this is a memoir of her death.

Over a hundred years before their virtual disappearance, Jews were officially admitted into Székesfehérvár, *székes* meaning 'seat', *fehér* meaning 'white', *vár* meaning 'castle'. The seat of the white castle, between Budapest and Lake Balaton, was royal, the town having seen the crowning and burial of many kings, and a few queens, over half a millennium.

Walk up meandering Fő Street, Main Street, with its King Saint István museum, antique Black Eagle Apothecary, historic fountain and snaking tourist train, and you cannot help but feel the weight of its heritage, passed on in digestible royal moments from Prince Géza, who established his royal residence in 972, to the nation-defining Golden Bull laws issued here in 1222.

When József Hirschhorn, Mária's father, arrived in the 1840s, he would have known where he had arrived. He couldn't have missed the history but also the historical moment, the possibility of living in a place that had once taxed Jews just for entering. The town was irresistibly pretty, too, and expanding if not yet booming as it would after the building of the railway station in 1861. József would have settled here with the rest of his life in mind.

The sidestreet he found was Várkapu – 'Castlegate' – Street, at the northern end of Main Street. The approach to its right angle is guarded by the statue of the heroic sixteenth-century fighter Várkocs, who defended the town against the Turks. Behind the guardian, beside a second-hand book store, is number 6, part of a one-storey building running the length of the street, green shutters flapped permanently open, the door timbers and brickwork exposed, the winding stairway worn and waved by footfall, its wooden handrail smoothed and shined by hands. József arrived in the years before the Revolution of 1848. This was a national struggle against Habsburg oppression, and would involve the citizens of Székesfehérvár. It was also supported by Jews, though it failed to bring the hoped-for emancipation. In fact there was rioting against Jews, some people fearing the new freedoms, the new equalities. The fears would persist. In 1919, in advance of Hitler, the Bishop of Székesfehérvár would claim that the Jews were 'eating us up'. He would liken them to a bedbug epidemic against which people had to defend themselves.

Three years after the revolution, in 1851, József established a decorative sign-painting business, one that would sustain him and his family, via one of his sons, into the twentieth century. A trace of it remains in an advertisement in a local commercial directory:

JÓZSEF HIRSCHHORN AND SON, *diszitőfestő*.

Soon after the business was established, József married Betti Grosz. The first of nine children, Malvina, or Milli, was born in 1856. After that, for the next two decades, there was no stopping them: Fani, 1857; Regina, 1859; Gyula, 1863; Zsófia, 1864; Samu, 1867; Mária, 1869; Bianka, 1874; Lilla, 1875. Lilla lived only months, and Bianka only four years, but the rest grew generously, their working hands enlarging, the bodies of the females increasingly amorphous from relentless child-bearing.

There's a picture of a battalion of sisters, including Great-Grandmother Mária; her two brothers, Gyula and Samu, absent. The picture is undated but, judging from the ages of the women, it's the late 1920s. The sisters are dressed in black, most likely on the occasion of the funeral of Mária's husband. He died in 1929 and was buried in the Jewish cemetery, his tall, rounded white stone still rising above the weeds and dandelions on the main gravel thoroughfare used by locals as a shortcut. The sisters are standing on a semi-vacant, semi-industrial lot somewhere nearby. All are in their sixties, give or take. They are double-chinned, heavy-jowled, wide-hipped. They are not wanderers. They are not lost. These women all set down their bundles long ago. They made their home. They are of their land. They are deep-rooted, bound to the earth like trees. It would take organized violence, rifle butts and cattle wagons to shift them.

*A battalion of sisters: third from left is my great-grandmother, Mária,
née Hirschhorn, with her siblings in Székesfehérvár on the occasion of her
husband's funeral in 1929. She would be deported from here in 1944.*

Back in 1894, aged 25, Mária married Gyula Berger, who was both
a *schuster*, a cobbler, and a maker of boots and shoes with his own
business. There's a later picture of him, post-1918, in the doorway of
his shop, flat-capped, aproned, Mária just in front with an apprentice,
and four of their children.

Mária, like her mother, gave birth many times. Irma, the first child,
died in 1895, aged 21 days; another, Nándor, died aged six in 1903.
But the rest – my grandfather Nándor who was born in the same
year as, and named after, the dead child, his younger brothers László,
Imre, Pista and Gyula, and the only daughter, Márta – all grew up
Hungarian in a Hungarian town. Some of them would change their
name from the Germanic Berger to the Hungarian Bokor.

Religion, too, was ebbing. At a certain point, in 1863, the Jewish
community of Székesfehérvár, like many others across the country,
split. Orthodox and Neologue Jews would build their own syna-
gogues, much as they would across the country. In Székesfehérvár's
register of 'Israelite' births, deaths and marriages, the birth of the
first Hirschhorn daughter, Milli, is listed in both Orthodox and

Neologue sections. It's as if her parents were undecided, on the cusp between the traditional and the progressive. Milli certainly made racy progress. At the age of 37, she divorced. Then she remarried a non-Jew, a 23-year-old former soldier and photographer called Henrik.

By the time Mária first conceived in 1895, religion was less important to the family than making a living. Four decades later, the majority of the town was Neologue. God, in Mária's letter and in the aunts' messages, is the God of last resort. It's the one people count on when there is nothing else to count on. More typically, it was Mária's brother-in-law, Ignácz Berger, who embodied the entrepreneurial spirit: he was one of the first van drivers in the seat of the white castle. God moved in mysterious ways; Ignácz moved for a living, and was available for hire until the business ended in 1926. He and his wife, Ilona, who wrote a celebratory message and who appealed to the God of last resort, would both accompany Mária on her final journey.

But back then, the whole family was moving on or ahead. Business was the method, based on education. Mária's own education is questionable, as the numerous spelling mistakes in her original letter suggest. I cannot claim to have noticed them. Only my mother could completely decipher the handwriting, and notice the spelling. The mistakes are as much part of Great-Grandmother Mária's voice as the things she chooses to commit to paper. She was used to speaking, not writing. Or writing Yiddish, not Hungarian. There's a picture of her in the 1930s, sleeves rolled up, the history of the weather she has experienced in her face. She's standing over a wooden washtub in the back yard, rinsing clothes. She didn't live in a *shtetl*, and she wasn't born in one of those semi-mythical Yiddish places, literally 'little towns', that dominated the pre-urban culture of East European Jews. Yet somewhere behind her is the story of those Jews – Ashkenazi, Germanic, medieval, biblical. It's in her forearms. It's in her capable hands. It's in her spelling. It's also in the fact that two of her sons, Nándor and László, were educated at *kereskedelmi*, business school. They weren't scholars but they could spell. They weren't religious but socialist. They would outgrow the provinces and head to the capital. They had aspirations.

One of their brothers, Gyula, symbolizes their outlook. He became a representative of Ford, taking advantage of renewed international investment in the almost bankrupt town after the First World War. There's a picture of Gyula standing in shirt and tie outside his shop opposite the Székesfehérvár courthouse, spare mechanical parts in the window, distinctive italicized 'Ford' logo above him. There's also an exceptional picture of him at the same location, sitting astride a brand new motorcycle. It's a 500cc D-RAD R9 from Berlin's Spandau-based Deutsche Industriewerke. Only 10,000 were manufactured in 1929.

It's safe to say that such a machine did not belong to him but must have been ordered by a wealthy customer. Its tyres are in perfect condition. They have yet to experience friction. It was delivered there, not ridden. What does belong to Gyula is his aspiration. He's posing, hands on the handlebars, sporty skullcap on his head, dressed for adventure, looking straight at the camera. In his eyes there is a proprietary hope. Behind him is the courthouse, the seat of the law, the security of home, the stability and order of society. Ahead is the future, a place to travel to on a gleaming machine. Gyula would not go that far. The law would not allow it. Neither would the new social order. He would end up in the same place as his mother.

The sisters, the shoemaker, the van driver, the business students, the Ford representative, the motorcyclist: fixed moments in the life of a *polgári*, 'petit bourgeois', family. Fixed moments in fixed places: László's yellow-brick school; the courthouse on Zichy Park; 5 Sas Street, 'Eagle Street', the home of József and Betti Hirschhorn in the centre of the old town where several of their children were born; 12 Gyümölcs Street, where Mária and her husband lived from soon after their marriage in 1894, where some of their babies were born and even died, now a horse-riding outfitter. Fixed moments in a fixed place. The wanderers had arrived out of the fog of their ancestry with their ornamental Germanic names. Hirschhorn did not originally mean just 'deerhorn' but also implied 'dweller at the sign of the deer'; Berger could come from *Berg*, mountain, but also from *Burger*, citizen, even castle-dweller. They came to the seat of the white castle to make homes and to make babies.

The ride to nowhere: Gyula Berger, one of my paternal grandfather's
brothers, posing on a new German motorcycle (not his) in Székesfehérvár
in 1929. Along with his wife and daughter, he would be deported.

They certainly kept the midwife busy. The same local woman, called
Jármut, delivered a few Bergers and Hirschhorns, and the midwife's
daughter might have carried on in a kind of genealogy of genealogies. The last birth in Székesfehérvár in the late Thirties was that of
Évi, daughter of Gyula the motorcyclist and his wife Irén. There's a
picture of the little girl in a ballet costume and pose. Where her father
and mother ended up, so too did she.

Walk up meandering Main Street; look at the archival photographs:
street names might have changed, but the topography of the town,
despite war fronts moving through it several times, is almost unaltered.
It's possible to navigate the streets with a century-old map. What was
then, still is now. The family inhabited the streets. Mária went to the
weekly market, where horse-drawn carts brought the produce of the

countryside, or to the bigger market on the rough ground of Széna Square. She took her children to Zichy Park where a band would play in the summer or to the skating rink on Nagy Sándor Street. They had a certain faith, and Mária went to the Neologue synagogue, which was destroyed in the war, in the vicinity of Main Square. They paid their taxes. They advertised their businesses in commercial directories. Like other citizens, they tried to get on.

In a small town, with a pre-war population of under 50,000, there was a relatively small number of Jews. The official pre-deportation list recorded 2,064. People knew each other, and many of the *polgári* families resembled each other, in size and circumstance. Fixed moments in a fixed place. Then the Germans arrived.

Székesfehérvár, after the 19 March invasion, became a fixed place of a different kind: Zone III, District II. Gendarmerie District II covered the town and a half a dozen other centres, and was one of ten policing districts across the country, each under a pro-Nazi colonel of the gendarmerie. The districts were then subsumed within larger territories that were, according to the leading scholar of the period, Randolph L. Braham, part of 'the masterplan for the dejewification of Hungary'.

Zones, districts, responsibilities, registrations of people and property, money affairs, marshalling, moving, concentrating, timetabling: the bureaucracy of the process is reflected in some way in every line of Mária's letter. The emotional starting point is her son, Laci. He's been on her mind, as if the trouble she can't see is necessarily worse than the trouble she can. He's in Budapest, and Mária has clearly heard of arrests or actions that have already taken place. Another son, Pista, has written to her about the 'severe curfew' in the capital. A third son, Imre, is 'out', she writes, apparently referring to an arrest or period of detention. This was almost certainly in Székesfehérvár. Imre Bokor's wife, Ella, definitely survived the war. She would emigrate to Sweden in the late 1940s, accompanying her 12-year-old ballerina daughter, Marika, on a ballet school trip.

But Mária's sons are not the letter's chronological starting point. That is elsewhere. It's in the reference to the previous weeks. 'For weeks now we've been in such a state because every sign indicated G.' The lone capital can stand only for one thing: ghetto. The abbreviation, too, can stand only for one thing: the fear of the unmentionable whole. There is a certain shadow of superstition or religion, as if the mighty powers of good and evil cannot be named. She fears naming her fears in case she invokes them.

Yet the rest of the letter is full of the detail of struggle: the raids, the loss of property, the loss of home, the wellbeing of her children. In a short space, the two months from invasion to letter, the 75-year-old woman got used to a certain level of abuse. But she knew there was worse. If 'G' wasn't actually the worst, then it pointed that way. In fact, as she writes, all the signs point that way. The chronology most of all. Mária fears the ghetto because, by now, on Thursday 25 May, she is halfway there.

Yellow stars had been introduced in the provinces days after the invasion, the first step of the process. Some saw poetry in the bureaucracy. On 11 May, Toldi Arpád, a former gendarmerie colonel, became prefect of Fejér county, which encompasses Székesfehérvár. Where once *ködös*, 'foggy', Jews whispered about business, he stated, now Hungary's future would be 'merry, innocent children'.

The prefect of the county is quoted in the only book on the 'Tragedy of the Jews of Székesfehérvár and Fejér County, 1938–1944'. The writer, Anna Gergely, is a historian and scientific secretary at the King Saint István Museum on Main Street. Among the Roman stones and the treasures of the county, in the middle of the history of the Middle Ages and the Ottoman Empire, is her file-filled office, the colour of grey excavated stone. Red-haired, bespectacled, Gergely is one of, as she puts it, 'very few' Jews left in town. She has seen the dwindling number dwindle. First there was war, in which she, too, lost family. Then there was the general dissipation during the communist era, in particular during the Kádár regime. Then there has been a general assimilation to the point where, as she puts it, burials are the main, and in most cases the only, religious choice.

In the Jewish cemetery where Mária's husband lies, I saw fresh flowers at one grave, the sole burial of 2008. Fixed moments in a fixed place. Gergely has tried to fix these moments in other works, such as a series of biographical sketches of preeminent Székesfehérvár Jews. Gyula the motorcyclist was not one of them, yet Gergely is very much taken by the photograph of him, the solidity of the machine, the definiteness of the location.

Two days later, I stumble on another fixed moment. In a wood-panelled sidestreet cafe, the Ribillio, named after a former owner's parrot and meaning 'chaos' or 'brouhaha', I discover Gergely with the Chief Cantor, a cantor being a leader of the congregation. In the brouhaha of history, it feels like stumbling on a quiet, determined, ongoing discourse between fewer and fewer people.

Somewhere on the general territory are Mária's footprints. I tried to look for them in Auschwitz–Birkenau, also known as Auschwitz II. I looked by the railtrack. I looked by a broken crematorium. I remember my father telling me that he wondered, as he looked at a pile of shoes displayed behind glass, whether those of Gyula the motorcyclist's daughter, Évi, were among them. In Auschwitz I, in the camp's main administrative building, I naively asked a Polish guide why the steps were worn by footfall when relatively so few would have used them. 'You're forgetting the 25 million visitors,' she said. 'One million this year...'

I tried to look for Mária's footprints on the cemetery path and around her husband's grave. Or the adjacent grave, her older brother's, Samu, later Sándor, Hirschhorn. I even placed a stone, a pebble, on each grave. It's something I know Jews do at the graves of their ancestors. It's partly folkloric, East European; partly a visible mark of remembrance; partly to keep the soul in place with a stone, to keep it from moving, from haunting the living. It is not a formal act of the faithful but it has more than a hint of the religious. I placed a pebble, allowed myself some religion, much like Mária. 'We can put our hands together that we got here,' she wrote. But I'm not looking for religion, neither in Auschwitz nor in Székesfehérvár. Nor am I looking for history. I just want to see her footprints.

Mária's letter, according to Gergely, falls between key dates, 23–31 May, the period during which Jews had to move into yellow star houses. This required the cooperation of non-Jewish families who had to move out of the designated addresses. The difference was that their costs, from electricity to packing to transport, were covered. Mária didn't have a choice. She just had to come up with the money.

Already there had been 'raids', the so-called *razzia* or, as Mária spells it, *razia*. The word, originally Arabic, meant robbery, seizure, pillage. Gendarmes, in their boots, cock feathers in their hats, would turn up in the night in search of 'concealed weapons'. They would tap the walls, examine the floorboards, bayonet the furniture, and make threats. Of course, what they really wanted was valuables, the mythical wealth that was secreted somewhere clever.

The state seized what it could, even warning non-Jewish citizens in early June that goods taken ad hoc from Jews had to be given up to officials. The Gestapo, installed at 5 Kégl György Street, across the road from Gyümölcs Street, controlled the acquisition of Jewish property. Arrests, beatings and torture helped them to acquire things more efficiently.

In the two days prior to her letter, Mária's flat was requisitioned by her non-Jewish lodger for three non-Jewish families. These families had to move out of their own homes, now designated as yellow star houses, to make way for Jews. Later, once the Jews had gone, they could move back. Mária's property, her family's property, had to be registered. What she could take or carry with her was, she writes, piled in the corridor or in the courtyard. She likens it to Teleki Square in Budapest. But even in Teleki Square furniture was not piled to the sky. The rest of what she owned was left either with the *hitközség*, the Jewish community organization, or at the 'Epinger' brick factory.

Eppinger, which Mária misspells, was a Jew, Ignác Eppinger. His was just one of a number of brick factories arcing around the edge of town. The history of any town is the history of its brick and stone and building rubble. The relationship of the brick factory to the centre is a constant, and its relationship to transport is a given. During the war, the brick factory was therefore an obvious choice for a new role. It was where people could be concentrated before deportation, including brick factory owners. Ignác Eppinger, with his family, would end up in the same place as everyone else.

Mária knew the fine lines between bricks. Her only daughter, Márta, was seriously ill, but there had been no contact with her for three weeks. The reason was that Márta's husband was a non-Jew, a Catholic. Sanyi Szieber was fair, muscular, young. Márta was dark-eyed, black-haired, high-boned. In their one pre-war picture, the couple have an unaffected glamour about them. In May 1944 they all knew that Márta's racial identity was not erased through marriage. The couple's status was uncertain, so it's understandable that Sanyi was frightened of contact with his wife's family. Still, knowing that they were forbidden from travelling, he took the risk of going to the capital to see his brother-in-law, Pista, whose own movement was restricted by a severe curfew. The two of them talked about money. But back in Székesfehérvár, with its atmosphere, anyone could have known about Sanyi and his wife. Anyone could have seen him, denounced him. It's equally understandable that, however much it hurt not to be able to visit her sick daughter, Mária accepted the situation. They all lived with it; some of them died with it. Looking back, there is one small irony in the balance of things: Sanyi worked for the railway that would take his mother-in-law.

Raids, intimidation, registration, a forced move to a designated house: Mária appeals to her God, hopes it won't get worse, just wants to be left in peace. At least she has a roof over her head, she writes, unlike many others. It's impossible to know whether she had to move again to the 'G', but it's likely that, within days of the letter, she had a new address. Along the way, she shed her belongings. 'If we will ever see any of it again, God knows.' The ghetto 'collection' houses were spread out, some clustered in the streets near Zichy Park, such as Kigyó Street, others in those nearer the station, such as Lövölde Street, their locations familiar to any local.

Then, on Tuesday 6 June 1944, at 5 a.m., the police came knocking with rifle butts. Ten minutes were allowed for everyone to gather. Courtyards filled with people. The procedure was recalled and recorded in different parts of Fejér county by the few survivors. People were allowed a pack, some food, some clothing. Some heard they were going to work. Wherever they were going, there were fresh searches. The pens, watches, wallets, rings and penknives missed by previous *razzia*s were discovered.

Specifically, there were body searches. Women gendarmes searched the women until it was realized that these searches weren't sufficiently thorough. Local midwives were deployed. Those who had delivered children now relieved the mothers of their final burdens. According to one survivor's account from DEGOB, a Hungarian acronym for the National Committee for Attending Deportees, which was established in Budapest in 1945, the searches were crude. Only two pairs of rubber gloves were used for several hundred women.

The town's Jews, in that repeated collective gesture of the Holocaust, were then marched, this time in the direction of the railway station. Somewhere in the crowd was Mária. With her was her son Gyula, his wife Irén, their daughter Évi, her brother-in-law Ignácz and his wife Ilona. Mária's older brother, Samu Hirschhorn, also known as Sándor, had died in 1922, but his wife, other Bergers, Imre Bokor, as well as Mária's friends, members of the Keller, Schwarcz and Deutsch families, were all there.

A mayor of Székesfehérvár, G. Emil Csitáry, witnessed the scene and wrote of it between 1964 and 1970 in his memoirs: 'I'll never forget,' he recalled, 'when the Jews were escorted in rows of four...' He and his wife stepped into the doorway of a building, from where they *kukucskáltunk ki*. They peeped out. They peeped out as their doctor, a good friend, passed by in a row of four. Those who watched those who marched sometimes waved. Or they laughed. Or jeered. Or they did not watch. They looked away. Or they did look but in particular ways. They peeped out.

The crowd went beyond the railway station, which stands alone at the southern end of the town, to a brick factory, not to Eppinger's but to the Szabó brick factory and tile-works. This was the main collection point for the surrounding areas. The only shelter on the dusty open ground was the pillared structure supporting a roof beneath which bricks would normally be dried. It had rained earlier, so the first to arrive huddled near the centre.

Over the next two to three days, around 2,800 people were gathered here, including those from outside the town. On 10–13 June there was no food and nobody was allowed to leave. Some were beaten. Some died. Some committed suicide. Early on Wednesday 14 June, the whole camp had to stand in line. According to László Kiss, who recorded his experience in his 'Auschwitz Diary' in 1945, everyone was led to the railway station. The train was meant to depart in the afternoon but an air-raid warning delayed the entrainment. It wasn't until later that people were finally, though efficiently, wagonized by the SS.

According to Kiss, there were sixty-five to a car, with twenty-five to thirty cars attached to two engines. Windows were nailed shut. The numbers, according to Gergely, were forty-seven cars with sixty-five or more to a car, forty cars for the healthy, two for the sick, two for

Hungarian gendarmes and three for food. Either way, there was only one train for all of them, after which the brick yard was empty and ready for disinfection.

At around 6.30 p.m. the train pulled out of the station on a route that would circumvent Budapest. The heat in the wagons soon became intense. People couldn't relieve themselves. The train's speed varied, from 'express' to very slow, as it made its way along the eastbound Pusztaszabolcs line before turning north in its orbit of the capital. There was a stop for water at the pretty town of Kassa, now Košice on the Slovakian side of the border. As the Hungarian state railway train was handed over to German guards, its prisoners were searched again. From there, the direction was north-west to Auschwitz.

On Saturday 17 June, the train arrived in the vicinity of the main camp, Auschwitz I, stopped for a short while, then continued to Birkenau, Auschwitz II, the *Vernichtungslager*, the extermination camp. Reports of the time of arrival vary between noon and 4 p.m.

Polish Jews in striped uniforms pulled people from the wagons. Men and women were separated. The SS captain and physician Dr Josef Mengele was present. He was particularly looking for twins. There were several sets of them from the Székesfehérvár transport. As for the rest, the selection was either for work, to the right, or for death, to the left. Old women, children, mothers who refused to be separated from their children, went to the left. It is likely, on this basis, that whereas Mária, Gyula's wife and child and so on, went to the left, her sons, Gyula, Imre and so on, would have gone to the right.

There are two SS photographs that are thought to have been taken at some point between May and June, during the arrival of Hungarian Jews. They show a walking group of roughly 35 women and children between 'Krema II' and 'Krema III', crematoria II and III, on their way to the former. According to Jean-Claude Pressac in his 1989 book *Auschwitz: Technique and Operation of the Gas Chambers*, this group has about two hours to live.

The only person who peeped beyond this and recorded it was a French Jew called David Olère. He was the only artist in the 'Sonderkommando', a group of prisoners tasked with clearing corpses from the gas chambers. Some of his sketches, produced in 1946, have a photographic accuracy. One shows the undressing room of

Krema III, with naked victims and armed guards. At the far end, off to the right, is the gas chamber. Another sketch, 'Gassing by Zyclon B' (*sic*) depicts the anguished faces of the dead, apparently witnessed through the gas chamber door in which there was a peephole.

After the war, people apparently asked Olère if he knew what had happened to their relatives. He replied by showing them a sketch of Krema III. From its chimney, with its lightning conductors twisted by heat, a cloud of smoke composed of faces, naked bodies and undifferentiated corpses belches out. Through the peephole of Olère's work, it is possible to see any one of the victims in any one of the faces. Mária died on 17 June 1944, possibly before the early evening but no later.

There is a list, the 'Székesfehérvár Martyrs List', that records the majority of those deported. On it are several family members. But there is another list, written in advance of this semi-official one. Mária's letter is that list. It's her personal list of people, each name implying a fate, each name implying other names. Without knowing it, on 25 May 1944, some 23 days before her death, Mária was already engaged in necrology, in compiling a list of the dead.

I turn behind me to where I've left the letter, to look again, to check one more name, a final spelling. But the letter is already retreating from the light. Seeking shadow from peeping eyes, it folds back in on itself along its fold lines.

My maternal grandmother, Bözsi, with her two daughters, Zsuzsi and Ági, in her Budapest flat in 1987, the year before she died.

The Slipping of a Wig

THE THINGS WE DON'T KNOW about some people represent them better than the things we do. In the case of Bözsi, my maternal grandmother, the linear trajectory of her life was as slippery as her slipping wig. There are myths and truths and imaginings. There are the unverifiable details that populate the spaces between dates. Neither of her daughters really knows of her childhood or can say for sure what is or is not true. There is no surviving letter.

It's not that she ever claimed to have altered the course of the stars. But mention her name to family members and there is likely to be a smile, a certain shared smile that evokes a listener's experience of her dubious moments, her unsubstantiated stories, her claims. 'She had delusions of grandeur,' says my brother, smiling. She could be infuriating, irascible, bullish. She interfered. She smoked hard. She played cards. She had a voice like dredged Danubian mud, and a laugh like an out-of-petrol Trabant. She is remembered as someone who always managed to get things when things were needed and, according to my cousin Nóra, to have a special bite to eat on the table whenever anyone turned up. She is also remembered for the fear inspired by her pea soup, at least the quantity of it that she made you consume. For all this, she is remembered with love.

But there is magic in mystery, and her claims beguile like legends. How she escaped deportation; how she was a great pianist; how she was a skilled motorist; how she created meat stews during the war when there was no meat; how she dispensed medical advice to her 'patients': her claims are her claims, and her moments are her moments. If there is one explanation for all of it, one clarification that has lasting resonance, it's the one that she herself consistently gave: '*Az ujjamban van.*' 'It's in my fingers.'

Her fingers always seemed boney, spidery, alive with a restless energy of their own. Maybe they could span an octave. Her pink painted nails complemented the blonde curls of the slightly bouffant wig that she wore later in life. She loved playing cards, particularly canasta. Beneath a painting of a reclining nude with a hole in her elbow that Bözsi always said was a bullet hole from 1956, she would snap each card onto the table during a game, bending it. She would laugh her raspy laugh as she won a hand, and drum her fingers across the invaluable joker. Her wig could slip but not her fingers.

Bözsi, like my mother's sister, remained in Hungary. Unlike my paternal grandmother, Lili, who came out to Britain a few years after the events of 1956 and with whom it was the familiarity that hid so much, Bözsi was always the 'other' grandmother. She was other-worldly, distant. Yet she was larger than life in spite of the distance, perhaps because of it. When the two grandmothers went down the road together to buy a loaf of bread, which they did on one of Bözsi's rare visits to London, Lili came back complaining of her sore feet; Bözsi came back with an anecdote about the baker. It was their difference in outlook.

She died in 1988, just over a year before the big changes in East Europe in 1989 and the first free elections in Hungary in 1990. The date of her birth was a secret throughout her life, a shifting set of numbers between loose parameters, the degree of accuracy depending on her audience. According to my cousin, Andris, she once changed her birth date on some identity card or other and, once her husband, Ernő, found out, she was made to change it back. Of course, there's always the possibility that she changed the date from one already falsified.

In fact, she was the youngest of three children. Margit was born in 1897, and lived a hundred years. Géza followed in 1899, and died in 1978. Bözsi, according to her birth certificate, was born in 1905. But the '5' is smudged, its arc clumsily looped. It could be a '6'. Whoever did it, did it deliberately. A single digit separates reality from fiction.

The births of the three siblings, two in the nineteenth and one, apparently, in the twentieth century, might have determined the differences between them. Or it might have been their wars, their revolutions or their politics. Or it might have been their birthplaces. Whatever it was, my mother has often wondered how grandmother Irén 'spat out these three', each of these three being feisty, argumentative and spirited. Or, according to my mother's sister, Zsuzsi, 'fiery'. Whatever the adjective, there was always a certain rivalry.

Is personality a genealogical issue? Or is it accidental, circumstantial, experiential? It's not merely events that cause stories. The desire to tell them plays the greater part. In Bözsi's case, it was desire and pride. Mere facts couldn't get in her way. Nor did the depressive or melancholic disposition that oppressed several of those around her, including my other grandmother. For Bözsi's daughters, it was her spirit and humour that kept her young. And perhaps her name. Her name was Erzsébet, Elizabeth. The diminutive of that is Bözsi. But she was also known as Böske. Finally, there was a diminutive of a diminutive, Böbi. Each has its own identity, its own place in her chronology. But when it comes to creating an impression, does the order of things matter?

I last saw her two years before she died. In Újpalota, an outlying north-eastern district of the capital, she was working in a street-corner kiosk, a *trafik*, as a newsagent and tobacconist. Surrounded by newspapers and magazines, titles and headlines, her wigged head looked like a glossy front cover brought to life. She was laughing with the customers, yacking, advising, recommending. For someone always keen to create an impression, the kiosk might have been a demotion. Worse, it might have felt like exile to a remote outpost with no return ticket.

This wasn't Bözsi's way of seeing the world. She passed off everything she did with the same pride and optimism, as if everything she did – or that happened to her – had status. Her news was the news that mattered. This was her inner compass. Her chin was always up, pointing ahead. Maybe it was because she began her life displaced. Her verifiable beginning was off-centre, just like her ending in the kiosk. She was born not in Budapest but 150 miles to the south-east, in what is now the Romanian town of Arad. But why there?

Arad, on an alluvial plain on the eastern edge of the Great Hungarian *puszta*, is in a historically much disputed territory. It sits, mostly, on the north bank of the almost looping Mures River, a river that connects two grandparents from different sides of the family. On the south bank, in the loop, is a citadel, now a military compound, that carries the traces of the town's struggles, its victors and its prisoners, a trans-Europe embracing the changing administrations, the switching sides, the arrivals and departures of Hungarians, Russians, Austrians, French, Serbs, Jews, Romanians. Arad is dated and dateless. Europe's international relations may have changed forever but, as the train crosses the border, the Hungarians search the Romanians and the Romanians search the Romanians.

On Arad's main street, the Bulevardul Revoluției, with the train station at one end and the nineteenth-century state theatre at the other, there are small banks and money-changers every few steps. There are mobile phones and false nails and an eclectic collection of trams from a pre-war era. In a shop there is a thin language book that translates into Romanian the surprising fact that 'Lancashire has unsurpassed polyglots.'

A century ago, Arad's identity was sharper. It found its true self during a population boom. A threefold increase in inhabitants was accompanied by a cultural enrichment, particularly in music and literature. The town was one of the net beneficiaries of the 'decentralization' of Hungarian literature, with many writers decamping to the countryside. The tenuous connection to Bözsi becomes clearer.

Her father, Jakab Kranner, a name later Magyarized to Jenő Karczag, began his working life as a printer's apprentice at the Kunosi or Kunossy printing company. At the turn of the twentieth century, when he was around 30 years old, Arad must have seemed like a good prospect. The little man, with a face like a hamster (according to my mother), of whom everyone was scared (according to my aunt), who was a *kis ördög*, a 'little devil' (according to the writer George Pálóczi-Horváth, a friend of my father who died in the mid 1970s), and who knew how to shout (according to anyone else), made it his business to get on. In the one photograph of him, a head shot, there is no suggestion of his proportions or height, but there is a pugnacity about his parted and slicked black hair, his potato nose and hooded, light eyes. There is a self-importance in his bow tie and in the gold watch chain that hangs from his lapel to his breast pocket. He would work his way up to become the printing firm's manager.

In the early 1900s, before 1905 or 1906 or thereabouts, little Great-Grandfather Jenő brought his wife, the significantly larger Irén, to Arad. Their address was 2 Deák Ferenc Street, on a corner just off the main boulevard and across from the neoclassical theatre. But the building that keeps this sidestreet – with its crumbling grandeur, reliefs and lions' heads – shadowed is the one opposite number 2. The Hotel Ardealul, built in 1840 and originally called the White Cross, was a cultural centre. Inside, beneath its grand, creaking, winding, red-carpeted staircase was a concert hall where Liszt, Brahms and Strauss all played. This and another hotel, the Vass further down Deák Ferenc Street, hosted the great Hungarian writers of the day, such as Zsigmond Móricz and Endre Ady. The latter's poem, 'The Arad Thirteen', preserves the memory of the 1848 revolutionaries executed by the Austrians.

The Hotel Ardealul's concert hall is now the 'Viva' disco. Visiting regional football teams have replaced the international visiting artists. The Austro-Hungarian culture that came has all but gone, except in the fuzzy photographs of promenading gentry hanging along the hotel's corridors. In 1911, Bözsi's birth address, 2 Deák Ferenc Street, now Mihai Eminescu Street, became home to one of the key literary magazines of Arad's golden age. A Jövő, 'The Future', published its first edition here. Perhaps Jenő was involved with the printing, perhaps not. Either way, Arad left its imprint.

All this amounts, at the very least, to proximity, and proximity is always a good starting point for the tellers of tall tales. A mystical osmosis takes place, a rubbing off, an exchange of atoms. Characters, perspectives and points of view flow together. They cease to be distinguishable. The new narrative is imprinted through repetition. Bözsi operated on this territory. She could utter the longest meaningless word in the Hungarian language: *megszentségteleníthetetlenségeskedéseitekért*. The Guinness Book of Records tried to define it as 'for your unprofanable actions' but, with its multiple suffixes queuing to be heard, the 'word' has a musicality beyond meaning. Beside it, claiming a closeness to artists barely registers. One way or another, there was more to her 'art' than airs and graces and a long, meaningless, word.

There are clues. One is my mother's memory of a brief period of pre-war pianino practice. While she clinked the keys with all the subtlety of a child, Bözsi would be cooking in the kitchen with the door open, listening. A moment later she would come in, wooden spoon in hand. 'Can't you hear that's F-sharp?' she would ask, passing the spoon to her daughter. '*Igy kell játszani!*' 'This is how to play it!' She would demonstrate the notes. Then, according to my mother, Bözsi would add with all the subtlety of 'a typical Jewish mother': 'I gave up my career because of you.'

Was there a career to give up? On Bözsi's father's side the artistic connections turn out to be actual. By the time Jenő moved to Arad, two of his three sisters, Ilona and Rózsi, were established dancers with the Hungarian State Opera. The 'skilful Kranner girls', as they are referred to in a 1956 history of Hungarian ballet, had distinguished careers spanning over 20 years, even though Rózsi's was effectively ended when she fell into the working parts of a mechanized carriage lifting her above the stage, and broke her leg.

The guardian of the ballerinas' story is Mari, my mother's cousin and the daughter of Bözsi's sister, Margit. Although she now lives in Canada, she still spends summers in her Budapest flat where, with the reverence of a museum curator, she preserves her 'treasures'. In a corner of the bedroom there is a group of three objects that belonged to Ilona, known as Lonci: a tinted photograph of her with her perfectly coiffured red hair; a bronze statuette of her as a ballerina on a pedestal; and her thin-framed, wicker-backed wooden chair.

According to Mari, the two ballerinas – Rózsi blonde and blue-eyed, Lonci dark – were both beautiful and childless. Perhaps as a result, Lonci loved Margit dearly, taking her on many outings, including to the famous Sliac spa in what is now Slovakia. Perhaps this was the birth of the rivalry between Bözsi and her sister. One was 'adopted'; the other wasn't. Certainly there is pride in Mari, handed down along with the heirlooms.

The skilful Kranner girls married 'fantastically', as Mari puts it, and their lives do seem impossibly glamorous. Rózsi's husband was

Ilenczfalvi Sárkány Béla, a landowning baron and high-ranking soldier from a Protestant family with a long lineage. Lonci married an exceptionally wealthy director of a bank, so wealthy in fact that the couple habitually travelled without luggage between their identical homes in Budapest and Vienna, each of which contained identical personal wardrobes.

Meanwhile, Jenő brought his family back to Budapest in 1912, after which he was also involved with the opera. In fact, the Kunosi printing company, back in 1897, had been responsible for printing money for the opera. For this 'offence' it had found itself in court. The company's defence, reported in the Budapest newspaper *Országos Hírlap*, was that the money was actually, and quite obviously, 'play money' for use on stage. If this wasn't allowed, went the argument, what about a king's 'crown' or official 'uniforms'? The court deliberated but, just in case there was a catch, fined the company anyway. At the opera, Jenő tried to keep his eye on the real money: as publicity director he was in charge of advertising on the safety curtain.

Bözsi was brought up by a father for whom illusion, presentation and advertising seem to have been vocational. Even the possible cause of his eventual demise has something of the theatrical. As Mari puts it: 'According to family tales, a big luggage piece fell on his head during a train trip as a result of sudden braking.'

Jenő died in 1937. My aunt, then aged six, and my mother, aged three, have a common memory of seeing him just before the end. He was frighteningly pale, shrunken and wrapped in a white sheet. Whenever Bözsi's career ended, it was well before then. There is only one photograph of her seated at a piano or clavier. It's undated but must have been taken in the mid to late 1920s when she would have been, must have been, in her early twenties. The sleek, short, side-parted hair, the make-up and the long, dangling bead necklace are all of the period. She has turned left towards the camera, her right elbow perched above the keys, her fingers touched to her cheek. She is clear-eyed, assured, yet the portrait is mannered, studied. It is the sort of 'convincing' portrait of a pianist one might invent or imagine without any musical knowledge and without any meaningful relationship to a piano. It could be a pose because it is a pose. Or it could be a moment in the life of a pianist just like a bronze statuette captures a moment in the life of a ballerina.

But the photograph has another context. It appears in the top left-hand corner of a sheet of frayed yellow paper that never seems to have had a home. It has floated on family currents between London and Budapest, lost more often than found. The page is entitled, '*BÖSKE KARCZAG PIANISTIN*'.

Around the pianist's portrait are eight reviews extracted from leading German-language, Austrian and Hungarian newspapers. At a concert in the dramatic resort of Semmering in the Austrian Alps, known for its pioneering mountain railway, the 'hugely talented young pianist' wowed both the audience and the notoriously difficult-to-please Viennese critics. 'Her natural fire captivated her audience,' wrote the *Neue Freie Presse*. The audience was 'beside itself with pleasure', insisting on two encores, observed the *Pester Lloyd*. For *Der Tag*, 'her beautiful, soft and elastic touch revealed a real talent'. For the *Pesti Napló*, what mattered was her 'strong personality, her beautiful touch and the poetry of her performance'. Yet, for *Die Stunde*, 'she does not play for the audience' because 'her art is the complete expression of her inner feeling'. The *Budapesti Hírlap* went slightly further than the rest: 'From her burning musical spirit flames rise to the heights...'

Beyond the heights it's difficult to rise but, clearly, the Austrian hills were alive that night with the sound of Böske's incendiary performance. If there is one false note, one F-sharp, on this single page of extracted reviews from an unknown publication, it's that it was printed by the Kunossy printing company. That aside, there are other musicians mentioned. Böske was not alone. Those performing with her included the Austrian opera singer Richard Mayr, who had a long and illustrious career, and violin virtuoso Paul Wildner.

Between the loose parameters of dates, and another floating fragment, part document, part memory, it's possible to establish that, in early 1920, Böske attended the Jámborné Riesz Olga Music School at 64 Andrássy Boulevard, one of Budapest's grandest thoroughfares. Then, according to the archives of the Ferenc Liszt Academy, from 1921 to 1924 she was enrolled as Erzsébet Karczag, as student number 267. This was where any serious and talented pianist would have trained, and would still. This was where her fingers found themselves and launched a career, at least for a few years. In 1930, she reached the plateau of the *Ungarischer Künstler Almanach*.

In this almanac of Hungarian artists is an objective truth: 'Böske Karczag – *Klaviervirtuosin.*'

Perhaps it was this career that made her sister, Margit, jealous. There was her brother, too. Géza, in Mari's words, was 'a devoted socialist'. In fact, she says, 'He was such an aggressive leftie that my mother [Margit] could not invite him to parties given for her friends because he attacked everyone who was not socialist.' Maybe he disdained his sister's bourgeois musical pursuits. 'Maybe,' according to Zsuzsi, 'he was macho, a little man with a lot to prove.'

Bözsi certainly had a view on where his aggression came from. Years later, when my mother, aged eight, asked Bözsi why grandmother Irén had such big breasts, Bözsi replied, 'Because Géza bit her nipple and they grew.' But it wasn't sibling rivalries that ended her career.

In 1929, Bözsi married Ernő Semler. Böske Karczag, in her mid twenties, became Bözsi Semler, one diminutive replacing another. Their eldest daughter, Zsuzsi, was born in 1931. Motherhood could, of course, curtail a clavier virtuoso's career. Even marriage might have changed everything, especially because the Karczags looked down on the lower-class Semlers. Ernő, a silversmith by trade who worked for a jeweller's and later became a jewellery store manager, was not the type to scale the Alpine heights of art. Nor did he have the land of a baron or the identical homes of a banker. Nor a car.

None of the above seemed to distil Bözsi's spirit. She used to claim that, back in Vienna, she'd been a skilful driver. 'Of course I drove a car,' she used to say, adding that she preferred to drive at night because there was less traffic. Or because, according to my mother, it was easier for the traffic to avoid her. Still, Bözsi was in love in Vienna and that, combined with her musical fire, was the sort of combustion that other road users would have feared at any hour. Later in life she was known only as a skilful backseat driver.

Whether she could operate a car or not, whether she was Böske or Bözsi, married and a mother, she still had her fingers. Her next claim, her account of how she escaped deportation, is connected to them. It's also connected to Vienna, at least to the road that leads to it from Budapest.

In November 1944, Ernő having been taken on forced labour, Bözsi, her two daughters, her mother Irén, Ernő's mother (also Irén) and 56 others were living in a flat at 40 Pozsonyi Street. It was not a yellow star house but a so-called *védett*, 'protected', house. How Bözsi managed to gain a place in a building that was under the protection of the Swiss legation is unclear. If once there was a document to accompany the protection, it no longer exists.

The address is a few doors from where my aunt still lives, on a long, shaded street running from Margit Bridge parallel to the Danube on the Pest side. At the time, the area of Újlipótváros became known as the 'little ghetto' for its concentration of 'protected houses', houses that the Arrow Cross government thought it could trade for international recognition. The Arrow Cross had respect for this protection only when it suited them.

Some time in early November, they came knocking at number 40. It's likely that there was a round-up, and a bit of a *razzia* thrown in, too. They most likely took more than one person, not just a former pianist with a poetic touch. But none of this has come down. Family history is sometimes prismatic, splitting light in all directions, and sometimes there is tunnel vision, light from a single point. In the story, it feels as if there was nobody else involved. 'This is where they took her from,' says Zsuzsi. According to her, Bözsi said to the Arrow Cross, 'You can't take me. I have two girls and two grandmothers to take care of.'

Did she say this to them? Or did she tell them, ask them, plead with them? The verb is unclear. Although I can hear Bözsi's voice, I can't hear her uttering this. It's possible that a hundred mothers said, asked, pleaded the same thing, each in her own voice, each referring to her own daughters and grandmothers.

Bözsi knew how to ask for things. She knew how to ask for money. She cried when Ernő had to go on forced labour but, before then, they'd had a good few 'screaming matches over money', as their daughters remember. So she could have asked or pleaded to stay with her children like a hundred others. Before Bözsi left, she told Zsuzsi to take her sister to nearby Pannónia Street. This is where Bözsi's sister, Margit, lived. Then she was gone. Where did they take her? Where did she go?

How she came back, how she 'escaped', is something I have always known because it has always been there as a 'fact', a piece of information, a story, a memory that has been as definite, as objective, as an heirloom. She once told me the story. I was in her flat in the mid 1980s, having just returned from a long overland journey through Asia. It was winter, a typically bitter Hungarian winter, and she served up litres of her pea soup. Maybe that's why I only remember the opening words – '*Mikor elvittek…*', 'When they took me…' – and the bit about the shoelaces. Because that's what it had to do with: the tying of her shoelaces. I remember that, in the telling of her story, her fingers tied imaginary laces in mid-air. She imagined it, reenacted it. At the time, in November 1944, she pretended it, faked it. That was how she claimed she did it, how she escaped, by pretending to tie her laces. So, as if it mattered, I go in search of where this might have happened.

The major deportations that had swept away Hungary's provincial Jews had been stopped in Budapest in late June. By November, at a time when the Germans were losing the war and the Russians were closing the ring on the capital, a new use was found for the undeported. The 6th of November saw the first forced march of tens of thousands of people the two hundred miles to their final destinations in Austria or Germany. They were to build earthworks and fortifications to defend Germany. Many would die en route, on what became known as 'death marches'.

But what was this route? When those who were deported, or when those who knew those who were deported, talk about deportation, they sometimes make a gesture. An arm briefly rises towards an unknown point. It's a 'long road' gesture, a 'God-knows-where' gesture accompanied by a jerking of the chin towards an imagined or reimagined place very far away. It's not the direction; it's the distance. Bözsi, according to my mother, 'came back filthy'. Or 'filsi', as she pronounces it. 'Everyone was filsi at that time,' she says. But this was different.

She and Zsuzsi seem to remember that their mother mentioned a brick factory, which goes with the territory. In the case of the capital, there were many of these, not just one, dating back to the 1860s. Given the context and the objective, it is likely that anyone taken from the Pozsonyi Street neighbourhood would have been marched across the river. Margit Bridge, already mined, had been destroyed in a gas explosion on 4 November. So, in the mud, rain and cold, they marched across the pontoon that replaced it. Then they would have turned north-west onto the Bécsi Road, the Vienna Road.

The road goes through Óbuda, 'Ó' meaning ancient, with its first-century ruins from the Roman province of Pannonia. At the base of the steep Óbuda hills was a cluster of brickyards, the birthplace of the modern capital. None of the brickyards remain. The last and biggest, which became the biggest of the transit camps, was the Nagybátony-Újlaki brick factory, which closed in the early 1970s. Beyond a sidestreet called Tégla Street, Brick Street, in among trees and weeds that separate traffic from service road, is a sooty stone. It's more of a large pebble on the site of the brick factory to commemorate the tens of thousands who came, who stayed a few days, who tried to huddle around the brickyard burners for warmth, who passed through en route to far away.

Bözsi, according to her daughters, was gone for three days. But her story is not that she sneaked away from a particular place. Instead, while being marched in a column, she fell back, step by step, to the last row. Then she stopped, bent down, and pretended to tie her shoelace. Or her shoelaces. With her skilful fingers she pretended as long as she needed, until either the column puddled past or she became invisible.

Nobody knows how long she was marched or how long it took her to return. Once separated from the rest, she unpicked the stitching of her yellow star and removed it. Returning the way she came would not have been easy. The road was long and muddy and crowded. Outbound columns were forced to cover ten, fifteen, twenty miles a day. There was little traffic in the opposite direction. Was she reminded of Vienna? What did she think about? Did she hear music? Maybe she recalled the Sunday lunches before the war when she made *mákos*, *túrós* and *meggyes rétes* – poppy seed, cream cheese and cherry strudels – lifting and smashing, pulling and stretching the dough on a wooden slab in the kitchen. 'That's what gives it layers,' she would say. And in case these weren't enough, her mother, the ever-larger, powdered and perfumed Irén, would come with cream cakes from the patisserie two doors away.

Somewhere along the Vienna Road, Bözsi tied her shoelaces. Then she came back 'filsi'. But she did come back. She came back for the return of her husband, who survived forced labour albeit with chronic and persistent sciatica. She came back to feed her daughters. At the end of the war, they remember there was a *pörkölt*, a traditional Hungarian winter stew of beef or pork, paprika, onions. Mari remembers one, too. They differ over who made it but it was either Bözsi or her mother or both. Whoever it was, Mari remembers it as 'the best *pörkölt*' of her life, although the meat it contained was of questionable origin. 'I still suspect,' says Mari, 'that it was carved from one of the horse cadavers to be found all over the streets.' And when Bözsi and the girls moved back to their former flat at 77 Baross Street, the roof and top floors had caved in on account of Allied bombing. Bözsi procured chickens, and turned the dusty open-air *rom szoba*, the 'ruin-room', into a farm. How she got the chickens is a mystery.

Four decades later, in her Budapest flat in communist Hungary, she had to share a telephone line with an unknown so-called 'twin'. Sometimes you would pick up the receiver and there would be a conversation going on. That was how the system worked, or didn't. Cheekily, I asked her if she was ever tempted to listen in. 'Yes, of course,' she replied. And do you? I persisted. 'No, of course not.' Why not? 'Because,' she laughed, 'they might listen in to me.'

Her personal narrative was in flux to the end. The chronology was sometimes confusing, but not the impressions. Many of her generation of women, though resilient and resourceful, were oppressed into deep and lifelong silence. My other grandmother, for instance. Bözsi would not go quietly. Her last job, post-retirement and just to keep her busy, was in the grey, baroque Trefort Street outpatient clinic. She was employed as a filing clerk. That was her employer's first mistake. The second was to give her a white coat. It wasn't long before she was diagnosing complicated ailments and, at least verbally, prescribing remedies. '*Jött egy betegem…*' she would begin. 'There came a patient of mine…'

Just before she died in 1988, she asked for my cousin, Andris. He happened to be out of town but returned as quickly as he could, arriving at the hospital, where he worked as a doctor and where she lay, at 8 a.m. She had died an hour earlier. Maybe she would have told him a final secret, the code to her life.

Bözsi's sister, Margit, when she died in 1997, aged 100, did tell Andris a final secret: during the war, Bözsi had stolen a ring from her. This story has buzzed around the family like a heard but unseen fly. Occasionally it lands and there is silence. Then it takes off again. I last heard it from Margit's granddaughter, Ági, only recently, in another century. Who knows? Andris says it's possible. Zsuzsi says that, if there was a ring, it was highly unlikely to have been Margit's to begin with, that someone else's ring was handed down or on and it went to Bözsi not Margit.

When my mother saw Margit just before the end, a kind of penultimate end, she made a point of asking her why the sisters had never got on. After a pause, Margit replied, 'Bözsi had big hands.' Who knows what this meant? Was this a reference to hands that could play the piano? Was it jealousy over hands that could span an octave? Or hands that stole? Maybe she meant to say 'head' instead of 'hands'. Maybe it was all of these things, a statement of general sibling rivalry to the very end.

The fingers of Bözsi's story have come together from London, Toronto, Budapest, Vienna and Arad. Parts of it are even true. Of course, she continued to appear and reappear in other people's stories. After the war, when my mother tried and failed to get into drama school, Bözsi was devastated. She wanted to pass on the flames, the heights and the poetry. In many ways, she did. She definitely did not go quietly. Yet what is missing most in her story is the sound of her music. As her wig slips, what remains is her compelling voice, her infectious laugh and the drumming of her fingers across a joker.

Barefoot from the Wilderness

S HE FAILED to get into drama school but she is full of drama. It comes in the form of remembered verse, lyrics, poetry, songs, ballads. These arrive in Hungarian, occasionally in fragmented Russian, sometimes in hand-me-down German, with Yiddish words bubbling to the surface that she's never seen written down. They range from revolutionary rallying calls to socialist realism to children's ditties to the alternative lyrics of 'Gloomy Sunday', which involve a rough encounter with sexually transmitted consequences.

These ordinary mysteries of memory point to my mother's first 20 or so years. It's a period that joins the dots of Hungarian history as well as family chronology. It joins the orthodoxy of her grandparents to the siege of Budapest. It joins the German soldier who hid in the cellar to the two Russian soldiers who came in search of alcohol and women. It joins the survivors who came home from distant places to the communists who made schoolchildren rewrite history. It joins the rabbi who thought she was wonderful to the world-famous Hungarian footballer who called her a cunt.

There are many ways to describe a mother. And there are many more ways to describe a particular mother, my mother. One is that she is small like her mother, has always taken care of her hands like her mother did with her own hands, and that recently in the middle of Oxford Street she missed her mother and had to buy a bottle of 4711, an eau de cologne, because it reminded her most of the smell of her mother. Another description belongs to my father, who remembers how, when they got married, she had grown into a beautiful woman pursued by men from Buda and Pest.

Perhaps most of all, my mother draws together the story of the women of the family. She has cared for my father following his stroke, just as her sister, Zsuzsi, coped with her husband, Tomi, following his tragic accident. The women cope; the men disappear. My mother's first performance at the age of 12, one that would later inspire her to try for drama school, was prescient. It was at Uncle Lakner's Children's Theatre one Sunday morning in 1946. Uncle Lakner had not survived Auschwitz, leaving his daughter to run the theatre. The audience was mostly Jewish although, according to my mother, this was never mentioned. The poem she recited was entitled 'A Message to Distant Fathers'. 'There were tears everywhere,' she recalls.

Of course, her own father, Ernő, had returned from forced labour. The person who really went missing from her life, or from whose life

The Semler girls: my mother and my aunt just before the Second World War. After 1956, most of their lives would be spent apart.

she went missing, who either way 'became' distant, is her sister, Zsuzsi. That happened a decade later. Nobody in 1946 suspected the existence of a road that led to 1956. Still less did they suspect the fork in that road. If the drama of my mother's memories joins the dots of Hungarian history, if it tells the tale of her first 20 or so years, then the tale would be meaningless without Zsuzsi.

After 1956, the dark-haired, dark-eyed sisters would write letters to each other for over 30 years, from London to Budapest and back. These messages to distant sisters no longer exist. They were thrown away by the blue-eyed Bözsi, who was always openly privy to their content. In fact, the letters were addressed to her, too, and she kept them, ribboned, in a drawer. Apparently, one day, she decided to save space. Instead, she created one.

Maybe there were more specific reasons why she got rid of them. Maybe she had personal or political fears about who might end up reading them. Still, this thoughtless erasure is an erasure of common memory, at least the spontaneous detail of it, the moment of it. The space leaves a life to be reconstructed like the *Hampelmann*, the matchstick man, in a German ditty that, ironically, Bözsi taught my mother: line by line, dot by dot, *punkt* by *punkt*, with all its facial punctuation marks.

The tale of two sisters, who married two best friends, has its own punctuation marks. These are not dots and lines but rubble, the rubble of the siege of Budapest and the rubble of the revolution. Rubble defines their liberation as well as their separation. They picked their way through without knowing where they had come from or where they would end up.

When does their common memory begin? When does the younger sister's memory catch up? When do their common memories end? Is it possible to find spaces between memories, especially memories that have been repeated often enough to resemble recitals? How do we tell collective family stories?

On their mother's side was the drama, the grand stage, the performance, the concerts, the operas and the sibling rivalry. On the other side, their father's side, there are two details that always grabbed my attention, as they once did theirs: one was the madness of one of their grandfathers; the other was the hairy mole that both sisters saw and feared on the face of a great-aunt. Their mother's side always looked down on their father's side. Their mother's side used to say that Ernő's own father, Bernát, had 'arrived in Budapest barefoot'. In other words, he had arrived with nothing but God.

The sisters, my mother the younger by three years, my aunt the taller by three inches, both remember Grandfather Bernát as a severe, and severe-looking, man. In the only photograph of him, he seems to want to leave that impression: a pince-nez, which is too large for his face, magnifies his glaring, scrutinizing eyes above a white and whiskery moustache. His orthodoxy is difficult to forget: wrapped in his prayer shawl, he would *daven*, pray and sway towards a wall, murmuring in Hebrew. He had come to the capital with nothing, barefoot, and had made his way.

He sold biscuits for a living, and chocolates wrapped in silver paper. Eventually, he came to own a small chocolate manufactory. Nobody can remember where this was. No matter, because this confectionery represented and provided some of the comfort and luxury of urban life. It was proof that Bernát had made good in the big city.

But tragedy seems to have stalked him all the way from wherever he had come. His daughter, Rózsi, Ernő's sister, married a gambler whose debts he eventually had to underwrite. Meanwhile, Rózsi's son used to unwrap the sample chocolates, eat the confectionery, then carefully rewrap the paper. Bernát would have to present the chocolates to prospective clients and endure the embarrassment of explaining away what was missing. By the time his son-in-law's gambling debts were paid off, Bernát's bank account was as empty as a silver-wrapped chocolate.

Rózsi, remembered as a hauntingly stick-thin and dark figure, had to work to support them. She became a manicurist. In 1944, while on her way to or from a client – although who wanted a manicure at that time is unclear – Rózsi was taken off the streets by the Arrow Cross. She disappeared without trace.

Bernát, by then in his eighties, went mad in the same year. From his well-appointed flat in Csokonai Street, he and his wife, Irén, had had to move to the nearby but, even today, much shabbier Német Street. The flat they shared was tiny. 'They used to wash, cook and pray in one room,' Zsuzsi remembers. 'It had an overpowering smell of cabbage and urine that neither of them noticed,' my mother remembers. One day, for no particular reason that anyone can think of, Bernát decided to chase his wife around the kitchen table with a big knife. Round and round they went, so the story goes. They completed several circuits until, presumably, Irén's screaming attracted attention.

From this state of mind in a shabby flat, perhaps clinging to the remnants of his religion, Bernát made one final move. Or, rather, he was moved. Lipótmező lunatic asylum, far out on the hilly western edge of Buda, became his new, and his last, address. This was where he died in 1944. By then the Germans had invaded and Ernő, afraid of the dangers lurking on the street, did not allow his daughters, Bernát's granddaughters, to attend the funeral in Budapest's Jewish cemetery.

Somehow, it seems, Bernát Semler ended up where he began, in a place unknown and apparently unreachable. Yet the prints left by his bare feet must lead back to a place beyond the horizon, beyond the bend of time, to the place the sisters sprang from.

One day or week or month some 65 years after his incarceration, I make the journey to the defunct, nineteenth-century madhouse on the edge of town. Built in 1868, it became the largest institution of its kind in Hungary. From the main road, a long path leads up a hill into a wood. The building is shrouded in trees, and only its rooftop moulding and coat of arms can be seen. At the barred gate, outside his lodge, sits a languid porter. He tells me the obvious, that the former neurological institute is closed. Usually, in such circumstances, one can come to an arrangement. But he's insistent. 'It's *hermetically* closed,' he says. 'There are dogs,' he adds.

I wander away, looking for an alternative. Nearby, a woman carrying a bag of yellow peppers offers one. She mentions a residential block in a sidestreet, with its overgrown garden that adjoins the institute. At the back of the garden there is a fence, and in the fence, she tells me, you will find a hole. Doesn't all family history have holes, holes that prove something is missing, and holes to look through, through which to catch a glimpse of a part of yourself?

Minutes later, I am crouching at the hole, looking through. The patients and the madness have gone. They have been scattered by time like the breeze has scattered leaves across the path. The vast three-storey building, its yellow paint flaking, its windows dirt-streaked, betrays no confidence. But it's just possible to stand there long enough to feel what a great-grandfather might have seen in his final days, what he would have remembered, what he would have wanted others to remember as he neared his end. Did he know where he had come from? Then a guard dog starts to yowl and it's time to leave.

Back in my aunt's flat, I'm stroking her dog to stop it barking. 'Bernát,' Zsuzsi remembers, 'had a brother who had two sons and a horse. The sons were both black-eyed and had long black moustaches. I saw them once in about 1940 or '41 when I was nine or ten.' With these words she conjures apparitions. I can see them on a long road, travelling out of the past towards the present. They carry their bundles yet they are all weightless. A day later, the vision is given some weight in the form of another memory. This time the memory is my cousin's. 'I heard from Bözsi,' Andris remembers of our common grandmother, 'of a man called Mór. He might have come from Szatmár.' This is a reference not to the town, now Satu Mare in Romania, but to the north-eastern Hungarian county. Then he remembers a list of inky dates and places left by our common grandfather, Ernő, on a piece of paper. And, indeed, a written name or two seems to confirm that the apparitions once lived and breathed and walked.

Narrow down the territory, and the territory expands. Look through a hole in a fence or squint through a microscope, and life teems. This distant territory, this county, comprised dozens of settlements, rural, widespread, tiny, many of them as vanished from the map as a manicurist from a Budapest street.

The road to this vanished place leads east across two rivers, first back across the Danube, then on towards the Tisza, the Danube's longest tributary, which crinkles into the Ukraine. The road crinkles, too, back into the past, to a place that my mother never knew and that Zsuzsi barely glimpsed.

The last town of size in this direction is the seat of Szabolcs-Szatmár-Bereg county. Nyíregyháza, its suffix meaning 'church', is in the northern part of the Great Hungarian Plain. Here, the remaining *Izraelita* archives are held in batches according to settlement. Among these other written names, I find a trace of a solitary Mór or Móricz with a variant spelling of his family name: not Semler but Zemler.

Móricz Zemler is listed as a trader of small and mixed goods. In other words, he would have sold anything going. He is also listed as an inhabitant, in 1900, of Cseke. The place name is etymologically linked to 'crossing', as in the crossing of a river, such as the Tisza. How did the Semlers, or Zemlers, arrive at this crossing? Did they cross barefoot? Cseke still exists, known also as Szatmárcseke. The road to the past becomes clearer, just as the places on that road become ever smaller.

Cseke, first mentioned in the fourteenth century, lies right on the border of the Ukraine. Its bus timetable is intuited by the village drunk, and it would lie undisturbed in the mind of the population at large were it not for a unique connection to one of Hungary's most famous poets. Ferenc Kölcsey lived and died here. It was on this land that, in 1823, he composed Hungary's national anthem, the *himnusz*, and he is buried in the strangest of Finno-Ugric cemeteries, characterized by carved, pointed, inscribed wooden stumps. One of the village streets is named after him. It's a street where, it turns out, some of Móricz's relatives also lived, and died.

The wooden stump of the family tree has grown new roots and branches. These now extend from the siblings Mór and Bernát to their father, Herman, who was born in 1843 and died in 1908, and beyond, to Herman's father, Farkas Zemler, my great-great-great-grandfather, born two centuries ago in 1809.

Barns, woodpiles, a horse dripping saliva, yowling dogs, big knives, and country words forgotten by shoe-wearing metropolitans hundreds of miles distant: Cseke has barely changed. The village drunk swears he knew a Zemler. Perhaps he did. But, looking around, I feel I do now.

Once upon a time, a Zemler hung corn on his porch. He worked land with his hands. He might have owned a boney nag. He sold 'mixed goods'. He wore a *cájg*, hard cotton pants, and an *ujjas*, a jerkin, with a *surc*, an apron. He had a *bankli*, a workbench, at which he sat on a *hokedli*, a stool. As the sun went down on the upper Tisza, he contemplated his day's trading in the surrounding settlements. Come Sabbath, he would observe the rites and rituals of his religion.

Móricz had a wife called Bimbi. They had four children, a son who died almost at birth, a daughter called Rozália, and two other sons: Gyula, who was born in 1900, and Sándor, born four years later. These must have been the black-eyed, black-moustached sons glimpsed by

Zsuzsi. Móricz died in 1944, the same year as Bernát. There is no mention of him chasing his wife around a kitchen table with a knife, and he apparently died of entirely natural causes. By contrast, the black-eyed sons most likely died of entirely unnatural causes, swept up along with so many other rural Jews. As for the boney nag, who knows? Maybe it provided a meal or two.

But there is still the question of the aunt with the fearsome and hairy mole. From a few hundred miles south towards the Serbian border, from an equally remote part of the country, came this woman and her mole, the hairs of which would brush the sisters' cheeks when she kissed them. She and her sister, Irén, who was chased around a kitchen table, had similarly arrived in Budapest with nothing. They had come from the small market town of Hódmezővásárhely. Through Irén's maternal line emerge the links in the genealogical chain. Buried in the concealed Israelite cemetery behind the crumbling railway station is a man called Ábrahám Grünhut. Born in 1809, died in 1877, this man was my great-great-great-great-grandfather. What makes this unheard-of individual remarkable is that he was the area's first rabbi.

'Bingo!' says my mother when I tell her. My equally unreligious brother is overjoyed. 'You want me to FedEx you a Keppel?' Rabbi Grünhut, it seems, initiated community activity at a so-called 'kosher pub' at 2 Mózes Street, where in the 1840s the local landowning baron had granted a small number of Jews, especially the ones 'of good behaviour', a dispensation to produce alcohol.

So a barefooted Zemler, with a belief in God, left the countryside for the city, and went mad in a lunatic asylum. And an especially religious Grünhut tried to pull together a rural community that would be all but wiped out. In a mirror image, a distant descendant, Ernő, would be made to leave the city for the countryside. This coming and going, this searching for yet never finding a place, this 'crossing', is the point where the sisters' deeper roots begin to fade, and their independent memories shoot from the earth.

One baking day in May 1944, Zsuzsi distinctly remembers her father's footprints in the asphalt as he went off on forced labour to dig earthworks for a rural airport. Ági, aged nine, doesn't remember the footprints but says she will 'never forget leaning out of the second-floor window' and seeing her father, who was dressed as if for a hike, with 'tears streaming down his face'. She remembers when he returned, too, a year later, when the war was over. The two sisters had had the worst argument of their lives over something that neither can now recall. They ran apart, Zsuzsi upstairs to a friend's flat. A little while later Ági saw two men approaching. At first they looked like soldiers but in odd patchwork uniforms. Then she recognized one as her father. Before rushing to greet him, she had to find her sister. This was something that she felt the sisters had to experience together. When she found her, she told her, 'We're never going to argue again. Daddy's home!'

They have a common recollection of what they did between their father going and returning, when their mother was taken. Instructed by Bözsi to go to her sister Margit, a short distance away, they both remember a much longer journey, a bubble of time involving subterfuge and cover stories. Number 40 Pozsonyi Street, from where Bözsi was taken, and 22 Pannónia Street, where her sister lived, are parallel. The walk might take an unhurried adult five minutes. But they remember the rubble from damaged buildings, the bombed-out basements, broken windows, the intense smell of burning, a dead horse, dust clouds, everything crunching underfoot. The girls were little and the buildings big. 'We picked off our yellow stars,' they say. 'We put scarves on our heads.' Zsuzsi told her sister that she had a new name, a non-Jewish name. She was now Teréz Kovács. If they were stopped by anyone for any reason, they were refugees from the countryside, from Erdély, Transylvania, true Magyars, and that they'd been bombed out of their home.

They remember the sanctuary of Margit's flat. Number 22 was, in fact, a German-protected Christian house, and when Jews had to move out of it into yellow star houses, non-Jews moved in, including many workers of the Budapest transit authority who were also members of the Arrow Cross. However, Jews were allowed to remain in two flats. These, according to Margit's daughter, Mari, were craftsmen, such as tailors and shoemakers, who were useful to the Germans. Margit, who had married a Christian in April 1944, survived the war effectively hidden among the enemy and exempted from wearing a yellow star, even though her own daughter still had to wear one. The treatment of miscegenation varied from one building to the next. At some point, Mari recounts, the Jewish craftsmen were taken away by the Arrow

Cross only to be brought back, 'saved' in Mari's word, by the decent non-Jewish concierge who was actually accountable for them.

It was into this delicately balanced atmosphere that the sisters entered, and to which Bözsi would return after her escape from deportation. It was also where, after a Christmas 'celebration', including a tree, on the traditional Hungarian evening of 24 December, the siege of Budapest began. The Russian forces had encircled Budapest; the Nazis, psychopathically, refused to give up the city. The ensuing battle, with the civilian population caught in the middle, was to last over a hundred days, with the Russians paying a heavy price to liberate the capital street by street. Only the battle of Stalingrad is comparable in its intensity.

The girls, Ági, Zsuzsi and cousin Mari, had experienced heavy Allied bombing, both British and Russian, especially from September 1944, but this was close-quarters artillery. Windows blew out. Buildings collapsed. One night early in the siege, Bözsi's and Margit's brother, the devoted socialist Géza, turned up. He'd somehow managed to escape from forced labour, and had found his way back to Pannónia Street. 'We were side by side on a mattress trying to sleep,' the sisters remember. 'Our heads were by the window and Géza immediately insisted that we turn the other way.' Minutes later, 'the building next door blew in or up causing a huge big vase to fall onto our legs. We were lucky that we changed position.' It was, says my mother, 'good socialist advice'.

The following weeks were spent crowded into the stinking cellar, with its smells of mould and human decay, now and again catching glimpses of German boots. Few German soldiers trapped within the city would survive. One came and went, a frightened phantom, hiding out for half a night. 'Of course, by then,' says my mother, 'they'd become very polite.'

Actually, it was the liberating Russians who were less polite. The Hungarians had been German allies. The Russians made little distinction between Hungarians and Hungarian Jews. As such, many Hungarians, especially women, would come to learn their first Russian words as victims. When *baryshni*, women, were asked to peel *kartoshki*, potatoes, it usually meant rape. In addition, tens of thousands of Budapest's citizens were rounded up for *malenkaya rabota*, a 'little work', which came to be a euphemism for deportation to forced labour camps in the Soviet Union. Like many women, Bözsi dirtied herself up to make herself as undesirable as possible.

My mother remembers the young Russian soldiers with hard faces, who'd fought their way into the capital, coming into the flat to search it. They picked up an unusual-looking box torch, which they couldn't figure out how to use. 'Before Bözsi could say anything, I helpfully showed them the button that opened it, and they gratefully pocketed it.' Then, in a cupboard, they found something that really interested them: hair tonic and eau de cologne. These they immediately poured down their throats without blinking.

Then the shooting and the bombing and the shelling stopped. The Germans had gone, so too the Arrow Cross, and it was Russian soldiers directing the traffic. Budapest was in ruins, razed, its bridges flotsam, having been systematically destroyed by the Germans who, by mid January 1945, had nothing better to do.

Ernő, Bözsi and the sisters returned to their pre-war flat at 77 Baross Street, where Bözsi would keep chickens under an open sky, where Ernő would secrete bits of jewellery in the stove because certain things could only be paid for in precious metals as inflation soared.

Day after day, month after month, people returned from distant places. Those who had survived in the capital waited for them, looked out for them, hoped for them. In fact, initially, the sisters were among them. My mother remembers a friend at number 77 shouting, 'The Semlers are back!' Then, she remembers, 'A red-haired girl with ponytails called Vera ran down from the fifth floor. The first thing she asked us was, "What happened to you?" and I remember trying to think what to reply. Then I said, "Nothing."'

Nothing. A self-censorship with one word. An erasure of memories like letters thrown away. Perhaps it was easier to be a witness to the successive homecomings of others. It was the homecoming of a third party that led to Zsuzsi's first meeting with her future husband, Tomi. After the war, my father's best friend, with whom he'd been hidden in the cellar in Népszínház Street, went back to his family home virtually next door to the sisters at 81 Baross Street. Tomi used to come to number 77 to ask after his friend and classmate, Imre Kertész, later to become the Nobel Prize-winning writer. Imre lived a floor below the sisters. In the summer of 1944, aged 15, while on his way to do forced work at the oil refinery in south Budapest, he'd been taken off a bus by Hungarian gendarmes and deported to Auschwitz. 'Tomi was very skinny,' Zsuzsi remembers. 'I wouldn't have paid much attention to him but I was very fond of Imre and also wanted to hear anything there was about him.'

Imre returned in late spring. 'He looked dreadful. His knees were so swollen,' says Zsuzsi. In his novel *Sorstalanság, Fatelessness,* first published in 1975, there is an oblique reference to the sisters who lived upstairs, and to Baross Street, 'weatherbeaten but full of a thousand promises'. The book deals with the going, the returning, and what people would ask when they saw him, and what he would say when they asked, and what, if anything, he would remember.

My mother remembers that, one day, her classmate and best friend shouted to her that her sister had returned. She, too, was swollen. She, too, had been to Auschwitz, arrested originally for political reasons. 'She showed us her number,' my mother says. 'I'd never seen anyone who'd been there. We'd all heard something about it by then but she was the first we saw.' Then there were the ones who had been there and came back but never really returned. A woman called Klári, who'd been there, too, and had lost her entire family there, did come back one day. And on one other day, a year or two later, she jumped from a fifth-floor window.

There's a film by Miklós Jancsó whose title captures the stories of displaced people flung far and wide wending their ways back: *Így Jöttem.* 'This is how I came home.' There is obviously no film for its opposite: this is how I left and never came back. It's almost as if the countdown to the terminus of 1956 began once everyone who was going to return had returned, when there was nobody left to wait for.

Of course, nobody knew that the hours and the days were being counted, but someone, somewhere, was counting. It's an impression I have had when talking to so many about that period. As Zsuzsi, neither a fatalist nor religious, said to me, 'It was written.' Look at any history book on the subject of 1956 and there is always a counting down. It's as if there were nothing but 'key' dates between the Russians liberating the country and the Russians invading it. Was it written? Was there a counting down? Each date seemingly falls with the precision of clockwork. What were the ticks of the clock in the life of a girl who, like many other Hungarian girls, came of age just in time to escape? What were my mother's 'key' dates?

21 MAY 1946 – RELIGION AND POLITICS

After her performance at Uncle Lakner's Children's Theatre, there is a recollection of the school rabbi. In her school remembrance book, alongside her classmates' drawings and made-up verses, the rabbi wrote a message that began, 'My dearest child, Ágnes, the enchanting smile on your beautiful face...' Unfortunately, aged 12, my mother and her best friend thought the rabbi was on the dingy side, 'a bit smelly' in fact, and 'terribly dandruffed'. At that point, as my mother recalls, 'What did being Jewish mean anyway?' Her older sister was already much more interested in politics, in socialism, in debating issues, in asking big questions, such as, 'What did things really mean?'

1947 – ROMANCE

Colour and light returned to the life of the capital. Some sunbathed on ruined bridges. Some went dancing. The sisters were given a holiday in the form of a campsite in the country where poets came to read by firelight, where girls could stick their bare buttocks out of windows and poke fun at boys. Although my parents had met at Swedish gymnastics when my mother was four and my father eight, they met again at the swimming pool, in the sunshine, when my mother was thirteen and my father seventeen. He was with his friend and classmate Imre Kertész, and they invited her for a coffee. Then there was the first party at 77 Baross Street, when the sisters' parents were out. My father was there, apparently with an accordion that he attempted to play.

1948 – US AND THEM

The light began to change as the communist era took hold on every level, from political posts to the military and state security. 'Parents began to teach their kids how to lie,' says my mother. 'Our parents told us many times: "Never repeat what you hear at home."'

1949 – REWARD AND PUNISHMENT

Hungary was declared a People's Republic. The sisters had special functions at school. It was considered a great honour to be responsible for culture, and the sisters' role was to draw attention to Soviet plays and communist books, and to help organize relevant outings. There were regular meetings over these issues, which were held in the school gym. But such positions in the new order were often double-edged. 'At one meeting, in front of everyone, we were asked to stand up,' says my mother. 'We were simply told that the role had been taken away. It was awful, embarrassing.'

It was especially bad for Zsuzsi since her university application was imminent and the support of the Party was essential. Days later, the sisters plucked up the courage to ask why, when they were good students, this had happened.

'Because you're different,' came the reply.

'How exactly?'

'Your uniform is pressed every day,' came the reply.

The inference was clear: they were too bourgeois. Bözsi and Ernő were not just upset. They were frightened. Again. Ernő was always an optimist but his view was clear: 'If you push it, things will be far worse.' During these years, such scenes could be played out in virtually any setting. Hundreds of thousands would be charged with some offence or other against the state. There were internments. There was forced labour. There were expulsions to remote rural villages. There was the first 'show trial'. It was a period that many Hungarians recall with the phrase *csengőfrász*: 'bell fright'. A black car would arrive after dark or before it was light. Its occupants, secret police, would ring the doorbell, arrest someone, then drive at speed to 60 Andrássy Boulevard, formerly the Arrow Cross headquarters, now the headquarters of a new power, complete with underground cells.

As a result of what happened at school, Zsuzsi never got to study what she wanted, which was medicine. By accident rather than desire, she managed to get a place studying engineering, which she hated, followed by a career in engineering, which she also hated. Even today, she does not forgive 'those who caused us problems'.

1951 – THE TRUTH OF HISTORY

The beginning of what my mother calls 'the worst years'. There is a Hungarian verb of the period that, in many ways defines it: *csirizni*. The verb is derived from a noun, a floury, watery paste with which pupils were instructed to stick together certain pages of their history books, according to the prevailing view. A few months later, the same pages of history would carefully have to be unstuck using a warm knife. And all the kids would have to give Stalin a present on his birthday.

1952 – THE VISION

As school ended, the class was taken on a trip to a special town. The year before, Dunapentele had been renamed Sztálinváros, Stalin Town, only reverting to its present name in 1961. Some 45 miles south of Budapest, the name-changing Dunaújváros still carries the traces of the country's first town developed along ideological lines. It was intended as a socialist paradise of workers' apartments, bespoke culture, and of course its primary industrial objective, the still-predominant ironworks to the south with its unmistakable pillared entrance. It could have been a poem by the Russian revolutionary poet Mayakovsky come to life, especially the one half-remembered by my mother: 'Iron-Smelter Ivan Kozirev's Narrative about Moving to a New Flat', which reveals the proletarian worker's happiness at using his new, state-provided hot and cold bath taps. Some people were forcibly relocated to Sztálinváros. In the case of my mother and her classmates, they went on a compulsory excursion to carry bricks, pick carrots and to sing to the locals. They were sent there 'to help to build the future'.

1953 – THE ILLUSION

Stalin died and the tramlines were finally lifted from beneath the war rubble on Baross Street. Whatever future she was helping to build, and whatever its direction, my mother failed to get into drama school. This was despite the Hungarian phrenologist who fingered her skull and told her she had a great soprano voice. The real problem was her lack of enthusiasm for Soviet plays at her drama school audition. Then she failed to finish university because she innocently asked her literature tutor 'if literature itself would be discussed alongside Marxism and Leninism'. The frightened tutor informed the party secretary. The party secretary ordered my mother out of the building. So, instead, she began a course in photography, and would soon be doing darkroom shifts for Magyar Foto.

1954 – THE SEEDS OF FATE

She started going out with my father. Flowers started to arrive at 77 Baross Street. Ironically, the concierge told her, 'I didn't know you'd become an "actress".' It was also the year Zsuzsi married Tomi. Perhaps because of this, Ernő and Bözsi began to fear the possibility that their younger daughter would marry my father. The thing was that, whereas Tomi had had the opportunity to study, my father hadn't. Tomi had the strong prospect of becoming a doctor. My father had few prospects at all.

The situation had arisen because, though bound by friendship and the common experience of losing their husbands, from which neither ever recovered, the boys' mothers had very different circumstances after the war. Tomi's mother, Panci, could rely on the relative wealth of her parents, which was secured by their gentleman's outfitters on Baross Street. They also took especial care of her, having lost their other daughter and her family in Auschwitz.

Lili and her parents, by contrast, had nothing, and my father had to work to support himself. In the late 1940s, his grandfather Móric would come to meet him after school. My father would exchange his school bag for a case of sample handkerchiefs that he would endeavour to sell to a certain Mrs Ramschburger. Odd jobs had kept him going until he decided to be a journalist. Worse, he was trying to make inroads as a freelancer at a time when freelancing was virtually unknown. 'We love you,' Bözsi would tell him, 'but you can't marry her.' Ernő even took my father for a private tête-à-tête in a desperate effort to dissuade him. Needless to say, their words fell on deaf ears.

1955 – THE LAST OF THEM

The last of my mother's grandparents died. Irén, Bernát's wife, had lived at 77 Baross Street since the death of her husband. She was a witness, of sorts, to the developing romance between my parents. In the late evening of her life, she'd sit in the hall in the dark to make herself as inconspicuous as possible, while pretending not to hear anything when my father came by. During the day, she'd take her string bag to trade whatever she could to make ends meet. Some of her 'goods' might have included dried beans from a Jewish relief agency or black-market alcohol. One day she failed to return home. The sisters went out to look for her. They eventually found her in the mortuary. Apparently, she had fallen out of the number 6 tram on a bend. Maybe she was weighed down by beans. Maybe, in an ancestral irony stretching back to Rabbi Grünhut and his alcohol dispensation, she was holding a bottle of fruit brandy instead of the handrail. Either way, the generation associated with religion, string bags and the wilderness was gone.

1956 – THE MAKING OF A MARK

Early in the year, my mother found herself standing by a goalpost in the national stadium. She had a camera in her hand, and she was making her own way. As a trainee for *Képes Sport* – 'Picture Sport' – the leading weekly magazine, she took pictures of the Red Meteor women's handball team, 6,000-metre cross-country championships and just about any other breathless event with an Exacta Varex camera, which she could use one-handed though it was 'heavy as mud'.

For her first big football match, her editor told her, 'You're small, so just get to the goalpost and shoot anything you can.' She obeyed. And that's when it happened. Ferenc Puskás, after whom the national stadium would one day be renamed, was already a legendary talent who scored vast numbers of goals with his favoured left foot. 'He was running towards the goal with the ball,' as my mother tells it. 'The crowd was screaming. As he shot he carried on running and had to jump over me.' On the other side of her, 'the fat little chap', as one English commentator called him, turned back. 'With his hands on

My parents coming out of the registry office on the corner of Andrássy Boulevard, Budapest, 9 September 1956. The Hungarian Revolution erupted the following month.

his hips, he looked down at me and said, "I've seen a few big pricks in my time but in a woman never such a total cunt." '

She'd made her mark on the national game. Some of the action pictures taken of Puskás by the 'total cunt' still survive in the magazine's archive. With hindsight, they seem like my mother's final 'key' moments. The Zemler who walked out of the wilderness, the father going, the mother going, the mother returning, the father returning, the Nazis, the socialist uncle who saved her from a falling vase, the Russians, the communist vision, the budding career, the poems and ballads and verses of empire and of totalitarianism all flowed together.

9 SEPTEMBER 1956 – THE RISK OF HOPING

Despite the protestations of her parents, and still pursued by men from Buda and Pest, she married my father. There's a picture of the couple, each of them dressed in a one-off black suit for all special occasions, striding arm in arm out of the registry office on the corner of Andrássy Boulevard. They're smiling radiantly at the camera. They're smiling at the future.

Around them is an unseen crowd of well-wishers and relatives: their mothers, Lili and Bözsi; my mother's father Ernő; Zsuzsi and Tomi; my mother's cousin, Bandi; and so on. The branches of the family tree came together that day. The men and the women drank together. Some got drunk. There's a picture of my father, pissed, garrulous, surrounded by family, friends and flowers.

But the smiles, the drunkenness and the togetherness belie the future. The truth is that there was no time for a honeymoon. In fact, there was barely time to recover from the hangover. Wherever my mother had come from, whatever songs and poems and verses she would remember, however she had come through the consecutive totalitarianisms of the preceding years, the events of the following month would change her and the family, in fact all families, forever. The revolution was coming.

1956

A Revolution in a Family

D RAMATIS PERSONAE:

ISTVÁN, *father*
ÁGI, *mother*
LILI, *my father's mother*
BÖZSI, *my mother's mother*
ERNŐ, *my mother's father*
ZSUZSI, *my mother's sister*
TOMI, *Zsuzsi's husband*
PANCI, *Tomi's mother and Lili's best friend*
BANDI, *my mother's cousin*
JANCSI, *family friend*

*

'What's all that noise?' Bandi asked.
   'Shooting,' my father replied.
   'Why is there shooting?' Bandi asked.
   'There's a revolution,' my father replied.

*

It was the evening of Tuesday 23 October, the evening the shooting started. My father, who had been freelancing for Hungarian Radio since 1948, was trapped like the rest of the journalists in the Radio building. Since the communist takeover, the Radio had been an organ of the state run by Stalinist executives. Outside there were protestors demanding that their grievances be broadcast. Guarding the building were agents of the hated AVH, the Hungarian secret service. Nobody knows who exactly fired the first shot. With the political and social situation changing hourly, the phones at the Radio had been ringing all day. My father just happened to answer a call. The caller just happened to be Endre Gömöri, a friend, senior colleague and his wife's cousin.

As a child, Bandi, the diminutive of Endre, had been the one who had sneakily rewrapped the silver-papered chocolates belonging to his grandfather, Bernát, having eaten the contents. During the war, he'd survived on his wits, often with a false name and false papers, and once or twice disguised in an Arrow Cross uniform. In October 1956, Bandi, some eight years older than my father, was an established foreign political correspondent. He was calling from Poland, where he'd been sent to cover the rebellion that had begun in the summer and which had ended with a new government, rather than being crushed by the Soviet military.

As they spoke, neither knew that one would end up staying in Hungary, and one would escape.

The question of who started the shooting at the Radio building on Bródy Sándor Street is disputed to this day. What is beyond dispute is that, as a result of the next few days and weeks, there were those who stayed, and there were those who went. Half a century on there is still a pair of verbs that defines the nation: *menni*, 'to go', versus *maradni*, 'to stay'. The verbs define the nation, and its families, including mine. Since I can remember, the other side of the family was always the one that chose the other verb.

In Hungary, in the autumn of 1956, everyone was given the same choice. The revolution, in that sense, was egalitarian. Each choice was accompanied by a story, and stories of the revolution were sprayed like bullet holes across the country. There were a lot of bullet holes. Some, especially in the capital, are still there. You can see them on random buildings, around window frames, above doors, on fifth-floor balconies, at street level, at head level, from any angle, as if the whole city were pockmarked or porous, as if the whole city were a giant sponge.

Sure, Budapest, where my family was, looks better than it did. Redevelopment, renovation and renewal made a difference, especially after the new millennium. It made a cosmetic difference to some of the buildings, but not to the people who lived in them. The revolution gave everyone a choice and it forced everyone to choose. This means that there was a revolution in everyone, ten million of them.

Some people, caught up in grand events, cannot help claiming, especially after it's all over, that they were somewhere special or that they did something special. They talk themselves or write themselves into history. One of my distant relatives, Ádám Bíró, writer, editor, collector and teller of jokes, whiskery and twinkling, whom I met once in his poetically weedy and broken-down holiday home in the village of Leányfalu on the Danube, and who escaped from Hungary as a boy in 1956, told me that many of the people he knows of that generation claim to have been somewhere special at a special moment: 'They all say they were there. It seems everyone was a revolutionary and that the whole of Budapest was right there in the square when Stalin's statue was torn down. And you took photographs? I ask them. "Of course," they reply. And you still have them? I ask. "Now? Oh, no. It was so long ago," they reply. "They're gone... Lost..."'

The revolution in my family, and therefore in so many others, involved more words than bullets. Between them they did not throw a petrol bomb or shoot a Soviet soldier. None has ever claimed to have been in the square when Stalin's statue was torn down. There are no 'lost' photographs from the events of October and November because none were taken.

But it just so happens that there is a bullet hole in a 'lost' painting. And that there was a tank shell on a 'lost' date. And that my father was in one of the most famous locations of the revolution on its opening day.

And then there are the words. These words, the words that were exchanged between family members, the final words, and the *final* final words that led to irreversible decisions, are just as important and difficult to pin down as anything else. Everyone had a revolution. It's just that not everyone had the same revolution.

According to the 'souvenir' version, the T-shirt version, the version packaged for Western tourists, the revolution was a freedom fight against tyranny, a spontaneous people's struggle for liberation fought against a superpower. There are two famous images of the struggle. One is *Time* magazine's January 1957 cover. It's a romanticized drawing, not a photograph, of a shock-haired freedom fighter with a bandaged hand clutching a weapon. *Time*'s 'Man of the Year 1956' stares bravely at you, eyes challenging you. The other image is that of the *Pesti Srác*, 'the boy from Pest'. His statue stands outside the Corvin Cinema, which saw some of the most intense street fighting. The boy is improbably young and carries a rifle. He symbolizes the innocence that fought against overwhelming odds, and died. There is truth in both images. Estimates vary but around 2,500 people were killed and up to 20,000 wounded by an army that brought tanks onto civilian streets and shot civilians at point-blank range. Who could call this anything other than an outrage?

But this is a family story, and the revolution in a family is not necessarily about grand statements, nor about multi-point declarations made by students, nor about which communist leader announced what and when, nor about how workers' councils were formed, nor about a prime minister declaring withdrawal from the Warsaw Pact, nor about whether there should or should not have been outside intervention by the Americans or the British, nor about the essential character of the revolution. The Russians of course claimed it was a fascist counter-revolution, but, as one old Hungarian, leaning out of his Budapest window, put it to me: 'How can the people have carried out a counter-revolution against themselves?' To unravel that logic would be to solve all manner of puzzle. It's easier to say that it's true, a people can't. But perhaps a family can. It's not that families wanted to. They were forced to.

This is one of the enduring differences between the sisters. One went; one stayed. Neither knew until the last minute what each would do. One of them, post-1956, never had to look out of her window at the exact places where things had happened, where things had been done, at places cast in remembered pain. The other has always lived in these places. It's what happens when a family revolts against itself, when it counters its natural instinct to stay together. The outcome in my family, as in so many others, is that it split.

How did this split happen? How was one verb chosen over the other? Who was standing where? And when? And who said what to whom in this family revolution?

After the war, given all that had happened at the address, Lili had been desperate to leave Népszínház Street. People didn't buy or sell flats. Rather, they put an advertisement in a newspaper and exchanged them. Lili had managed to exchange hers for one on Baross Street, somewhere she had aspired to live for a long time. A second-floor flat with a street view in the huge, green–grey, four-storey, turn-of-the-century corner block that is number 109 became home to my mother and father after they got married, and of course Lili.

Bözsi and Ernő had moved a few hundred feet from 77 Baross Street to nearby Mária Terézia Square, but Zsuzsi and Tomi lived further up the street at number 81. Their flat was divided into two, with Tomi's mother Panci and her parents Aladár and Berta living next door. This was the way people lived, with mothers and fathers and sons and daughters, with the family the war had left, and with the ever-present possibility of dramatic entrances and exits on a claustrophobic family stage.

The first family move was an exit, actually a belated holiday. Zsuzsi had been almost too ill to attend her sister's wedding back in September. Because of an operation, she and Tomi had delayed a short trip to Prague. My father, with an ear closer to the ground, warned them that something might be about to happen. The events in Poland since June, the student activism in various Hungarian towns, the literary Petőfi Circle's criticisms of the Communist Party, all pointed to greater expectations and an increasing national temperature. On 18 October Zsuzsi and Tomi went anyway.

Within days, a mass demonstration was being organized by students in combination with writers' groups. The Petőfi Circle meetings had 'built up without government reaction', according to Jancsi, a friend of the Semlers' and colleague of my father's whose life was to become inextricably bound to the family. 'Initially, there were only a few people at the meetings, and everyone waited for speech-makers to be arrested.' When they weren't, subsequent meetings had 'hundreds queuing... It was a fantastically exciting time.'

A march of mostly students and writers was planned to the statue of General Bem, the national hero of the 1848 Revolution, which stands on the Buda side of the Danube, opposite parliament. The 23rd was unseasonably warm, as the weather had been for weeks before. Many of the Radio's employees would have agreed to broadcast students' demands, including news of the march. But those in charge were frightened, and they were controlled by the secret service.

My mother went to meet my father at the Radio building, a short walk from Baross Street. From there, they went to join the march. 'It started on the Pest side,' my mother remembers. 'There were windows opening, people coming out of offices. It was swelling all the time.'

The crowd was around 20,000 strong by the time it reached the statue. There, in the afternoon, the actor Imre Sinkovics read the famous but banned 'National Song'. Written by Sándor Petőfi in 1848, the song calls on Hungarians to resist slavery. Back then the Habsburgs had been the oppressors; now it was the Soviet Union. 'People cut out the communist symbols from the Hungarian flag,' my mother remembers. The gesture would be repeated many times.

From Bem Square, the marchers headed across the river to link with demonstrators outside parliament. My mother accompanied my father back to the Radio. At that point, the area was calm. By early evening, the crowd outside parliament had grown ten-fold. Cause and effect is disputed, but there was heat in the crowd following a separate pro-communist broadcast. A delegation wanted to broadcast people's demands, in particular the 'Sixteen Points' called for by students. The first of these was that the approximately half a million Soviet troops stationed in Hungary since the war should be withdrawn.

The AVH used tear gas to try to disperse the crowd around the Radio building, but failed. Most likely the first shot was fired by an agent of the AVH, a guard who simply panicked, or a rumour of a shooting actually sparked the shooting. Hungarian soldiers who arrived to reinforce the AVH instead backed the crowd. Some even handed over their weapons.

There is a well-known photograph of the Radio building taken a day or two later. It shows the facade, now completely renovated, with its small first-floor balcony overhanging the narrow street. The whole of it is covered in bullet holes, flaking plaster, damaged brickwork, its broken windows gaping.

Inside, it seems that most of the journalists ended up under the same desk at some point. 'I was under it when Bandi called from Poland,' says my father. Jancsi saw one of the party secretaries, George Garai, a friend who was involved with the Petőfi Circle and who would escape Hungary, under it, too: 'He was hiding there. We were trapped in the one room all night until the morning of the 24th.' My mother also found temporary sanctuary under it 'when there was shooting everywhere'. Between the phone call and the first light of dawn, my parents managed to leave the building through the back entrance, which is now the car park. They returned to 109 Baross Street.

Secret service agents had fired on demonstrators; Hungarian soldiers had fired back; cars had been set ablaze; communist symbols had been desecrated. Between 9 p.m. and 10 p.m., László Solymár, a family friend, had passed Stalin's statue: 'I saw two or three men working on it with oxy-acetylene torches.' Eventually, Stalin would be cut down completely, leaving just his boot, before being paraded later that night. By 2 a.m. on the 24th, Russian tanks were rolling into Budapest.

When, sometime the next day, Zsuzsi and Tomi called from Prague to find out what was going on, my father simply told them not to return. He simply told them, and they agreed. At that point, they were ready to leave. At least, they were ready not to return. They even went to the British embassy. But the embassy turned them away. As the border was sealed, their family, in particular Tomi's mother, Panci, began to worry about how they would ever return.

Over the next few days, most people took to their cellars, just like during the war. In Bözsi and Ernő's flat at 16 Mária Terézia Square, a bullet of no specific origin aimed at an uncertain target found its way in, and holed a painting. That was always Bözsi's revolutionary story, her close escape, with a suggestion of what might have happened, a story that came with a distinct shrug and a nod towards the Almighty, and a characteristically hearty laugh. I first heard the story in my childhood, although obviously that was not the first time she had told it.

The framed painting in question was of a naked woman in a dark green–grey forest. She was sitting, right three-quarter profile, with her knees drawn up, her left elbow resting on her left knee, her gaze directed down towards her right arm, which supported her. Her right elbow covered her private parts, and it was this elbow that had suffered the wound. In the mid 1980s, I remember seeing the painting, with its clean round hole through the elbow joint. By then, both Bözsi and the painting had moved to a new flat. Today, nobody knows where the painting is. Zsuzsi believes she gave it to Andris years ago; Andris doesn't remember ever having had it. It is a lost painting.

And, inevitably, there is doubt over Bözsi's claim. The painting, according to a plan of the second-floor flat that I ask Andris to draw from good memory, hung in an alcove of the living room above the bed. The nearest windows looked out onto a garden. Even today, the whole configuration, as my cousin points out, including the wall of an adjoining flat, makes the inward passage of a bullet extremely tricky, so tricky in fact that we start to compare it to some of the world's trickiest bullets, such as the ones fired in Dealey Plaza, Dallas, in 1963. But of course, across the whole of Budapest, bullets were finding their ways into the unlikeliest of places, not least into innocent civilians.

Two days later, on what came to be known as Bloody Thursday, AVH agents shot into a crowd of demonstrators on Kossuth Square near the Parliament. The fighting spread across the country but, by 28 October, it seemed to be more or less over. There was a new government, and the Soviet forces seemed willing to withdraw and to negotiate. Many were jubilant. It seemed that the revolution had succeeded in some of its key aims.

A steady stream of people came to 109 Baross Street, because it had a telephone. 'Many people didn't have one,' my mother remembers, 'or they didn't have one that worked.' Everyone was keen to get in touch with relatives from other parts of the country. Zsuzsi and Tomi were still stuck in Prague. At least some hope and normality began to creep back into the life of the capital. On 4 November, however, all that changed when Soviet forces, which had initially withdrawn, returned in force with tanks, artillery and fighter jets. In fact, in the previous days they had completely encircled the capital.

Baross Street, wide as a boulevard, runs south-east out of Pest like a radial from a central ringroad. Its neighbouring radial, Üllői Road, is much bigger, providing heavy armour with an obvious route into the city. This area, in the vicinity of the natural defensive courtyard of the Corvin Cinema as well as the army barracks, would see heavy fighting. It was almost as if wartime rubble had barely been cleared from the streets before tanks started to fire into buildings and petrol bombs were thrown down onto them from upper floors.

Bözsi and Ernő had been staying at number 109 for one or two days, partly to assuage their worries about Zsuzsi and Tomi. The living room and Lili's adjacent room looked out onto Baross Street. Their windows had to be avoided because of the gunfire. At the back of the flat were the bathroom and kitchen, separated from the study by the hall. It was in the study that everyone gathered, since it provided the most protection from the street. It had two doors, one to the hall, next to which were piles of books, the other to the living room, which was kept shut.

One day, on a date nobody can remember, Bözsi was cooking some soup. There seems to be no reason to remember such a thing, and nobody who was there can remember what sort of soup it was either. But Bözsi is remembered as standing by the kitchen table. This had been brought into the study. There was a little food, crockery and cutlery on it. There was also a small burner on which the soup could be heated. Lili was sitting in an armchair near the door to the living room. Behind her was the pile of books.

Then, wearing a distinctive green overcoat, Jancsi arrived with George Garai. 'We were ducking tanks in the street,' he recalls. 'There was rubble everywhere and a lot of shooting.' On the opposite side of the room from the kitchen table, my father was standing by a small cabinet on which stood the radio. He was trying to listen to a BBC broadcast. Jancsi removed his coat and came to stand near him, leaning with a hand onto a writing desk. The desk was new. It was the first writing desk that my father had bought. His only other recent purchase, two days before, was a book of Greek mythology. There was conversation about the situation, the atmosphere on the street, about Zsuzsi and Tomi. At some point George Garai left. At some later point, my mother was somewhere in the middle of the room between the kitchen table and the writing desk. She was, she remembers, 'desperate to go the toilet' but 'too scared to go across the hall alone'. Her father, Ernő, offered to accompany her to the door. In the end, it was my father who started to go with her towards the hall.

Everyone remembers this moment, and where they were: Bözsi stirring the soup, Lili sitting, Jancsi leaning, the BBC broadcasting, my mother desperate for the toilet, Ernő hovering in the middle of the room, my father crossing it. 'Then "BOOM!"' as my mother puts it.

The blast knocked my father to the floor. Thick dust filled the room, followed by the sound of apparently indiscriminate gunfire. The wall to the study had partially collapsed. It seems a tank shell had come through the toilet window, its trajectory taking it over the roof of the lower building next door into the exposed main wall of number 109. Along with the toilet, the bathroom and kitchen had been destroyed. My father got to his feet. '*Kifelé!*' he remembers shouting. 'Everybody out!'

Through the overpowering dust, people felt their way down the hall to the front door. It seemed at first that nobody had been injured, that everyone had been accounted for. They were lucky to be alive. One of them, Jancsi, was exceptionally lucky. A metal fragment had struck the hand with which he'd been leaning against the desk. His thumb was broken and the wound was bleeding heavily. As he says, 'Another five centimetres...'

On the street they looked for an ambulance. In fact, there was one close by. For some reason, instinctively perhaps, my father refused to allow Jancsi to go with it. Moments later, as it drove along Baross Street, it was hit by machine gun fire. A second ambulance, a converted bus with a red cross painted on it, took Jancsi to a first aid station. Since there was no cellar at number 109, the others made their way to 81 Baross Street, where the next few days would be spent underground with other residents. My father went in search of food; my mother couldn't speak for three days. She had what she calls 'lockjaw'. Meanwhile, she remembers, there were many children in the cellar who wouldn't stop singing a ditty that included the line 'Let the little devil take you...'

The detail is remembered but the date is lost. In a revolution whose every minute has been pored over and interpreted, the tank shell through the toilet window seems like a particularly family affair. Other families had their own events, the key dates that changed their whole outlook, often their whole genealogy. The tank shell damaged not just a home but the idea of it, what home meant. It caused a change of direction. But the date has blurred. Lili might have had a date for the ending of happiness, but not for this. From following events, however, it's possible to narrow it down.

Jancsi – whose green overcoat was sensitively returned to his mother by George Garai with the words, 'Don't worry' – was taken from the first aid centre to the 'Heroes' Ward' of a Budapest hospital. 'It was dangerous,' he says, 'because I might have been construed as a fighter.' In the bed next to him was a young Russian soldier. 'A Russian speaker asked him who he was. He thought he was in Egypt fighting imperialists.'

A surgeon asked Jancsi what his line of work was. He replied that he was a journalist. 'In that case,' said the surgeon, 'I'll save your thumb.' To achieve that, bone had to be chiselled out of Jancsi's leg, without anaesthetic. The operation was a success but Jancsi's allergic reaction to a tetanus shot paralysed him for several weeks.

Given that Jancsi, on George Garai's advice, escaped from Hungary on 8 December, the date of the tank shell is likely to be during the initial period of the Soviet return. On the morning of 4 November began the military operation named *Vikhr*, 'Whirlwind', which in turn began with the code word *Grom*, 'Thunder'. Archival photographs of the period 4–6 November show the effects. Rubble, damaged buildings and burnt-out Soviet tanks, as well as anecdotes and eyewitness accounts, all point to heavy fighting in the area on those dates, including the heavy shelling of buildings on other parts of Baross Street.

Unlike with Bözsi's bullet, a shell would have had little trouble in striking the exposed wall of number 109. But then there's the question of what fired the shell. Was it a tank, such as a T-34 or a T-54? Both saw action. Or was it an ISU-152 self-propelled gun, famous from the Second World War but still deployed in 1956? And to whom would these have belonged? The T-34 and ISU-152 were both available to the 33rd Mechanized Guard Division. This division, which entered Budapest on 4 November, was tasked with securing the south-eastern part of the capital, and specifically capturing the Corvin stronghold around the cinema, the nearby Kilián Barracks, east and west railway stations, the Radio building and various others in the relative vicinity of Baross Street. And so on and so forth. Whether it was a bullet or a tank shell, there is a gentle curve of evidence, of facts and micro-facts, that tends towards certainty but never actually reaches it.

In the end, there was a martial shell fired into a family flat by a Russian who thought he was either in Egypt fighting imperialists or in Berlin fighting fascists during an operation codenamed Whirlwind. Is it possible to pin anything down?

A few days after the whirlwind and thunder at number 109, something else happened that is as difficult to pin down: Zsuzsi and Tomi returned to Budapest by boat along the Danube. 'Why did you come back?' my mother remembers asking her sister. During that period, they must have been the only Hungarians to escape into Hungary. It was as if they had to return to say goodbye.

Bandi, who had been told to stay in Poland by his boss at the Radio, finally returned to Budapest on 4 November on a military aeroplane that was transporting blood. The next day, Soviet forces occupied the Radio building. In the next few weeks, all of them, Bandi, Zsuzsi, Tomi and the rest of the family, would discuss escaping. Meanwhile, thousands were escaping. For many, the sight of Soviet armour on 4 November had been enough. By noon, over 5,000 people had crossed into Austria. They were granted automatic refugee status under the Geneva Convention. Ten days later, in the midst of the continuing exodus, the Austrians noted the ever-increasing level of prevention by Soviet and Hungarian paramilitary forces along the border.

At 81 Baross Street, shortly after Zsuzsi and Tomi's return, there was an incident with some armed revolutionaries. They wanted to come up to the flat because it was a useful vantage point from which to target Soviet tanks or troops below. Tomi, obviously worried about his mother and grandparents in the flat next door, didn't want to let them in at first, Zsuzsi remembers. But they came in anyway, threw some petrol bombs out of the window, left a trail of broken glass and stole two suits.

What is a revolution? What, for that matter, is a revolutionary act? People were fleeing the country in droves, and the family was still uncertain. At that point, Zsuzsi and Tomi wanted to leave the country much more than my mother or father. So, too, did Bandi. His wife, Klári, now in a tranquil care home on a quiet Buda hill and surrounded by the prizes that Bandi would win later in life, distinctly remembers this. 'We were preparing to go,' she says. 'We got our one-year-old girl onto our papers, and that's what we were talking about, going.' Despite his existing professional status and his love of radio, there was the concern that the things Bandi had already said and written would come back to haunt him. He had received warnings from a 'central control committee' in the postwar days when there had been a greater degree of openness. Now nothing was certain, even as the fighting came to an end.

The revolution is often assumed to have been over once the last of the armed resistance groups called for a ceasefire on 10 November. But the civil, social and industrial unrest continued. There were strikes; there were arrests; there were incidents involving Soviet troops firing on civilians. Budapest journalists went on strike on the 16th; Budapest traffic stopped between 2 and 3 p.m. on the 23rd to com-memorate the events of the previous month. The Prime Minister of the 'revolution', Imre Nagy, hadn't resigned but had been replaced by a Soviet-backed hardliner. In late November, János Kádár was increasing, not decreasing, the pressure on 'counter-revolutionary' elements. In this atmosphere, on 2 December, the first Sunday of the month, my father was involved in a radio broadcast that would make family decisions unavoidable.

When a workers' council was asked to come to parliament to talk to Kádár, its representatives were told that it was in everyone's interests to return to work. The workers' representatives agreed to go back to work, but only if they could keep their weapons by their sides. Kádár, my father remembers, with his coat draped over his shoulders in the freezing building, seemed to agree. But then my father was ordered to edit the recording to remove all mention of weapons, as if the agreement simply had to do with a return to work. Spontaneously, he and a tape editor connived to produce two versions, one for the censor that had no mention of weapons, the other as recorded for broadcast. They deliberately finished the edit late to give the censor no chance of stopping what went out on air.

Within days, a friend called from the Radio. 'He told me,' says my father, 'that two people had been arrested and that I should try to leave immediately. I also heard they were looking for me at 109 Baross Street, but of course I was no longer there.'

At number 81, the conversations became that much sharper. It was, by now, very late and very dangerous to leave the country. There were the stories of arrests and shootings at the border. For my father, there was no choice. He had to leave. Out of the rubble of number 109, he salvaged one or two things: a briefcase and the book of Greek mythology. The new writing desk would never be used. On 5 December my mother returned her camera to *Picture Sport*. Her editor was the same one who'd assigned her to a goalpost. 'I told him something silly, that we had a coal delivery and I couldn't come in the next day. He said, "Really? Good luck." He knew I wasn't coming back.'

That evening the family gathered at number 81. Everyone seemed to want to wash themselves. 'Neurosis' is how my mother remembers it. The neurosis wasn't general but specific, a form of terminal anxiety, a preparation for the end. Wood was piled into the stove to heat water so that those leaving would be able to depart clean and those staying would be clean enough to say goodbye.

It's just that not everyone was certain of what they would do. 'We were there when they decided,' says Klári of my parents. Bandi, whose wartime lack of fear was legendary – he'd dined in disguise next to SS soldiers – was uncharacteristically scared of the consequences of leaving. 'There was also the practical problem of escaping with our one-year-old,' says Klári. As an odd afterthought, Klári adds, 'And Bandi was still hopeful of the situation.' It's odd because, whatever the choice, hope was rarely a factor in either direction.

My father wasn't hopeful. He spent much of the evening trying to fake papers that would give the impression of a round trip on official Radio business, with his wife accompanying him as a photo-reporter. There were items of stationery stolen from the Radio, a piece of rubber, some ink, and halved potatoes into which letters had been cut. The 'stamps' were then 'smudged,' says my father, 'to give them a realistic Hungarian feel'. He even took the precaution of booking a small hotel on the intended route. Why would anyone who was escaping, went the logic, book a hotel? And, to sustain the illusion of swift return, they would take no luggage.

These plans and some of the phoney papers were meant for four people. Because of course Tomi and Zsuzsi were meant to go, too. They, too, had made preparations. But there was a problem. 'Lili,' Klári remembers, 'was very brave about it.' She would later feel differently, but both mothers, she and Bözsi, seemed more able to accept what was happening. In fact, Lili had been questioned on one occasion by two men in suits. They had asked her where her son was. She had told them that she didn't know. On 5 December she cried but she understood the danger. It was Tomi's mother, Panci, who had a problem.

She was next door with her mother, Berta. Everyone remembers Tomi going back and forth between the flats several times. Each time he seemed a little less certain. Panci was distraught. 'You're leaving your mother and grandmother?' she would ask over and over and over. There were other things, too. Tomi was a doctor and had done nothing to warrant arrest. Even though initially he had been the keener to leave, he was the more frightened of the road ahead, especially as Zsuzsi still hadn't fully recovered from her operation. So he went back and forth between the flats. *Menni? Maradni?* To go? To stay? Each flat represented a verb. He went over to his mother one last time. When he came back, everyone knew that all his coming and going would result in staying.

What is a revolutionary act? Is it simply an act that is the consequence of revolution? Somewhere on a typical rug on a typical floor of a typical flat on Baross Street are the footprints of someone who almost went but stayed instead. 'We've talked about it so many times since,' says my mother of her conversations with her sister. 'It never leaves you, the "what if?". For the last fifty years we've talked about it.'

Whatever the decision, it would have been crushing for someone. At six the next morning, on Thursday 6 December, St Nicholas's Day, Ernő ushered them to the door. He was red-eyed from crying. 'He couldn't bring himself to say anything,' says my mother. 'He just said, "Go."' So my parents left Baross Street with its mothers, a father, a cousin, a sister. They didn't know whether they would see each other again. Neither of them really remembers the goodbyes.

Ten years later, in 1966, the émigré writer Arthur Koestler would note that Hungarians had been 'strewn all over the world by that centrifugal force' generated when people are 'cooped up without means of expression in a small country'. As my parents boarded a westbound bus amidst the rubble of Deák Square, my father with just his briefcase and a book of Greek mythology, my mother with just a handbag, they had no idea where that centrifugal force would take them.

An Accidental Country

THE REVOLUTION OF 1956 is a reflecting pool in which people have always seen what they wanted to see. But those on the road towards a border only have one thing on their minds: how to cross it. Nothing is reflected; everything is projected. The empty future counts, not the past with its tangled roots, its overgrown graves, its complex genealogies, its heirlooms and sentimental souvenirs, its friendships.

Around 200,000 Hungarians did cross a border, mostly the Austrian border, like the retreating armies of a former empire. In 1956, where else could they have gone? Not, as first choice, to the Soviet Union, Romania or Czechoslovakia. Yugoslavia was a geographical possibility but, for the majority, there was no second choice. Austria was the door to the West, and that was that. As the old joke goes: a Hungarian tries to escape to Austria. He is caught and given a short prison sentence. On his release, he tries to escape again, again to Austria. He is caught and given a short prison sentence. On his release, he tries to escape a third time, this time to the Soviet Union. He is caught and given life in a lunatic asylum.

Many who had escaped in early November crossed to the Austrian village of Andau, the closest crossing point west of Budapest. Andau became famous for its narrow footbridge over its canal, the Einserkanal. Tens of thousands escaped across the bridge – or, as James Michener put it in his sensational 1957 book *The Bridge at Andau*, the bridge 'across whose unsteady planks fled the soul of a nation'. But there was no point in following the footsteps of successful refugees as the border patrols had become equally successful at following the same footsteps. In late November 1956, they blew up the bridge.

The bus my parents were on would take them to the town of Győr, halfway along the road to Vienna, halfway to freedom. But the route would not be that easy. They didn't stay in the hotel that had been pre-booked. My father simply pre-paid it to reinforce the idea that they were coming back. Then they took a train west, to the border town of Sopron.

The carriages seemed to be full of people, hundreds, up to a thousand, thinking the same thing. Some nervously shared information about their intended routes. There were stories of those arrested being deported to gulags. Inevitably, the train, like any border-bound train, attracted the wrong attention from the border police and the Soviet soldiers supporting them. In other words, the great liberating army of the Second World War was fielded to keep the great civilian army that it had liberated from leaving.

My parents' original plan involved a contact at Sopron station, someone who knew someone who knew a way across the fields to Austria. But the train was stopped en route to Sopron. Hundreds, the vast majority of passengers, failed to show good enough documents, precise enough papers, give convincing enough reasons, provide sufficient corroboration. They were all arrested.

My mother was sitting in the compartment. She was reading the book of Greek mythology. My father stood in the corridor. He was waiting. There was only a flimsy, phoney document with the Radio stamp, allowing a journalist and a photo-reporter to travel by bus, train and car, that separated my parents from those without any meaningfully ambiguous papers at all. There was also a second ragged piece of paper in Hungarian and Russian that was meant to be a *passe-partout*, allowing the bearer even greater freedom of movement in the name of Hungarian Radio. But, when the mixed Hungarian and Russian uniforms came, the book of Greek mythology turned out to be just as important. They were impressed by the radio journalist referring to them as 'comrades', and by this radio comrade's wife who was just sitting there studying weighty myths without a thought for border control because, of course, she and her husband were going back to their pre-paid hotel in Győr.

'It would have been the biggest dilemma of my life,' says my mother, 'if they had been taken off...' It is more than likely that, had Zsuzsi and Tomi been on the train, they would have been arrested. A doctor and an engineer without a good enough reason to be travelling to Sopron, with a little less luck, with a little less face or front or chutzpah, would never have completed their journey. And then what? A million tiny things had to conspire in 200,000 fates in order for each to result in escape. 'If they had been on the train and then taken off,' says my mother, 'I don't know what I would have done.'

As it was, my parents were allowed to continue, along with around 20 or 30 other passengers. The contact who was meant to have met them at the station was long gone. The train was, after all, hours late. Uniformed men filled the small station. They slouched around or they drank in the station bar.

Fifty years on, the station has been renewed but its *büfé*, buffet, is a time capsule serving beer and greasy frankfurters. On the otherwise deserted Platform 5, waiting for a lazy branch-line train across the border, I get talking to a man called Dezső. He's drinking beer and eating a frankfurter. In 1956 he came through Sopron. Then, with his wife, he made it across the border to an Austrian village. For him, for them, that was good enough. For around three decades he lived, worked and brought up a family in what he calls 'the first village'. Then, when things opened up, he decided it was time to go further afield. He went back to Sopron. He went back to work and to speak Hungarian. His German-speaking son, he grins, prefers the Austrian side. Centrifugal forces work in mysterious ways, sticking people flat, throwing people wide, spinning people around.

My parents had it in mind to go further than the first Austrian village. But first they had to get there. In full view of the soldiers and police, a phone call had to be made to the contact. The contact gave them an address. He emphasized that, if arrested, under no circumstances were they to reveal it. Somewhere in a forgotten Sopron street, at a forgotten flat, they spent half the night while the contact made calls.

Near dawn, the transport arrived that would take them closer to the border. It was an ambulance. The driver told my parents to hide under the seat in the back. Already two people were cowering there covered with a horse blanket. The ambulance then drove the three to four miles from town to a house or farmhouse in the village of Kopháza. There, an old woman kindly offered my mother her still-warm bed, which she declined. A while later, a younger old man turned up, possibly the old woman's son. He had clearly been drinking but announced that he would be the one to guide them. 'I know the border guards,' he told them with a bottle of *pálinka* in hand. 'I know where the mines are...'

The mines had actually been removed by this time, but it made a strong negotiating position. Then the guide's brother-in-law arrived with another group of refugees and the scene was set for some tough haggling. Who would smuggle whom? Who would pay what? How much would the brother-in-law get? In all cases, money or jewellery would do. By now, smuggling people across the border had become a small industry. After 23 October, there had been many stories of revolutionaries holed up in semi-rubbled bars actually leaving money for their drinks; of the bar owners never demanding money from revolutionaries anyway; of the population generally, which had never looted any of the shops damaged by fighting. But on the border, with one chance on one night, with the risks for those involved, there was no question of anything other than business. People weren't free to leave, and it wasn't free to leave. Pockets were emptied. Money was exchanged. Nothing was left. It was like the payment in full of all outstanding personal bills. It was like the final settling of the ancestral account. Slate: wiped. Balance: zero.

A long, anxious day followed while they waited for night. When it came, it was moonless. As arranged, the guide took the group out into the bumpy fields. The mud was heavy. 'If there's any shooting,' said the guide, 'just lie down flat.' Then, turning for some reason to my father, he added, 'And if a fox comes, just kick it in the head.' After a while, the guide pointed across a cleared stretch of no-man's-land: 'Austria,' he informed them. But they'd heard stories about people getting lost at night once the guide had turned back. Austria was a line of bushes, a clump of trees. Austria was just over there, they would be told. This is how some people never made it.

Sure, there were those who were taken off trains or rounded up in fields or arrested as they waited. Or they were shot. Then there were those who made it into the winter dark. They were told to cross a line of some sort, a treeline, a line of bushes, a fence, a wire or a canal like a line, or some other topographical feature that seemed line-like. Having crossed the line, they thought they were free. They thought they were in Austria, as if the line they had crossed was the border. But in fact they had simply crossed an imaginary line. Instead of being flung far and wide, they were spun around. They remained, accidentally, mistakenly, in Hungary. A million tiny things had to conspire in 200,000 fates. In the end, the revolution was egalitarian in this way, too: everyone who had experienced it, whether they stayed or they left, found themselves in an accidental country.

My parents and the rest of the group insisted that the guide stuck to the original bargain. So, running with heads down, he accompanied them into the midnight mud of a cleared stretch of no-man's-land. As the 8th became the 9th of December, my parents celebrated their three-month 'anniversary' with a kiss. Moments later, they were confronted by an armed guard. '*Guten Tag!*' said my mother. The guard, she recalls, responded favourably. This was definitely Austria.

The group was led into the first village. This must have been the village that Dezső once decided to call home. The name of the village, lost among the snatched memories of escape and rediscovered on a surviving train ticket, was Deutschkreutz. German Cross. It was in the territory of German West-Hungary until the post-First World War Treaty of Trianon gave it to Austria. Border villages don't have to escape. It's the borderline that shifts around them.

There's a tiny bar next to Deutschkreutz station. Music leaks from the radio. It's a song by the inimitable 1950s-born German pop singer Wolfgang Petry: '*Ganz egal! Ich liebe dich!*' 'It's all the same! I love you!' The barman gives me a glass of Rossbacher, the traditional Austrian herbal berry liqueur, and he waves his hand over the fields to where the historical border once was.

Hot cocoa rather than liqueur awaited my parents at the refugee reception centre to which they were taken, along with a brush for the mud on their clothes, some money for food and a train ticket on to Vienna. Whereas the bridge at Andau was reconstructed in 1996 to mark the fortieth anniversary of the revolution, there are no memorials in Deutschkreutz. Perhaps there is one: the remains of a kiss fluttering on the currents across the bumpy, muddy fields.

Today, to get to Vienna from Deutschkreutz, you have to go back to Sopron. It's more direct that way, more of a straight line than following the meandering borderline, which nobody really notices any more.

On 10 December 1956, my parents arrived at Westbahnhof, Vienna's West station. They crossed the space once crossed by the Bruckner and Rehovitz families; by my father's grandparents, Katalin and Móric; by Lonci the ballerina and her wealthy husband on their way to an identical home; by my mother's mother Bözsi and by my father's mother Lili when she was a child, her hand held by Uncle Józsi. Vienna is a family junction, a spinning dial of directions. Is where you come from more important than where you're going? In the case of Hungarian refugees, direction was more important than destination.

For several weeks, Vienna had been crowded with refugees. By December, the crowd had thinned considerably. Many of the countries willing to accept refugees, from Australia to Canada and from Brazil to Britain, had already absorbed their quotas. It would be a while before my parents found a way on.

In the meantime, they found a hotel opposite Westbahnhof. There was only one there, and there is still only one, the early twentieth-century Hotel Fürstenhof, a third-generation family business. Its dark, charmingly unchanged interior matches my parents' memories: long corridors; a room with a hand basin off a long corridor; a communal bathroom on one of the long corridors. Not wanting to go to a refugee camp, they booked a room in one name, and up to a dozen ended up sneaking in and sleeping there on the floor, the table and several in the double bed.

In the following days, they registered with the Bundespolizei and with the Intergovernmental Committee for European Migration. They went to the American Joint Distribution Committee and the Catholic Relief Services. They received a variety of papers, as refugees, *Flüchtlinge*;

as those seeking the right of asylum, *Asylrecht*; and as *Auswanderer*, emigrants. But they spent much of their time going from embassy to embassy to see which country would take them.

My father heard from another refugee that he could be paid for giving blood. With the proceeds, my parents went, on 13 December, to the Elite cinema. They remember Doris Day singing '*Que sera, sera*', most likely in Alfred Hitchcock's remake of his own *The Man Who Knew Too Much* which had been released that summer. They also bought, from a fruit stall by Westbahnhof, a strange, hard, hairy, brown sphere that they had heard about but had never seen: a coconut. Later, in the room at the Hotel Fürstenhof, a dozen Hungarians tried to break into it. But, mostly, they went from embassy to embassy to see which country would take them.

At a cafe that had by then a predominantly Hungarian clientele, they met Jancsi again. He had escaped two days after my parents. He, too, had got on a train but had got off it before the station. He had walked to a village. There he had met someone who walked him into the fields and pointed to a line of trees. 'I hoped,' says Jancsi, 'that he was telling the truth.' The line of trees that he had hopefully crossed had been the right line. Once in Vienna, Jancsi accompanied my parents, doing what they were mostly doing, which was walking around the embassies to see which country would take them.

My father recalls how beautiful Vienna was in the crisp winter air. They walked through the Prater district with its *Riesenrad*, great Ferris wheel, and the Burggarten, where Lili had once been kissed by an emperor. It was the first time he'd been abroad, the first time many Hungarians had travelled. Added to that, the refugees were young. Their average age was twenty-five, my mother three years below it, my father a year above. There was a sense of novelty. They were free. Only successful refugees, the ones who make it out, can look back on their journey as a kind of adventure. The world is gleaming and born again.

But my father also remembers how the atmosphere worsened, how the news from Hungary about arrests and executions got to every-one, and how the memory of missing family, of severed friendships, lingered. The adventure was far from over. Nobody felt entirely safe in Vienna. It was a junction, after all, not a destination. Everybody wanted more distance. So they visited the embassies to see which country would take them.

One day, around 20 December, while waiting at an embassy that my father remembers as Argentinian, Jancsi remembers as Brazilian and my mother remembers belonged to 'a country somewhere in South America', a rumour skipped through the queue. It seemed that two or three busloads of clothes had arrived from Britain, donated to refugees by students from Oxford and Cambridge universities. It also seemed that the British consul was minded not to allow the buses to return to Britain empty. As they rushed to the British embassy, there was real optimism. Britain would be perfect: it was still in Europe but there was definitely water between it and the rest of the continent.

When they got there, three buses were still unloading their cargo of clothes and medicine. They stood in line. Names were taken, identity papers checked. As my father's turn came, he began to look for his papers in all too numerous pockets. He gesticulated that he could step out of the queue while he searched and patted himself. But he was simply told that, if he said he had identity papers then he must surely have them. His word was good enough. The queue fell silent. Then it erupted in applause. My mother started crying. Accepting someone's word in this way was a new experience for all. In addition, the only people without papers were escaping Hungarian criminals liberated during the revolution, and the only people with unusual papers were secret policemen who'd escaped in the early days of the revolution. Another refugee, according to my father, was allowed through on the basis of the answer given to the question, 'Why do you want to go to Britain?' 'Because,' came the earnest response in broken English, 'I like Shakespeare.'

The buses departed almost immediately, none of the refugees having much in the way of personal luggage. The journey by road took in Ulm on the German Danube, where they stopped for an afternoon, and the Belgian city of Ghent, and it seemed like an extravagant sightseeing tour after the uncertainties of the previous weeks. Three days later, on 23 December 1956, the buses, with their unexpected new cargo, rolled through customs at Dover.

It suddenly felt a long way from Népszínház Street and Baross Street. Years later, when my father would talk for the first time to friends who had stayed in Budapest, they would tell him how they would sit in their old haunts, their old cafes, and mistake every other face for an old friend. Those who left would find it hard to shake off their memories, their emotional ties, their feelings for home. Those who stayed saw ghosts.

The journey out of Budapest can be pieced together from the fake Radio papers, a train ticket, a cinema ticket and one or two postcards kept by my parents as a montage of souvenirs, as mementoes of the honeymoon they never had. It was an adventure, and they had arrived in England. But when does an adventure end?

The three buses turned in different directions. The one my parents were on headed north. My mother recently said, for the first time, that it's criminal to force people out of their country. Once that happens, every country becomes an accidental country, a territory of and for transit, a waiting room not a terminus.

A Change of Identities

THERE'S A SHORT, personal, experimental film made in 1959 by the Hungarian refugee Robert Vas, who would commit suicide in 1978. *Refuge England* begins with a refugee's disorienting arrival and his search for an address. It ends with a set dinner table in a place the refugee can call home. But the difference between 'home' and 'a home' is like the difference between 'identity' and 'an identity'. Finding refuge in a country was one thing. Who to be in that country was another.

My parents had managed to avoid a refugee camp in Austria, from which some people found it very difficult to move on. In Britain, initially, there wasn't much choice. The bus came up from Dover and stopped briefly somewhere in south London to sort people for their onward journey. A dark and sinister building near the slopping river would be remembered by all of them even years later as 'Dickensian'. My mother thinks it might have been a Labour Exchange. Then the bus went north, deep into the English countryside. After several hours, they arrived at a place called Vellingorr.

Hungarians never had accents until they left Hungary, goes the joke. After that, they never lost them. Some are softened, mollified or subdued, but they are never transformed or erased. Occasionally, they might go a shade transatlantic, like those of the majority of Hungarians who passed through Britain on their way to Canada. But most Hungarians have been content for half a century to turn 'th' into 'z', as in 'zet's good' and 'zet's vut zey say', or into 'd', as in 'dis is de vey' and 'dey vill be dere'. There is also an 's' option, as in 'I'm sinking... I'm sinking about saying senk you,' and finally a 't', as in 'he's a real tinker'. One thing they are all agreed on is that 'w' is 'v' and that Wellingore is Vellingorr.

Wellingore didn't quite refer to the Lincolnshire village but to the nearby, semi-derelict, former RAF base. Once upon a time, some of Britain's great aerial heroes, such as Douglas Bader and Guy Gibson, had taken off from here. Then it had found a new purpose as a camp for former German and Ukrainian prisoners-of-war. On 24 December 1956 its freezing Nissan huts were temporary accommodation for Hungarian refugees.

There's only one photograph from the camp. It's of my father, beret on his head, cigarette hanging from his mouth, with Jancsi, bearded, both of them wrapped in scarves, their jackets buttoned against the cold. They're on one of the puddled concrete roads in front of the huts. Jancsi is carrying a teapot and a stove, my father three plates and three

Wellingore refugee camp in Lincolnshire, January 1957. My father (right) with Jancsi, an old friend, who had also escaped Hungary a month earlier.

mugs. The Women's Voluntary Service turned up on Christmas Eve with clothes and oranges. There were raised eyebrows, my mother remembers, when they saw many of the refugees sleeping together for warmth.

A tall man from the village of Wellingore also came. He wore a jacket with elbow patches and his spectacles were taped. He looked poorer than some of the refugees. He introduced himself as Peter Simpson, and he invited a few of the hungry Hungarians for Christmas dinner at his home the following day, my parents and Jancsi among them.

Until 25 December 1956, the refugees had only a second-hand idea of Englishness. They had read some Dickens in translation; in south London they had caught a glimpse of something 'Dickensian'; they had also seen the WVS at close quarters. Now they were about to experience English tradition, with the roasting and toasting and all the trimmings. They stood up for the radio broadcast of the Queen's speech, glass of sherry in hand. The refugees' English consisted of only a few words but they remember distinctly that the Queen welcomed the Hungarians. 'She talked about us,' says my mother. They all felt as if she were addressing them personally.

A fine dinner was served, as they recall. Peter asked if anyone wanted more. As politely as they could, they declined the offer, not because they didn't want any more but precisely because they did. The Hungarian ritual always involved repeated offers and repeated refusals before the host would play the trump: 'Have a little more, just to please me.' This is how Bözsi used to serve litres of pea soup, incrementally, just to please her with one more spoonful. But the English custom, as the refugees soon found out, was simply to acknowledge the refusal and to remove all the plates. 'It left your father somewhat pale,' my mother remembers.

Peter Simpson wasn't rich but he was better off than his elbow patches suggested. He was a principal probation officer, an occupation that was untranslatable and unexplainable. 'We thought,' says my mother, 'that he was trying or probing very hard to do important things in an office.'

His stone house, called Windyridge, was sprawling, mysterious, creaky, full of books and fireplaces and wormy cupboards. When it was sold shortly after Peter's death in the early 1980s, the auctioneers described it as 'a property of great character and charm in an unrivalled position between Lincoln and Grantham'. The unrivalled position was the windy ridge on the eastern lip of Witham Valley. A multitude of tall, short and wide doors led in various directions to a lawn, a rose garden, a kitchen garden, a summer house, a stone arch and a narrow stone workshop of great complexity where a taciturn friend of Peter's would build miniature steam engines. The local milkman was a former commando. The last stop on his round was Peter's house, where he would stop for a cup of tea on a long oak table dating from Charles II, warm himself by the Aga, and tell stories involving rope ladders and explosions.

People came and went. They just let themselves in. A black Labrador called Anna was the only creature who could traverse the house, its surprising staircases, its uneven floors, its crooked nooks, without the boards creaking and whining like an ailing galleon. And then there was Peter's wife, Rita, a former dancer whose chronic arthritis had confined her to silence in a ground-floor room. She once uttered the word 'croquet', and outlined its rules.

The man who tried very hard to do important things in an office became my 'godfather'. When I was old enough to begin to remember things, we went to visit him. In the mid 1970s, he still had elbow patches, the frames of his spectacles were still taped and people still just let themselves in. A certain view of England and the English had hard-wired itself into my parents' psyche: the English were welcoming and kind; the Queen knew everyone personally; it was essential to say 'yes' to second helpings.

A similar hard-wiring would happen to me. When I think of the English village in the English countryside, I think of Wellingore, wartime Spitfires barrel-rolling in the skies above. In fact, I remember planes in the skies above. They were huge delta-winged Vulcan bombers from another nearby base, RAF Waddington, and another war, the Cold War. In 1956, the Vulcan carried Britain's first nuclear weapon, a free-fall atomic bomb inspiringly called the 'Blue Danube'.

Englishness is many things, and Peter Arundel Simpson, also known as John, embodied several strands of it. There was his profound philanthropy. There was also a social conscience. Georgina Stafford was a former colleague of his at the London Probation Service, which had its roots in the Church of England Temperance Society of the 1890s. After her own 40 years of service, she remembers Peter from the early 1940s during their work for the London Juvenile Courts. 'He was very kind,' she says, 'and we were very green.' Peter, apparently, would explain the jargon of children and teenagers, many of whom survived in the dubious demi-monde that sprang up around London's air-raid shelters. It was in 1945 that he was appointed Principal Probation Officer for Leeds, a fact recorded in the one book on the subject, Martin Page's *Crimefighters of London*.

Alongside crimefighting, there was Freemasonry. I still have Peter's Masonic books, in the name of Brother John Simpson, initiated into the Amethyst Lodge, Cardiff, and advancing in 1922 to the 'second and third degrees'. There's the constitution of the United Grand Lodge, the by-laws of a provincial lodge, a Masonic apron, a 'hymn for invocation':

By the badge and mystic sign, –
Hear us Architect Divine!

When I think of the badges and mystic signs of the English in their village, I think of Peter Simpson in his house, a difficult marriage, paw prints on the edge of an oak table fit for tankards, people just letting themselves in, and a milkman's empty tea mug still steaming.

A second 'Englishness' came to my parents courtesy of the Labour Exchange. Jancsi and my father were found jobs at the White Hart Hotel in Leicester, Jancsi as a hall porter, my father as a barman. On 25 January 1957, the *Leicester Evening News* reported their arrival. In the paper's version, my father is the hall porter and Jancsi the barman. And they're no longer István and Jancsi but Stephen and John: 'In Hungary they were scriptwriters, but had to toe the communist party line. Able to speak English, they want to find jobs as scriptwriters in this country. John said, "I have an idea for a television panel game."'

Thus ended the news. According to my father, his first English words were delivered over a Leicester bar to the customers: 'Pint of best bitter?' But clearly his compatriot John had a different English phrasebook. This was, after all, the new age of television. Live coverage of the Queen's coronation in 1953 had boosted ownership of TV sets and, by the end of the decade, ownership had increased five-fold to around ten million. Leicester was educational: beer, television and a landlady called Alma Beck. It was from the partially deaf Alma's blaring new television that my mother learned her first English: 'Esso sign means happy motoring' and 'Don't say brown, say Hovis.'

Alma Beck, whom my mother remembers as 'lovely', now seems like a historical stereotype, a Mary Whitehouse lookalike in horn-rimmed spectacles, pastel blue twinset and pearls, matching hat. She's pictured standing in her garden, a pair of tortoises in the grass at her feet. When my parents first arrived at 17 Rosamund Avenue, a semi-detached house off the interminable Narborough Road South in suburban Leicester, Alma couldn't understand where my parents' luggage was. Assuming they'd left it in their car, she pointed to where they could park. By the time they left a month later, Alma had finally realized that there was no car and no luggage. So she would kindly send them parcels of clothes: 'Dear Agnes,' she would write the next summer, 'you must be very warm in your sweater by now...' During January 1957, she introduced my parents to fish and chips on Fridays, pork pies at any time and living with a cat generally. By February, Agnes and Stephen were in London.

A rooming house off Caledonian Road in north London is a snap-shot of another England, one barely known in the vicinity of secluded RAF bases or provincial towns. It was there that my parents became part of a new culture, immigrant culture, their story just one of many criss-crossing an ever-expanding city. In the context of the national narrative, their story was hardly an important one, and it is now hardly remembered. Like so many of those arriving in the capital, my mother saw an advertisement in a newspaper or in a window: 'Room for rent'.

Number 7 Rhodes Street, was a terraced house on a sidestreet of a sidestreet a few minutes' walk from the tube station. The landlady was English, her husband Jamaican. They lived on the ground floor. In the basement, sharing one room, were around a dozen Jamaicans, some related, some on their own. For £3 a week, my parents had a small room on the first floor opposite a small kitchen. Beside the kitchen was another small room shared by two Jamaican medical students.

The *Empire Windrush* had steamed in to Tilbury Docks from Kingston in 1948, the year that the Nationality Act had opened the door to Commonwealth migrants. This was colonial Britain, imperial Britain, Britain at the tail end of its empire, desperate for people, from nurses to engineers to drivers, to bolster the national economy. One of the passengers on the *Windrush* had been the calypso singer Lord Kitchener. 'London,' he had sung, 'is the place for me.'

Hungarians, on the other hand, were there accidentally, and without sufficient knowledge of English. Bözsi naively sent out her daughter's school reports so that she could show them to prospective employers. Even though there were jobs, the big employers could be heavily unionized. Added to that, the National Health Service and London Transport did not need ideas for television panel games.

The labour shortage was compounded by a housing shortage. Like everyone else, the Hungarians disappeared into the world of bedsits, hostels, rooming and boarding houses. It was around housing that social fault lines were emerging. In the summer of 1958, these were exposed in the form of the Notting Hill race riots. Hungarians faced the same social problems as everyone else. Some, inevitably, ended up in grim situations or even in court, such as the electrician and the labourer who had escaped in 1956 but were convicted of housebreaking in November 1959. The judge recommended their deportation.

At 7 Rhodes Street, which was only relatively recently erased by the car park and walkway of a local authority estate, all the migrants queued for the bathroom in the basement, thinking about what they had left behind and why they had come. One of the medical students bought my mother a pair of rubber washing-up gloves, my mother remembers, to protect her 'lovely hands'. The other student, realizing my father was working at home, brought him tea. What my father was working on, together with another Hungarian, Peter Sasdy, who had managed to secure a contract, was his first book.

Four Black Cars is a novel set during the revolution, the image of the black car inevitably associated with secret police and dawn arrests. The jacket blurb is a far bigger fiction than the story:

> The pen names Stephen Barlay and Peter Sasdy, the authors of the book, conceal the identities of two young heroes of the Hungarian Revolution. They were both conspicuous leaders of the Petőfi Circle, the headquarters organization of the revolutionists, and fought throughout the desperate battle of Budapest. Because they are both members of large and prominent families, some of whom are still outside the prisons and torture chambers, their identity must remain secret.

The book, originally written in Hungarian and translated by a third émigré, is nowhere near as sensational. In fact, the details are real, true, with autobiographical observation throughout, and several thinly disguised autobiographical incidents, a fire engine replacing an ambulance as the means of escape. In the blurb, which should be described as one conspicuous publicist's desperate battle for large and prominent sales, the exaggerations, embellishments and distortions belie a real fear. There could be, even would be, repercussions for those back in Budapest from the actions of a 'counter-revolutionary' escapee.

The fiction of a pen name was a small price. The greater price was my father not returning to Hungary for almost two decades. But by far the greatest price would have been the endangering of family members left behind. Getting on in post-revolutionary Hungary would involve having to make compromises, which is subtly different from being compromised.

Bandi, for instance, lost his job and would not be able to find work for years after the revolution. At least he was not arrested. Instead of the political reporting that fascinated him, according to his widow, Klári, he could only write about sport under a pen name until his situation gradually changed.

But the issues raised by dissidents cut in two directions. This was not just the era of a new multiracial Britain. The Cold War also contributed new faces. My father, who had been a Communist Party member in 1947, says that in 1958 he was approached, first by telephone and then in person, by a man called 'Wade' from a government department. He thinks it was the Ministry of Defence. 'Wade' was feeling around for information about Hungarian writers, which my father declined to give. 'Wade' did not seem to press the point, but there were other people feeling around, too.

The London of the 1950s was characterized by smog. The great one of 1952 had killed thousands and had stopped the traffic; 1956 had supposedly been the year of the Clean Air Act but my mother remembers how the air could sting her eyes. Smoke and fog suited the Cold War. It allowed people to feel around for other people. 'Wade's counterparts, in the form of Hungarian spies, agents and anonymous information-gatherers, were busy feeling around in the London fog, and then passing on what they found to their Hungarian controllers. The consequences are rarely easy to calculate.

Bandi might have lost his job but others had had it worse. One notable example was an older, by some twenty years, friend of my father. He was the writer George Pálóczi-Horváth. I remember him sitting in a dark brown leather-backed chair in my father's study, with his white shock of hair and the gravitas of a statesman, just before his death in 1973. I knew my father looked up to him. Pálóczi-Horváth, a staunch anti-Nazi from a prominent Calvinist family, had escaped from Hungary in 1941. He'd then worked with the British Special Operations Executive during the war, returning to Hungary in 1947 to become a leading journalist and fervent Communist Party member. Despite this, his own party arrested, tortured and imprisoned him in Hungary for over five years until his release in 1954. He escaped to London for the second time in 1956.

The Undefeated, his autobiographical book, came out in 1959, describing in detail his torture in the underground cells of 60 Andrássy Boulevard, formerly the Arrow Cross headquarters and then that of the communist secret police. Given the twists of communist politics, small things could have major repercussions. This is more or less what Martha Gellhorn said to me when in 1981, aged 18, I met her at a gathering hosted by George Pálóczi-Horváth's widow. Gellhorn, then 73, and instantly recognizable from photographs I had seen, with her strong cheekbones and rolls of fair hair, was standing, solidly, with a half-empty bottle of whiskey, the other half already inside her. I wanted to ask her about Hemingway. She wanted to speak about *The Undefeated*, which she had supported on its first publication, and later, too, on its republication. 'The stupidity of those years,' I remember her snarling. 'The stupidity of people…' And she knew about stupidity, having reported on half a century of it, from the Spanish Civil War to Vietnam to the civil wars of Central America. The specific stupidity of the Cold War was that anyone who had left Hungary in 1956 could be on the wrong side anywhere. Sooner or later, the Cold War was bound to turn up in London to search for them.

Unbeknown to my father, the Cold War did turn up, and then shadowed him for almost a decade, between 1957 and 1966. This only came to light after a recent application to see the records of the Állambiztonsági Szolgálat, the state security archives. An individual applies to the archive; the archive searches on behalf of the individual.

My father had to fill in the application but I was the one who requested the forms and asked him to do it.

Was there a moment when the contents of these documents were feared? Did my father think for a second that there would be something unpleasant revealed 50 years on? Did I? In Budapest, I remember asking Klári if she'd been to the state security archives to see what they had about her. 'Should I spend money,' she smiled, 'finding out who I was?'

The truth is, my father never feared the documents. But across generations there is a moment of indecision. There are stories of this sort, famous ones and less famous ones, of people finding out what their fathers did or did not do. The ugly power of secrecy is that it lasts, indiscriminately casting shadows across time, across generations. Did I fear what they had? There was an inexplicable moment.

As it turns out, the '*SZIGORÚAN TITKOS!*', 'TOP SECRET!', documents dispatched by the security service archives illuminate a system rather than an individual. Or, rather, they illuminate smog. The spies or agents who were either sent to or already lived in London went by various code names. One of these was 'Roger'. This 'Roger' was almost certainly familiar with a number of Hungarian refugee writers, perhaps because he was one. Or because he knew them 'from before'.

Either way, on 3 March 1958, 'Roger' reported to his Budapest handler, a certain Captain Virág – 'Flower' – at the Ministry of the Interior. The report detailed a conversation he had had with three writers. These included 'Barlay István', a name that is a curious hybrid of Anglicized pen name and Hungarian first name in the reversed Hungarian order. 'Roger' refers to an apparent 'sharp split' of Hungarian writers into two camps. He records some of the names in each camp, including George Pálóczi-Horváth, but not the writers' motivations, and he thinks that several of the writers, including my father, live in Paris.

In the following year, another top secret spy, code-named 'Lehel', reports back from his clearly state-sanctioned trip to England on 23 October. Eleven days later, on 3 November 1959, he bumps into two writers, 'Bokor István' with a former colleague from the Radio. 'Lehel''s main objective is surely to gauge dissident feeling three years after the revolution. He executes this diligently, and makes a remarkable discovery: 'They [the writers] are currently earning their keep through writing.' 'Lehel' then broadens his investigation: 'I asked them, "How are you?" To this they both enthusiastically said how well they were, how happy, and how freely they lived. I congratulated them, and said they were truly fortunate people.'

Three years later, in early September 1962, 'Lehel' is back in London. He manages to get 'Bokor''s telephone number from the same former Radio colleague. His earlier diligence is still in evidence: he dials the number but there's no answer. 'Finally,' he reports, 'a woman picked up the receiver.' The woman was, presumably, my mother. She informs him 'that Bokor is not here but abroad'. With that, the searing inquiry is over.

It's as if the two code-named spies, having to engage name-changing dissidents in casual conversation, are hesitant to find out anything that would adversely affect anybody involved. Neither seems to have been chosen for his ideological zeal. In fact, implicit in the low-grade information they provided is the ordinary person caught in the prevailing system. 'Roger' and 'Lehel' leave the impression that they existed somewhere between those compromising and those being compromised, somewhere between not wanting to report and not having the choice.

A covering letter from the state security archives mentions that attempts were made to identify 'Roger' but that these were unsuccessful, and that, in any case, contact between this individual and the inquirer would not be possible. Case closed.

Back then, the bosses opened files, and files within files, in the dense fog of a totalitarian bureaucracy. The mindset is captured in a London *Times* report from early December 1957: the Hungarian Minister of State had complained that 'some writers are apparently still in some doubt whether the October risings were in fact a revolution or counter-revolution'. His point was that the émigré writers needed to atone for their counter-revolutionary sins, and that 'Communist writers had to go into fighting action in the cause of the Party's views and policies'. The comment barely masked the real suppression. A year later, on 7 April 1959, Paul Ignotus, one of the refugee writers mentioned by 'Roger' in connection with the 'sharp split', wrote to *The Times* as the chairman of the Hungarian Writers' Association Abroad. The letter was about the continued arrest and imprisonment of writers, intellectuals and workers. It cited several specific cases, and ended with a plea: 'We, Hungarian writers, appeal to freedom-loving people throughout the world to protest on behalf of the persecuted...'

So when were such cases ever really closed? In my father's case, the last file or dossier to include his name, '*Objektum Dosszié* OD 2795', seems to have been closed on 24 May 1966. But, given that secrecy was the prevailing system, and that fog was the prevailing atmosphere, and that these issues are still sensitive, is it possible ever to know what is open or closed or what precise effect a passed-on word had?

With this going on in the background, it seems surprising that, in the wake of 1956, Hungarians could occasionally come out of Hungary not as escaping refugees but as monitored visitors or on some official business. There is the story of a certain Auntie Rózsi. As she made her way through customs at a London airport, she held up a conspicuous gold bracelet. 'Yoohoo!' she cried out over the barriers and the uniforms. 'I've got it! It's here!' There was the trip Tomi made to London for a World Health Organization conference in 1959. It was his first healthy glimpse of smoggy freedom. In fact, he lost his way in the smog. Both he and Auntie Rózsi had to return to Hungary. By contrast, 1959 was the year that Lili emigrated.

It's difficult to find anyone else who emigrated at this time. The 'coming out' years fell in specific periods: before the war there were people prescient enough or frightened enough by the gathering storm clouds to leave; after the war there were many, including many fascists, who ran from communism; and during the revolution the whole country seemed to flee. But 1959 was an odd year.

On a practical level, there were huge difficulties. Lili needed a passport, which were difficult if not impossible to come by unless the trip was official. According to the story handed down, the passport was obtained on the basis of an exchange through a contact in the security service. But the price was high. In return for the document, Lili gave over her flat at 109 Baross Street. There was no going back.

On an emotional level, she had to follow her son. Her surviving brother, Jenő, tried to dissuade her. This is what I am told one evening by András Rákosi, Jenő's elder son, whose round face and piercing eyes recall my faded impression of his father. It's our first meeting in 20 years. The last time we met we got drunk on William Pear *pálinka* on Castle Hill. This time we eat dinner on narrow Ráday Street. This street, now pedestrianized and lined with the terraces of small and traditional restaurants, was where Lili lived in the late 1920s. A picture exists of Sylvester Night, 1928, at number 11. Lili is seated at a wide celebratory table surrounded by family and food. It's not difficult to imagine her looking out of the first-floor window just across the street from us, wondering why we're talking about her.

András, now an accomplished pianist who lives, plays and teaches in Germany, tells me that Lili's departure was far from smooth. 'My father thought she shouldn't go,' he says. 'That's what I remember him saying. He thought she was behaving a bit like a monkey. He didn't at all mean it in a derogatory way or mocking way. It was just that she couldn't let go of her son. She had to cling to him.'

Jenő didn't find it easy to let his sister go but he understood, just as he understood years later when András left for Germany. The simple truth was that Lili, having also lost her husband and younger brother, couldn't face life in Hungary without her only son. Whether she could face life with him in Britain was another question. Still, she left her life because she felt her life was elsewhere. Aged 53, somehow too old to start again and too young to give up, she put on her dark grey two-piece and made the long train journey, carrying as much as she could. My mother remembers her arrival in Dover: 'She was carrying the essentials.' These included a pressure cooker and a marrow-slicer.

For the next few years, Lili would find work in the rag trade, as a fin- isher for an Austrian clothes importer. Looking back, she carried traces of far deeper roots. She was the descendent less of Hungarian nationals flee- ing Soviet tyranny than of the nineteenth-century Jew wandering across Europe, the *fusgeyer*, literally 'footgoer', who crossed borders to escape persecution and ended up in the West. Life was conducted in the old language and, as likely as not, a living was made using a manual skill, such as in the rag trade. Her road led, fittingly, to her first address in London, the one to which my parents had by then moved: West End Lane.

Not long after her arrival, she got rid of her dark grey two-piece. It was not that Lili was about to swing in the Sixties, but she went to the Bourne and Hollingsworth department store on Rathbone Place where she bought, my mother recalls, 'an extremely flowery blouse'. Her identity was changing. It was as if colour had seeped into the black and white of her history.

In fact, family history was almost in colour. There's the first colour picture of my parents, laughing, picnicking, in sunstruck yellow–green grass, their faces also yellow–green. They can't remember who took it or where it was. England. A London park. A patch of paradise. The brightness of its mood lifts it out of chronology. It belongs to a timeless space. But the Sixties did begin in black and white, with my mother taking up photography again:

PHOTO AS YOU LIKE IT

WHEN YOU LIKE IT

WHERE YOU LIKE IT –

IF YOU LIKE IT.

Following the ambiguous signals sent out by this calling card, it was inevitable that my mother would find a photographic studio in Soho. From the first floor of 29 Wardour Street, with its entrance on the adjoining archwayed alley that is Rupert Court, she could witness urban life and red lights. Prostitutes would walk up and down outside swinging the keys to their nearby flats. 'We timed them when we had nothing to do,' says my mother. 'The quickest was about six minutes.' They, my mother and another Hungarian photographer, did a fair amount of timing. Comart Studios managed to last three years, but it's their 'one and only big commission' that encapsulates the black-and-white Sixties.

The commission came through another Hungarian, Miklós Hargitay. Known as Mickey, Hargitay had been an underground fighter during the war, subsequently fleeing to America to make his name as a champion bodybuilder. In 1955, he won the title of Mr Universe. After that, while nightclubbing as one of Mae West's 'muscle-men', he had met and married the most platinum of blonde stars, Jayne Mansfield, who was best known for her outrageous cleavage. Both Mickey and Jayne had film careers, and a heart-shaped swimming pool at their Beverly Hills mansion. But it was in connection with promotional material for men's and women's bodybuilding equipment that the glamorous couple came several times to 29 Wardour Street in 1960. They stopped the traffic more effectively than smog. 'We really thought we'd made it,' says my mother.

Worldwide, thousands of photographs exist of the celebrity couple. There's Jayne in movie publicity stills, on the cover of *Playboy*, with Sophia Loren, and plenty of her, bikini-clad, held aloft by the barechested Mickey. But only two survive from their visits to the Wardour

Actress Jayne Mansfield in a fabulous test-shot pose at my mother and her partner's studio, 29 Wardour Street, London, in 1960. My mother is behind her.

Street studio. In one, Jayne is slipping off her white fur coat, holding it momentarily in her teeth. Her daughter, Mariska, hides behind her. Mickey watches her. My mother, smiling in a modest black dress, reaches to take the coat. In the other, Jayne is posing in the way that turned her into the star she was, her three-quarter swivel, brilliant teeth, dazzling hair and bust all synchronized for the lens. But it's just a studio snap by my mother's colleague, and my mother is also there, caught in the frame behind Jayne. She's standing with her head bowed as she looks down into the lens of a Rolleiflex.

The picture seems like a punctuation mark. Is my mother looking down a lens at the future, at celebrity, at London, at 'making it'? Or is she looking at her past, her whole story in a single frame: the tank shell, the escape, the accidental country, the camp, the Englishman's home, the Leicester landlady, other immigrants, the spies of the Cold War, a mother's journey, a flowery blouse, Soho at the beginning of the Sixties. Perhaps all of this is there in one frame, as if this is the barely perceptible point at which 1956 really ended.

One day, each of my parents filled in a wordy form. It was the 'Application by an Alien for a Certificate of Naturalisation'. The aliens had to be over 21 years old 'and not of unsound mind'. They had to be 'of good character'. They had to have 'sufficient knowledge of the English language'. They had to advertise their intentions in two local papers. And, within one month of the certificate being granted, they had to swear an oath of allegiance: 'I swear by Almighty God that I will be faithful and bear true allegiance to Her Majesty, Queen Elizabeth the Second, Her Heirs and Successors, according to Law.'

On 18 January 1963, the applicants, 'Istvan Bokor also known as Stephen Barlay and formerly Istvan Berger', and his wife, 'Agota or Agatha Bokor, also known as Barlay', became citizens of the United Kingdom. Naturalization documents are the final destination of all previous documents. All paperwork flows that way or it flies that way or it is carried, smuggled and dispatched that way. Naturalization represents the possible end to the question of identities. It's when an accidental country becomes home.

They never hesitated to call Britain home. They were no longer in transit, no longer seeking a place. It's just that the names they trailed behind them stretched far back. A part of them never left Hungary. Some people occasionally think that by going back they will find that part. Some people think it but don't go back.

The year of '56 had posed its three questions: whether to stay or to go; where to go; and, once you had got there, the question of who you were. But did anyone find final answers to these questions? Are there any? The questions posed in one year remain unanswered, year after year. Life is lived in relation to that one year. The next generations were by now in the air, in London and in Budapest. But every refugee has such a year, one that snags, one that only seems to elapse, as if it had reached a temporal border without ever managing to cross it completely. It's a year that glitches, that resolutely resists change, that lasts forever.

Parallel
Lives

A Tale of Two Doors

AS FAR BACK as I can remember there were two doors. Each led to its own world. Within a semi-detached house, the worlds were also semi-detached. Each had its own nouns, its own smells. When did we know, my brother and me, that these were not just doors but worlds? When did we know where we had come from or who we were? One door, downstairs, led to my grandmother's room. We always called her 'Lili', not Gran or Granny or a Hungarian equivalent. The other door, upstairs, led to my father's study. We always called him 'Dad'.

The doors might as well have been two different addresses. Addresses have genealogy, too, the paternal and maternal lines traceable through streets, numbers, flats and doors. Whose parent was dusty 134 Kölcsey Street in the village of Szatmárcseke on the Ukrainian border? Or 2 Mózes Street in the provincial town of Hódmezővásárhely? Perhaps together they begat shabby 11 Német Street in Budapest. And bustling 51 Mariahilferstrasse in Vienna met leafy 12 Gyümölcs Street in Székesfehérvár. One day they begat tram-rattled 59 Népszínház Street. Together with 77 Baross Street, 59 Népszínház Street begat 109 Baross Street. Number 109 was visited by a tank shell and thus came 17 Rosamund Avenue in suburban Leicester. Their descendants: a London rooming house at 7 Rhodes Street, and 56 West End Lane, on one of London's ancient drovers' roads. Finally came a grandchild:

the narrow black door of 38 Princes Court, a semi-detached house on an inclining cul-de-sac near Wembley, 'Vembli', High Street. Family history is an endless opening and closing of doors. The rest is just boxes moved, boxes left behind, possessions that one clings to and those that one sheds.

My grandmother came to Britain with a marrow-slicer and managed to turn her room into a fragment of the Austro-Hungarian Empire. The wardrobe, the side tables, the sewing machine, the chest of drawers and the rugs were accumulated bit by bit, not in Hungary but in Britain. Sure, the doilies 'came out', the traditional Hungarian tablecloths 'came out', and so did a picture or two. They came out like jewellery, like the bracelet brought by the certain Auntie Rózsi, which my mother would be photographed wearing to prove that it had 'come out', and which Lili would wear. But Lili brought something apart from the marrow-slicer. Like a folkloric riddle, this thing was bigger than any wardrobe yet easier to carry. What she brought was the perfect idea of what her room should look like and what it should feel like.

The arrangement of rugs on the floor could be found in living rooms across central Europe until the outbreak of the Second World War. And beyond. The rugs were dark and richly coloured, their edges aligned with the walls, their fringes straightened with a regular flapping of the corners. My cousin, Nóra, once saw my mother straightening the fringes of a rug in this way and told her to stop because it reminded her of her mother, Zsuzsi, who, like my mother, had got it from Bözsi. Lili got it, no doubt, from her mother, Katalin. This was less of a principle and still less an inter-generational conspiracy. It was part of their genetic code, their cultural hard-wiring. The fringes had to be straight. The alternative was chaos. Once upon a time, someone who couldn't own land had walked barefoot to a city. Until then, nobody had straightened the fringes of a rug.

Lili also brought with her cushions, not the actual cushions but the idea of them. Her room always had an unmatched variety with lush floral designs on the covers, some of which, using the skills passed on to her by her mother, she sewed herself either by hand or on her sewing machine. Even the furniture, wherever it had been acquired, had the personality of a disintegrating empire: the wardrobes creaked, the drawers snagged and the springs in the armchairs had turned in different directions.

In Lili's world, everything seemed to be as old as she could remember. We could only suspect what she could remember because she rarely shared her memories. At least, she wouldn't share them with us, my brother and me. In Hungary, her brother Jenő's sons, András and Feri, remember her remembering. When she later went back to visit, she would remember things about her childhood that we never knew. Perhaps there were things she could not make sense of: how, for instance, her family's home was lost in the Communist Revolution of 1919.

This must have seemed an incomprehensible irony, both to her parents at the time and to her later. After all, her father, Móric, and Uncle Józsi, had both done their bit for their country, as if to show they were true Hungarians, and Jews had helped to fund the war. Then came the Revolution of 1919, led mostly by Jews. Béla Kun, its figurehead, established a Revolutionary Council that nationalized all private housing: Lili and her family were forced to move into two rooms in a house belonging to a nameless 'count'. He, in turn, had to accept the situation. In some cases, a communist would be installed in a 'bourgeois' home to supervise the residents. A quarter of a century later, under Fascist rule, a 'house commander' would be installed to supervise Jews. How could Lili have made sense of such ironies? But it's also possible that she understood them all too well. Apparently, according to Feri, she referred to the 'Red Terror' and the 'White Terror', so perhaps to her there were no ironies at all, simply the single common denominator: the terror.

To her grandchildren in London, she told little, even when we asked, perhaps especially then. A half-light would catch the amulet she always wore. Inside its heart-shaped gold frame was a piece of her wedding plate. What would I say to her now in a language she barely understood, let alone spoke? What did I say to her then?

Back then, there were other fixtures in her room beyond the creaking furniture. These, too, had been accumulated in Britain. They came in the form of a group of women and a token man, which had come together in Britain. These Hungarians were not old friends 'from before' but immigrants. One or two had come out before the war, one or two after the war, and one or two were the mothers of those who had escaped in 1956. They came together in Britain in mysterious ways. They were pulled together like so many loose iron filings magnetized by experience. Like Lili, whatever they had left behind they had somehow brought with them anyway. They had survived similar circumstances, each in her or his own way. One of their fathers, for instance, had been killed at 59 Népszínház Street in 1944, something that only came to light much later. Several had lost their husbands as Lili had. But what are similar circumstances? In fact, they shared something more profound than their circumstances. It was the silence about those circumstances. They became equal in their silence.

They also became equal in front of the Chinese chiropodist who came to shout at them once a month while attending to their problem feet. During these 'corn parties', they would sit with their corny digits in bowls of warm water, awaiting their turn to have their cuticles scrubbed and scraped and picked. They did not share their histories with each other but they all had corns and bunions and calluses and ingrown toenails that seemed to come from wearing the same stubby, tight-laced shoes into which they squeezed. Lili had several pairs of these brick-like shoes in brown or in black. She was unhappy in all of them. So were the others in their shoes. These women had all walked the same walk along similar roads. Their bunions were their histories.

When they came to visit, my brother Robin and I would have to present ourselves to them in Lili's room. The atmosphere would always be the same: overpowering. As we'd push open the door, our throats and noses would be seized by perfume vapours, a heavy fug of powder, fragrance and, from the token man, ripe aftershave. We knew all of them as *néni* or *bácsi*, aunt or uncle. There were the Aunties Frici, Lola, Anni, Ilonka, Ella, the triplet of Bözsis, and Uncle Ricsi.

Frici was the shortest of them, shorter than Lili, and always wore the same benign expression; Lola was the tallest, quieter than the others, with swinging beads, and was the mother of my mother's photographic colleague; Anni had the most poetic face, the most empathetic, because she was a gaunt, throaty, philosophical smoker; the largest by far was Ilonka, who had come out before anyone else, spoke better English and had married big, jolly Johnny, a cement truck driver who would drop her off and pick her up; Ella was the notorious motorist of the group, who miraculously continued to operate her Mini way beyond her ability to see; there was a triplet of stout but unrelated Bözsis who came and went together and who agreed on most things; and finally there was Uncle Ricsi, always immaculately suited, cufflinked, shoes shining, who smiled a lot at the horizon and generally agreed with the Bözsis.

They'd be seated on the sofa or the armchairs, sipping coffee, pecking a cheese twist or a Linzer-style biscuit with a spot of jam in the middle. There was also a strange yellow, vaguely alcoholic liquid that none of them could pronounce called eggnog. At some point in the late afternoon they would eat *káposztás kocka*, cabbage in pasta squares.

Choking on perfume vapours, my brother and I would have to go around the group to greet each in turn. They would reach towards us, mouths opening. 'I could eat his little face!' they would say. Apart from Uncle Ricsi, who would carry on smiling. I got used to seeing my brother's features, and he mine, squeezed like plasticine between the women's painted fingers, his cheeks pulled and stretched, his head and chin compressed, his hair slicked and patted, his nose dinked and tweaked, one eye or the other bulging as a big powdery lipsticky kiss was planted on his forehead or near his mouth or on an eyelid. Face viced between hands, I would feel my gums separating from my teeth. I would try to hold my breath. On exit, we would compare faces to see who had the worst imprints. But as we'd go around, each of them would reach into her handbag, open her purse and press a coin into our palms. We discovered ways to work the room, how to turn our faces at the last second to avoid the clutch, the shake and the squeeze. But they would always succeed in grabbing us. 'I could eat his little face!' they would say, and put a coin in our hands.

Anni was the last of them. If it hadn't been for the other women, she would have been alone. When the others had died and she was alone, my mother invited her over for her favourite cabbage in pasta squares. 'Why do you want to make that?' Anni surprisingly asked. 'But I thought you liked cabbage in pasta squares,' replied my mother. 'Me? I always hated cabbage in pasta squares,' Anni replied. 'For the last thirty years I have hated cabbage in pasta squares.'

The women were bound by the values they carried with them. Anni ate cabbage in pasta squares for thirty years out of solidarity, out of common identity. For some of them, identity was language. The old ways of saying things. The old words. In Lili's case, there was little choice. Language was a barrier that refused to break. She often tried to learn new English words. She wrote them down in lists in the flowing, italicized, Austro-Hungarian handwriting of her childhood. But she had difficulty retaining the words. Beyond words, phrases mostly eluded her.

She once walked into a goods entrance because she found it very civilized that the English wished people a 'goods entrance'. And she would hurry into the garden to disperse gathering pigeons: 'Go avey!' she would shout at the English pigeons. 'GO AVEY!' But the English pigeons would stare back, unimpressed by her accent. And she would watch television without understanding the dialogue, just responding to the images. If a German soldier wandered across the screen in a war film, she would exclaim, *'Dögölj meg!'* Drop dead! And if she got angry, it was always in Hungarian. *'Kapsz egy nyaklevest!'* You'll get a 'necksoup'! This was an open-handed cuff on the back of the neck which made a loud skinny clack, and which she was adept at delivering until my brother and I outgrew her by the age of ten.

Lili even found a shambling market that resembled the one she had known on Teleki Square, next to Népszínház Street. In among the bric-a-brac and junk stalls and musty furniture of Portobello Road in west London, she almost found everything she had ever lost. During the early Seventies, she took us there, my brother and me, on most Saturdays. We, too, discovered heirlooms. The three of us each collected things that, even then, seemed completely random. With Lili it was stamps. With me it was military insignia and bullets from warplanes. With my brother it was old pennies.

I phone him. He's with his kids in heavy traffic on the motorway, somewhere between town and destination countryside. When I ask him why he collected coins, there's a long pause. Then he says, 'Why would I do anything so pointless? I really don't know.' Me neither, I tell him, I have no idea why I collected military insignia. 'Portobello,' says my brother. 'I bought a penny there. That's where it started.' After that, he looked through hundreds of buckets of pennies. He still remembers searching for rare ones, sequences in particular, such as a '1918 H' and a '1919 KH'. I still remember trying to find Royal

Flying Corps pilots' wings in wooden crates and Spitfire bullets in boxes in shambolic covered arcades. What were we really looking for among old things belonging to someone else's history?

Our collections were, of course, worthless. The coins seemed a better financial bet, but my mother found out the obvious years later when she heroically tried to sell them to a collector near Leicester Square. Lili's collection of stamps was meant to be different. It included Hungarian first editions that, she always claimed, would buy each of us a car when we were older. After she died, an expert called Mr Topper came to 'view' the stamps. He pored over them with a magnifying glass as Lili had done, and then took the lot for a tenner. 'Lili must have meant Matchbox cars,' says my mother.

All along, it seems, the act of collecting, sifting, searching had always been the captivating thing. Now, what I remember most about the trips to Portobello is the general industry of it, how we all tried to find something special, as if we had to stake some kind of claim.

Whatever coins, militaria and stamps we collected, we always ended up by the railway bridge on Portobello Road. Almost beneath it was a record shop selling reggae. Dreadlocked Rastafarians hung out there, in what became known as the 'dreadzone'. Next to the record shop was a Jamaican pattie shop. Clutching her Austro-Hungarian hand-bag, Lili would go in and buy bright orange patties, with either spicy beef or spicy vegetable fillings, which I still like to eat. Patties bring on nostalgia, like a Hungarian word, like the smells of childhood, like the first shoots of identity. In my teens, I would smoke marijuana for the first time at a basement blues party off Portobello. The Portobello of patties and Rastas and dub reggae plates has gone, except perhaps on some of the flashy floats of the annual carnival. But the sifting, the music and the patties became fused into a new and unexpected identity. After all, whereas Lili never completely understood that this, too, was Britain, and continued to feel an immigrant in the 'dreadzone', for me and my brother it was home.

The three of us went on many trips around London, but Lili was more naturally drawn to the Britain that most resembled her old world. On the periphery of her stamp collection would come her collection of Queen's Jubilee memorabilia, followed by souvenir spoons, mugs and plates from the wedding of Prince Charles and Lady Diana. As

a child she'd been kissed by an emperor. She had an enduring sen-
timentality for the benign indifference of a monarchy rather than
the ideologies that had scared her. The communists, the Nazis, the
communists again, two wars, two revolutions, the loss of her husband,
emigration to a culture she never understood and couldn't get to grips
with: royalty made sense of things. Someone was in charge, and had
been for a very long time.

Still, her fears lurked. It's not surprising that she ended up with a
hypochondriac's wardrobe stuffed with medicines. She had pills for
everything, and ailments of all descriptions, including ones yet to be
discovered by science. She rarely took the pills. They were there 'just
in case'. It was the same with a beautiful nightgown and bed jacket
that hung in her wardrobe. When my mother asked her why she never
wore them, she said, 'They're for when I go into hospital.'

The night she finally did go into hospital, in the summer of 1985,
I wasn't there. I was in another town being a student. In fact, I was
taking acid and wandering around in a cemetery. My brother was in
London but had friends visiting from out of town. Nevertheless, he
went to the hospital. Lili, already very weak, was surprised to see him.
'She asked me,' says my brother, '"What are you doing here? You've
got guests."' She hated to think that his guests had been abandoned.
She would never leave her guests to fend for themselves. She clung
to that principle.

She let go of everything else. Her mental letting go took place a
decade earlier. The evidence is two pieces of paper. One was the
potted life history that she wrote. Three short pages covered the first
part of her life, from her birth to the end of the war. She included
the key dates in between, such as arriving in Budapest, her marriage,
the taking of her husband, the ending of her happiness, the events
at Népszínház Street. It's clearly organized compared to the second
piece of paper, perhaps because she wrote it with a clear head, in
response to a question that she never verbally answered.

Either way, it was definitely written first. The second piece of paper
she dated 1976, although she put a question mark beside the numbers.
It's as if she wrote on the second piece of paper, a letter-headed sheet
with 38 Princes Court printed on it, and then, some time later, tried
to remember when she had written on it. There are several scribbles

on one side, as if she were trying to force ink to a nib. Then, with the page turned upside down, she wrote four disorganized lines in an uneven hand, one beneath the other. Straight away or later, she covered each line with a strip of transparent tape, presumably to preserve them, to seal them. If the first piece of paper is her life story, the second is her final will.

It begins, '*Ha el kell mennem…*' If I have to go…

If I have to go I ask you for a simple cremation and scattering. No religious
speech. What I ask is not difficult to arrange. Mother.
  Old documents in the writing desk first right drawer big folder
  Bank papers green bag in the machine
  (In my nightgown handkerchief my rings other in the machine)

Just in case anyone thought she was religious, she made a point of saying 'no' to religion. Sure, some denials are really affirmations. Saying 'no' to religion implies a proximity to it. Or a momentary thought about it, at the end. But the truth is that nobody ever saw her being religious, and she could not have imagined, not even momentarily, that her son would put on a religious funeral. As far as I could ever feel or see, the nearest she came to religion was when she cried during *Fiddler on the Roof.*

Still, there is something profoundly Jewish in these lines. If the lines aren't religiously Jewish, then perhaps they are racially. But by now this was not in her head either. Race was more of a memory than a reality, and she never experienced the racism in 1970s and 1980s Britain. So perhaps the Jewishness is about a mother leaving behind some guilt for a son. 'What I ask is not difficult to arrange,' she writes, as if this was all she was asking, all she, the poor mother, had ever asked from her only son. But, beyond the pathos, there's something else.

The Jewishness that surfaces really has to do with history, with the history of possessions and their places. Historically, where did Lili's ancestors hide their last possessions before their final journeys? They hid them in the old places. They hid them where they had seen their parents hiding them. They hid them in knotted handkerchiefs. They hid them in the wadded toes of shoes. They hid them under the pedal of a sewing machine or in the lining of a coat or in a certain part of a certain drawer or behind a certain tile or under a certain stone, and so on and on. They hid them to preserve them, not to seal them but to pass them on.

Sometimes we only open the door to someone after they are dead. Until then, we take their existence for granted. Lili took care of us, me and my brother, while our parents worked. She scraped mud from our football boots; she made salami and gherkin sandwiches to take to school; she worried in the winter when we refused to wear the blue berets she had knitted for us. She stared out of the window at the pigeons. She stared out for years, not knowing what to do with herself, not knowing what to do with her time, in this place, in this country.

When she went back to Hungary she travelled like a migrant, carrying as much as she could, acted like a displaced person forever trying to find her home, but she always arrived there like a prodigal spirit bearing as many gifts as possible. For two months prior to a departure, there would be a gradual accumulating of items from all over town, from the markets and budget stores. The clothes, utensils and presents would be gathered in her room until the accumulation reached a critical mass. Then would begin the grand *próbapakolás*, the 'trial packing' of her suitcase that would in itself last two weeks. The suitcase was bigger than her. It was always over the weight limit. Something always had to be left behind. Nothing ever seemed to be left behind.

In her stubby shoes, Lili walked the twentieth century. Some people thought she was sweet but dull, that she had little to say about the twentieth century, that she had little to say generally. In my teens I remember asking more than once, often, about her past. But she did not speak about it, and she never promised that she would one day. I have retraced her steps; I know her doors from the first to the last, and in the few words she left behind, it's clear how she felt about things, about her husband and the Arrow Cross, and why she shouted at German soldiers on the television, and why 'Tevye der Milchiker', 'Tevye the Milkman', could make her cry. Maybe she was dull. Or maybe she was just dulled by experience. And therefore silent.

In her uncomfortable shoes, she walked an uncomfortable century. It did not take miracles or religion to do that, and she did not believe in either. Maybe the socialism or atheism of her husband had left a mark. Maybe she had called on God and had not been answered. In any case, she never talked about religion, never lit a ritual candle, never put her hands together, and never appealed to higher powers. To walk her road, it simply took a fair amount of ordinary luck, ordinary bad luck, and ordinary hope.

Ordinary people are of second-class interest. Nobody ever thinks to ask who they are or were. Ordinary is ordinary, and seems to possess no mystery, no attraction. Yet there is always something in the ordinary mystery of Lili that I wish I knew. After she died and her identifying possessions – sewing machine, wardrobe, shoes – were disposed of, we continued to call her room 'Lili's room'. It's as if the ordinary memory of her is preserved intact under a strip of ordinary transparent tape.

What would I say to her now in a language she barely understood, let alone spoke? We would settle on Hungarian and I would ask her all the questions all over again. Maybe now she would even answer them.

The other door, upstairs, led to my father's study. We always called him 'Dad'. Perhaps not always. We grew up with two languages, and when I think of certain words, it is not simply a matter of knowing them. Certain words, like the Hungarian word for father, *apu*, feel so familiar that I know I must have used them before I knew them.

Downstairs was the mother in her world. Upstairs was the son in his. Inside his study the smoke was a constant, as thick as the fug of perfume in Lili's room on visiting days. It curled up the walls, yellowing the rows of paperbacks, yellowing the files and cuttings, yellowing the ceiling, yellowing the light. The sticky clacking of typewriter keys was also a constant, a sound that continued through book after book, year after year. The room was always full of codes, messages, words, notes, scrap paper, paper-clipped telephone numbers, paper-weighted reminders, heavily used carbon paper, crossings out, inverted marginalia, pencilled corrections that ran around the edge of a page and back to where they started. He drank espressos, and filled ashtrays with Woodbines, later with Gauloises. He would leave this yellowed yet ever-yellowing room on research trips. He would return with unusual items and gifts from far-off places, then resume his hunched position at the typewriter to generate more smoke and fill more ash-trays. The process led to what my mother called 'the funniest heart attack in the world'.

It happened in 1974, in between the writing of *Aircrash Detective* and *Final Call*, two books on aircrash investigation. One morning, a very big, very bright, momentarily very loud ambulance turned up in the little sidestreet. Dad was in bed. He was very ill, apparently, so my brother and I were told. Lili, her face doom-laden, went to open the front door to the crew. The two ambulancemen rushed upstairs to the bedroom. In the doorway, within reach of my father, one of them had a heart attack. The other ambulanceman, not being able to decide which victim to help, rushed back downstairs to call another ambulance. Meanwhile, it was impossible to stretcher out either the ambulanceman or my father. So they lay close to each other wonder-ing what to say or what not to say and which of them was worse off. After a nervous wait, during which two lives hung in the balance, the second ambulance pulled up. 'The neighbours were looking out of their windows,' my mother remembers. 'They must have thought: double murder at the Barlays'.' The crew of the second ambulance rushed upstairs and immediately grasped the situation. They stretch-ered out to the second ambulance the ambulanceman who'd had a heart attack. The surviving ambulanceman from the first ambulance, looking a little embarrassed, asked my father if perhaps he wouldn't mind walking down to the first ambulance on account of the general lack of stretcher-bearers. Though disappointed that his heart attack was substandard, my father agreed. He walked down, waved like a double-murderer at the neighbours, and climbed into the ambulance. About a week later, he returned. He went straight back up to his study, and took immediate remedial action: he never smoked another cigarette. Instead, he took up smoking big cigars.

Coffee and nicotine might have been the fuel for the work, but what was the engine? Necessity? Perhaps. After all, the refugee must work and save for the next generation. There is no money except the money he earns. The clock is ticking and failure is not an option. With that, in the case of my father, came anger and frustration, as if the refugee lagged behind everyone else, as if everyone else had had

*My father in his study in London, 1974. He was in the middle of his writing career,
a few months before having the 'funniest heart attack in the world'.*

a head start. But there was intense curiosity in him, too, suppressed by totalitarianism and liberated by flight from it.

In 1975, on its 50th anniversary, Hungarian Radio published a self-celebratory book in Hungarian, Russian and English. The English version referred elliptically to the organization's 'resultful history', as well as its 'Marxist–Leninist alignment'. Staying in Hungary would not have allowed curiosity about the past nor the general freedom to be curious. And of course freedom from necessity doesn't exist anywhere.

Psychologically, refugees have a variety of judges. There's the new culture, the 'host' culture, judging the value of the refugee. They have to justify themselves and show their worth. Then there are other refugees, between whom there can be competition to be the refugee who did best, who made the greatest difference. Finally, there are the people in the country of origin, those 'back home'. 'If you say you're doing well, people think you're boasting,' my mother once said. 'If you play everything down, people think you're lying out of pity or guilty feeling. You can't win.'

My father's choice of subjects, such as aircrash investigation, fire investigation, industrial espionage and human trafficking, held these forces in balance. He could venture into the world he had heard about in his youth. He could be fascinated by it. He could think about how the world would have been had he never left Hungary. He answered the phone in a Hungarian accent. 'Wembley 2363' was 'Vembli too sree seecks sree,' but he broke the language barrier to write the things he wanted to.

Smoke would sometimes seep beneath the study door and drift downstairs. Mornings in Wembley would begin the other way around, with smoke downstairs that would drift upstairs. School mornings would start with my father in his dressing gown, smoking in the cramped kitchen while reading the daily pile of newspapers and marking articles for excision.

Lili would make coffee, not the espressos she had known but the instant coffee she never mastered. It would always taste disgusting, with a wrinkled skin of milk sealing it that had to be pulled off, then flicked by me at my brother or vice versa until we were threatened with a 'necksoup'. Before we learned to tie our school ties, my father would tie them for us, each in turn. His fingers would smell of newsprint and, while his hands were occupied, he would park his cigarette in the corner of his mouth, inhaling smoke, exhaling smoke. His concession to non-smokers, and children, was to blow jets of smoke sideways or upwards or down through his nostrils, never straight ahead. But trapped at the end of a school tie, it didn't matter which way he blew.

Every morning there would be a certain tension. It wasn't just the universal morning tension where the members of a family, like game-show contestants, have to reach multiple destinations using the same limited resources. Bathroom. Breakfast. School. Work. The tension had more to do with mother and son, the mother pulling back, the son pressing ahead, Lili looking back, her son looking only ahead. Their perspectives met on the territory of their anxieties, their fears about the future. We didn't know then about such things, my brother and me, but we felt the pulling back and the pressing ahead.

One year, in particular, focused it all: the necessity, curiosity, past, present, future, the possibilities of identity. In the mid 1970s my father tried to go to America to do research. He felt strongly that escape from totalitarianism would result in freedom of speech and thought. These freedoms meant that you did not have to lie, that honesty was a given and that telling the truth would not, and in fact could not, bring trouble. This was why on his visa application form he had answered 'yes' to the question: 'Have you ever been a member of the Communist Party?' And this was why he had been refused repeatedly.

In May 1978, the US embassy finally informed him that he was now 'eligible for defector status under Section 212 (a) (28) (I) (ii) of the Immigration and Nationality Act'. It wasn't exactly freedom of speech, but a visa was a visa, and defector status was better than no status. After all, some had had it worse: after the war, in Hungary, an old friend of my mother's denounced a fascist. Years later, as he tried to gain entry to America, the fascist denounced him not as a former communist but as one who was still active.

Who was what? And where? And to what degree? Tomi, by then a chief psychiatrist in Budapest, posted out an article from a prominent cultural newspaper, *Élet és Irodalom*, 'Life and Literature', which he considered 'very important'. In other words, there was some hidden political message to it. 'But we couldn't get the point,' my mother remembers. 'Tomi said, "Is it possible that you've become so English that you can't read between the lines anymore?"'

The English had their own lines to read between, or at least to choose between. Unwittingly, as the first generation flees one country for another, they force upon the second generation the values of that other country. Growing up in the 1970s in London, you couldn't ignore totalitarian tendencies. They came at you armed and dangerous in the form of neo-Nazi gangs. What did I know then of family history, of reflections and resemblances and repetitions? Yet fascism and communism were terms very much on the general political radar and on the streets. In spring 1978, I remember going to Victoria Park in north-east London for the 'Rock Against Racism' gig. It was under this banner that many radical left groups coalesced. The main band, the band of the moment, was The Clash. The music was political, and the politics were in the music.

One of the things I hated and feared, hated because I feared, was the NF, the National Front, especially the skinhead gangs. These would hunt for 'yids n pakis n coons', though not necessarily in that order. If they weren't already chasing you in their Doctor Marten boots, also known as 'bovver boots', they'd stop you to ask if you wanted 'aggro', the abbreviation for 'aggravation'. 'You wan' aggro?' they'd ask. 'You wan' some bovver?' Or they'd chant in your face: 'A, G / A, G, R / A, G, R, O / AGRO!' And who would question their spelling?

In the neighbourhood, my brother and I were well acquainted with a typical representative of the NF skinhead. His name was Tommy. He was a lanky, spotty bone-head whose dark eyes scoured the street waiting for someone to look at him accidentally. If you failed to look at him accidentally, he'd provoke you to look. He had various methods. One was to walk into you. Another was to jump into your path like a low-budget horror movie. Then he would always pose the same question: 'Wha' you fuckin' starin' at?' 'Nothing,' would be the answer. 'Nuffink?' he would say. 'You callin' me nuffink?' And so on. The dialogue was always a one-way street. As my brother put it to Tommy one day, 'You're gonna lump me anyway so you might as well just get on with it...'

Which was a type of solution, but only a temporary one. As the local fishmonger's assistant, Tommy had access to knives, big ones, long ones, specialist ones. If you walked past the fishmonger, you never looked inside. You knew he'd be there, armed and dangerous in his Union Jack T-shirt partly covered by his blood-smeared white coat. The smell of dead fish was enough to scare you. The first time I ever saw him was the first (and last) time I went into the fishmonger with Lili. I remember Lili doing more pointing than talking. And Tommy, with his chewed down, fish-greased nails, did the gutting and the weighing.

From then on, there were incidents. He'd flick lit matches at your face or try to put a stick through the spokes of the bicycle you were riding or make threats involving exotic martial arts weapons such as 'Chinese death stars'. Some incidents also involved his older brother, who looked like him but was more the silent type and usually communicated in grunted monosyllables, such as 'Yid' and 'cunt'. It wasn't that we were afraid to hit back generally. There were ordinary childhood fights that came and went for ordinary childhood reasons. But the power of Tommy lay in what he represented. There was always the feeling that he could call upon a vast gang just like him, that they were out there merely waiting for a signal. It was as if the aspiring totalitarian had to be tolerated for that reason. His power lay in the fear in our heads. But of course it was true: he really could call on many more like him. We knew that because of the street fights that took place. Some of those fights are as disputed as the question of who started the shooting outside the Radio building in Budapest in '56.

Political movements changed that, not in one bold stroke but incident by incident, protest by protest, even if the change had more to do with the feeling of greater empowerment than its reality. As regards Tommy, the change came from an unexpected direction. Living down the road from us was a skinny, tall, blond-haired, very pale, very placid Jewish kid with whom we went to school. His nickname was Schniffer. Secretly, Schniffer began working out with weights. It didn't seem to make much difference to his appearance but it made a difference to his attitude. One day, Tommy was kicking Schniffer's bag along the street, as usual, because the bag no doubt symbolized a type of future that lay beyond Tommy's reach. But this was the day that Schniffer's arms, at least his idea of his arms, had grown big enough. The pale kid turned an incandescent red, began to scream expletives that none of us knew he was capable of, and actually went after Tommy. The bone-head, shocked for the first time in his life, confused about his identity on the street, turned tail and ran, his 'bovver boots' kicking up dust.

School, too, was a first-generation choice. My father had never finished school; my mother had never finished university. They wanted 'the best' for their children. 'The best' came in the form of a public school. The children of parents who could not afford the fees could take an exam and, if successful, would be accepted at a fraction of the cost. Both of us passed the exam, only to do badly at the school. I could never understand the preoccupations with English kings and queens, rugby and cricket, and the lethal combination of religion and milita-rism, in particular the latter, whose manifestation was a cadet corps.

In the same year that Tommy fled from our lives, 1978, we went to Hungary. We went by road. It was the cheapest way to get there, espe-cially if you had a car that could make good time through Liechtenstein and Austria and you had prepared enough green peppers filled with *kőrözött*. The car was a Cortina. It might have been second-hand but its colour was an eye-catchingly shiny silver. With its black racing stripes and sporty-looking hubs, it was a long way from the first car that my parents had owned in the late 1950s, an Austin featuring a hole in the floor and a dangling string that was a functioning part of the ignition process.

The Cortina was a spaceship, and its arrival in the then bumpy, potholed, one-road village of Dunaharaszti just south of Budapest was an extraordinary event. It was all there in the looks from the locals, the way they stood transfixed, staring disbelievingly at the spaceship. And then the doors opened and the pilot emerged. His tinted glasses and big cigar suggested that everyone's life was about to change forever.

It was the first time we had met Lili's younger brother, Jenő, and his two sons, Feri and András, in their sparse rural clothes in their sparse rural house. It was the first time I understood that we were different everywhere, and that there was definiteness in difference. We might have been relatives from abroad, from the West, but we, my brother and me, were the children of capitalism. We were assumed to 'have it all'.

People, of course, saw what they wanted to see. The reality was in the eye of the beholder. But for my parents there was something else. No refugee wishes to return to the old country empty-handed, as if defeated by his journey, as if a victim of the past, as if crushed by regret, and therefore coming home. My father, the refugee, dissident, defector, had returned successful, self-confident, with the car and the cigar, as if to prove that he had made the right choice, as if the future had delivered on its promise.

Feri and András were generous spirits, and we, my brother and me, perhaps could have understood just how easily we might have been them. But we were concerned with other things. In Budapest, we met my mother's cousin, Bandi. By now he was an important journalist, allowed to cover politics and politicians beyond Hungary's borders. Authoritatively, he told us, my brother and me, who we had been, who we resembled. Robin resembled our father's father, Nándor, with his broader, rounder face and darker eyes. I resembled our mother's father, Ernő, with his longer, angular face and lighter eyes. The resemblances, everyone agreed, were remarkable. 'It's almost as if they were here,' they said.

In 1978 they would not have been that old, these grandfathers, the former whom we had never known, the latter whom we could not remember. The resemblances didn't mean much to us. Nor did the names. Nor did the old photographs. Nor did some of the distant people mentioned. It was the year that Géza, Bözsi's brother, the feisty socialist, the forced labour escapee, the womanizer, the chief magistrate of two districts, died aged 79. The names, the photographs, the resemblances were an in-joke between adults. People nodded wisely, knowingly, philosophically. We were no more than a breath from our own history, but our heads were turned in a different direction.

My father went to visit Népszínház Street where he used to live, and my brother and I accompanied him. We saw the building, the high gate, the crumbling brickwork, the hallway, the staircase, the cellar, and the bullet holes that were still there inside the door. We saw my father talking to a woman. We heard about the concierge and the two boys, him and Tomi, hidden in the cellar. But the day was very hot and the details were opaque. We heard but could not imagine. We went to the Danube to swim with our cousins.

One morning, Tomi decided that I should accompany him to the Róbert Károly Hospital, where he worked. He had an anxious energy about him, hair always slightly spiky, dishevelled. Suited, he hurried up the steps of the entrance with me following. There was self-importance in him, too, a status that came from being chief psychiatrist. It was a position that had its own formality, not simply the formal 'you' with which he was addressed or the title of doctor but the word *úr*, 'sir', that came immediately after the title.

He walked me at speed through the geriatric ward. The lighting was low, shadowy. The bare room was overcrowded with patients, with smells, with noise. Some of the patients were in damp beds, many in barred cots. They drooled, they leaked, they groaned. Toothless, angled, stunted, they listened to each other's wailing and knew each other's body smells. The atmosphere of containment rather than care was like the relentless 'traffic of suffering' described in George Konrád's 1969 novel *The Case Worker.* Tomi stopped at one point to look at me. But I wasn't squeamish. Rather, it was his look that I remember. It said, 'This is the way it is. This is my reality.'

I also saw through another door. On an upper floor, on one of the ward corridors, was a large walk-in store cupboard. This, I remember hearing from one of the nurses, was where the 'treasure' was kept. It did contain treasure, the largesse of the medical profession: bottles of *pálinka* and wine, boxes of chocolates, home-made food, fruit, and sundry novelty items were piled on shelves. These were the gifts brought by the relatives of patients for the doctors. Urban patients sometimes brought items stolen from their employers; rural ones sometimes brought live chickens or a fattened goose, which had to be spirited out of the hospital. All these gifts were supposed to help smooth surgical and healing processes. In addition, they were a down payment against future illness. It was not that Tomi asked for these gifts or even took any of them home. He refused to. But, whether they were solicited or not, the system expected them, like a tacit social contract. Their distribution took place according to some system within a system.

Tomi could have had more lucrative 'private' patients. That, too, worked according to some system within Hungary, a country that was known ambiguously at the time as 'the happiest barracks in the communist camp'. For example, most people could afford a car, the ubiquitous, cheap and smelly Trabant, but the waiting list was ten years. Even once the car had been obtained, the owner had to live with the relentless jokes: How do you double the value of a Trabant? Throw a banana on the back seat; How do you triple its value? Fill up the tank with petrol; How do you measure its acceleration? With a diary. And so on. There were, of course, ways around such lengthy waiting lists, especially for Party members or those closely associated with them.

Zsuzsi told me the story of a former boss of Hungarian Radio, who subsequently became a political boss in the Hungarian Socialist Party. The woman also happened to be a patient of Tomi's. One day, Tomi, who always worked late, came home early to the flat at 35 Rottenbiller Street. Apparently, the political boss was coming to visit. Her son was ill and she wanted to befriend the doctor who would take care of him.

As befitted her status, she arrived with her driver-cum-bodyguard. It was of course the bodyguard who entered the flat first. He had a gun. With that already in hand, he stopped in the doorway and surveyed the hall and the living room. Almost immediately, he spotted something suspicious. On a side table near the entrance was a souvenir miniature sword from the famous Spanish steel town of Toledo. He picked it up, questioned the sword's provenance and its possible use. Only after he was satisfied that it posed no threat would he allow his boss to enter. She then dismissed him, according to Zsuzsi, 'like an aristocrat dismissing a servant'. That was the beginning of a very uneasy and very secret relationship, not because of the possibility of other 'weapons' but because Tomi was not a Party member and would never become one.

He didn't give in to the system, but he would find other compensations for his whole situation. Whatever those were, and they would come to light later, Tomi always regretted the decision made 20 years before on a typical rug in a typical flat on Baross Street. He wished he had left when his one opportunity had arisen. My father never regretted his own decision.

There's a picture of the two of them taken in 1938. They're aged eight, dressed in school uniform. In the afternoon sunshine, they're running, racing each other, through Mária Terézia Square. In other words, it's after school but before they get home, a brief period between two constraining regimes when a child is free and when everything is possible. Everything had been possible. But the two boys ran on separate paths, parallel paths, that became entirely separate ways. By 1978, they were separate.

In the act of looking back is it possible to resist looking for meaning? As Joseph Roth wrote in his novel *Job: The Story of a Simple Man*, 'How heavy were the destinies which had begun to collect.' It's all too easy to accept laden observations retrospectively, to accept that heavy destinies, like storm clouds, were collecting. It is especially easy in Tomi's case because of what happened to him a few years later.

A sense of destiny or fate was alien to my father. Unlike Lili, he broke through the language barrier with effort alone, and made a living in a foreign tongue. Shortly before his stroke in 2007, he was photographed for an entry in a Hungarian émigré writers 'who's who'. He's standing next to a pile of his books, including various editions and translations. He had shrunk a bit by then in width and length, but the pile and he still stand head to head.

The funniest heart attack in the world accelerated him. The stroke slowed him down. His anger disappeared. By then, what lay beyond the door upstairs had had its effect. Without knowing it, I would recreate his study, the paraphernalia of his working life, the desk with its special objects, the files, the scraps of paper, his old typewriter, and even some of the smoke.

How heavy were the destinies? I followed his footsteps and became a writer, just like my cousin, Andris, followed Tomi's footsteps and became a doctor. So first he was *Apu*. Then, perhaps from the day we went to school, he was 'Dad' just like everyone else's dad. Now, it feels natural to call him *Apu* again. Writing this, he has become 'my father'.

A Knock from History

ANDRIS TURNS TO ME AND SAYS, 'I didn't think I'd be able to come back here.' We're on the street where it happened. This coming back, this returning, is difficult. Especially to this place. It was difficult to ask him to return. I feel like I have already asked too many people to return to too many difficult places, to too many difficult recollections. But I needed to see it, the location, the exact spot, the pavement where it happened, as if the lines and cracks of a pavement can be read like a palm. Of course, what I'm trying to read is the past, not the future, who I might have been, not who I will be.

The pavement is a concreted path, spotted, stained, its aggregate stone chips embedded in history, and greyscaled like an old photograph. The sky, too, is greyscaled. I take photographs of the sky and the pavement to study their greyscales, to remember them. Andris stays in the car. He doesn't need to see this place. He doesn't need to hear the street name. Even the area is on an unnecessary route. Returning, remembering, not forgetting: for Andris, his sister Nóra, and his mother Zsuzsi, these are the last things they want to do.

Some say that what happened, happened out of the blue. Others say that what happened was waiting to happen. In fact, they say it was a very Hungarian happening. And some others say that what happened simply did happen. It did happen at a certain time at a certain place. The time was around 7.30 a.m. on 24 March 1988. The place was the pavement outside 18 Damjanich Street in the seventh district. That's where my cousin's father, Tomi, had got to with his dog, Roni, on their morning circuit. That's where he was when the sky fell in.

The family in London only heard about it. There was a phone call the next day from Zsuzsi. I remember my mother taking the call in the kitchen. I remember her crying. Because the phone call came out of the blue, the history and the causality are missing. It was sudden, like the event itself. Only the consequences weren't sudden. For Tomi, they were long and drawn out. The event did kill him but not immediately. For him, and for his immediate family, the process was worse. The process was in itself a place, with its own borders, its own topography. Two decades on, it is still a difficult place. To return to it is to complete a circuit, to connect with it.

From the pavement outside 18 Damjanich Street, I look up at the sky and wonder about what fell. The way it has been put since 1988 is that it was a balcony that fell. A balcony fell on Tomi while he was walking the dog. Was it out of the blue? Was it waiting to happen? Was it a very Hungarian happening? Whatever the answers, this is where it did happen.

Tomi and Zsuzsi lived around the corner on Rottenbiller Street, one of the district's many quiet residential streets. Every morning, Tomi would take the dog for a 15-minute walk around the block before going to work. He turned the corner into perpendicular Damjanich Street. He reached a certain point. A million things could have made him a moment late or a moment early. He might have turned into Damjanich Street and seen someone else already under a pile of rubble. Or he might have walked past number 18 before hearing a sudden and unusual sound behind him. He might have looked back and thought, 'That was close.' But he was neither early nor late. He was right on time.

On the opposite corner is an older, nineteenth-century building. Its corner balcony is held up on either side by a carved stone 'deus'. That corner and balcony have been crumbling for far longer than number 18, which is part of a block built in the mid 1920s. If a deus or two had come down, people would have said, 'It was bound to happen.' But the muscular, bearded Atlases continue to support their balcony just as the balcony continues to hope they won't get tired.

What happened along the opposite, even side of Damjanich Street is obvious, and yet not at all obvious.

What can you say? You can say that a tragedy occurred. You can say that a balcony fell. You can say that a man was crushed but survived. You can say that his dog escaped without injury. You can go further. You can identify the man, a chief psychiatrist, and the tragedy seems to inflate. Or it ripples out. Its shockwaves reach people distant from the scene, distant from the family. People can think of all that was lost. People can think that if it could happen to someone like him, it could happen to anyone. People can look up at the sky and wonder.

The less said, the better. Because of what happened, and because of what happened afterwards. Andris mentions an article that was written at the time. He's not sure where it is. I hear the same from Zsuzsi, that there was an article, a long one. But she can't remember which newspaper it was in or exactly when it was written. It's lost. Do they want it to be found?

Months later, the article is found. Only it's found in an unexpected place, not in Budapest but in London. My father remembers that he has it or had it, and that it was put in a file, almost 20 years ago, with some bank papers. He remembers correctly. It's there, folded and yellowed among the yellowed files and files within files. When I ask him why it was put together with bank papers, he says that there was a collection. After the accident, former early 1940s classmates from the Madách Imre School, flung far and wide after 1956, contributed towards the treatment Tomi received, some of which was in Britain.

The article, in the daily newspaper *Népszava*, is an odd one. It's retrospective, looking back at an event nearly two months old. The news is no longer news. And it's not a feature either. There's no attempt to reconstruct or to narrate. Rather, it quotes many sources at length, each providing a piece of a jigsaw. They come in the following order: the concierge of number 18; Zsuzsi, who is named formally as Mrs Dr Tamás Fenyvesi; the intensive care doctor treating Tomi; Tomi himself from his hospital bed; the seventh-district police report; an independent building surveyor's opinion; the district rights councillor; the high court judgment on the matter; and, finally, someone in charge of a department dealing with hundreds of other construction-related cases.

The quantity of information is for connoisseurs of tragedy, for those who like the forensic detail beneath the human interest. Even the reaction quotes, which can take a story from nowhere to the front page, have a procedural quality to them. But fact and feeling seem to flow together. Many words are italicized for no apparent reason, as if the sources were naturally self-italicizing people.

The concierge's opening statement establishes the first of many criss-crossing strands. At 7.30 a.m., according to her morning routine, she was about to let her child out for school. 'A huge *dustcloud* was coming into the courtyard,' she says. She ran outside as she was, in her nightie. 'In front of the entrance *under a load of rubble was a person*... I couldn't get *the sight out of my head* for days.' She then recounts how the emergency services were called and who did it, who came and when, to whom else she reported the event and what her exact responsibilities were.

Zsuzsi's strand, that of 'Mrs Dr Tamás Fenyvesi', begins around the corner: 'These morning walks were usually a *quarter of an hour*, as Tamás had to *hurry to work at the hospital*. After 20 minutes I felt a strange *uneasiness*.' The quoted 'Zsuzsi' doesn't sound like Zsuzsi. Maybe reading this, nobody will feel that they sound like themselves. Zsuzsi says she felt compelled to leave the flat to retrace Tomi's steps along his habitual route. She asked a few familiar dog-walkers if they'd seen him. One of them informed her that there had been '*some kind of collapse*'. She rushed there but found only rubble. She asked if the person caught under it had had a dog. Yes, they told her. Where did they take him? This they didn't know. But, in the meantime, an ambulanceman returned to try to identify the individual because he didn't have his identity papers with him. Zsuzsi says she 'found the strength' to ask the ambulanceman what condition he was in: '*Very serious*. Is he alive? *He hardly had a pulse*.' At least she found out where they had taken him: 'I called my son, who is a doctor, and he brought my daughter.' Eventually, at the hospital, they were told that the major issue was '*breathing*', and that if this could be solved then '*perhaps*' he'd live.

The italics are the only constant. They seem to comment on a wife's emotions and her husband's condition: shock, breathing difficulties, *breathing machine*, spinal injury, a crushed *thigh bone*, *infection*, *severe weight loss*, operations, sleeplessness, fear of death, complications, loss of feeling from the waist down.

Tomi must have known from early on what had happened to him. His initial reaction was to want to live. He wanted to be saved. After some sixteen days on a ventilator, his disembodied voice returns. It is inserted into the chronology: 'How to continue is the most important thing. If I knew *how long* this condition would last, and what would happen afterwards…' Tomi sounds as though he is putting general questions for the benefit of the journalist. He must already have known the consequences. According to one doctor, it was once Tomi's condition had improved and was no longer life-threatening that he began to fear the worst. He couldn't sleep, and was given medication for his existential fears, as if to sleep them off like a headache.

After the medical terminology come the police's and the building surveyor's. The building is picked apart like a body. According to the police chief of the seventh district, twenty square feet of plaster and concrete collapsed, causing a 'life-threatening *accident*'. An official inspection of the four-storey block almost a decade earlier reported no apparent problems beyond a certain amount of corrosion of the drains. The collapse proved that there must have been less apparent problems. Plaster was found to be in a relatively good condition, masking the fact that the concrete beneath had lost its consistency. In 60 years the building '*had not been renovated*'. The concrete became porous. Water seeped in little by little, rotting it. Twenty square feet fell from around the second window on the fourth floor.

One building department expert summarized it like this: 'What is *accidental* is that it happens so rarely.' In other words, the failure of balconies to fall is purely accidental in spite of the state's utmost effort to make them fall through neglect. The logic defines the event. It also defines the era, the era of 'deferred maintenance'. It was Tomi who told me the 'joke' about the state and a pot of paint: the state grants a contractor a pot of paint; the contractor takes half of it for his cousin, adds water to the rest which he gives to the painter, who takes half of it to paint his own flat, adds water to the rest and uses it to paint the building he's meant to paint; by the next morning, the rain has washed off all the paint. In the era of 'deferred maintenance', the extraordinary teeters on the brink of the ordinary.

Nevertheless, Tomi was compensated, not for material damage but for 'life damage', for the loss of certain life functions and for not being able to participate in life as he knew it. One day, in the flat overlooking the Danube that came as the principal compensation, Zsuzsi tells me she wonders *mi lett volna*, 'what would have been', if Tomi had had the accident in another country. At least there would have been more resources for somebody in his condition. In another country, of course, he might not have had the accident. Or he might have had it just the same.

The last time I saw him was in a place called Stoke Mandeville just outside London. There is a hospital there that specializes in spinal injuries. Tomi had some treatment, paid for by the collection. But he didn't want anyone to see him and he didn't want to see anyone. It was a terminal feeling, the feeling of the impossibility of going on. It was in his face. He revealed that he'd had a patient many years before who was a fortune-teller. She'd looked at his palm and had been so horrified by it that she'd been unable to tell him what she saw. To me, he simply said on one occasion: '*Ez nem élet.*' This isn't life. He said it without italics.

What was life? He regretted not leaving in 1956; three decades later he was in Stoke Mandeville for care. In the three years between his accident in 1988 and his death in 1991, there were incidents. Tomi once threw himself from his wheelchair, and he once cut himself deliberately around the abdomen. What were these acts? He was a doctor who could have killed himself efficiently. So these acts can be interpreted differently, according to the greyscale of a pavement and not with a one or a zero. According to my mother, Tomi didn't want to get used to his situation. He resisted. Was that obstinacy or fatalism?

Perhaps it was pessimism. He once wrote to a cousin of his on the cousin's 40th birthday. The breezy message was that life was over at 40 and that it was pointless going on because it was all downhill afterwards. 'Tomi was a very interesting person,' Ádám Bíró tells me one afternoon near the Rue des Arquebusiers in the third arrondissement of Paris where he writes and edits books. 'But that letter wasn't exactly a "happy" birthday.'

There was something else, too. His views on madness, on reason and on behavior, were concrete. Water did not seep into them and rot them. In the early 1980s, a former classmate from the 'B' class of Jews, later a fervent communist, was caught handing out illegal pamphlets. Clearly, he'd fallen out with whatever official version of Communism he was meant to support. Equally clearly, there was a minimum consequence of handing out illegal, self-published, material – what the Russians called 'samizdat' – or shouting anti-communist slogans in the street: arrest. Imprisonment, deportation and execution were by no means unlikely. But Tomi certified him as mad, and managed to have him taken into his hospital as a patient. Some say it saved the man's life.

That may be true, although conversations that I remember having with Tomi cast a different light. For him, it wasn't simply a pragmatic decision but a real one. After all, went the argument, if a human being knows absolutely that the consequences of his actions will be extremely self-damaging yet goes ahead anyway, is that not irrational? In other words, the man wasn't anti-communist. He really was mad.

On that basis, Tomi should have joined the Party, accepted gifts from patients, and done the 'rational' best for himself. But he didn't. So maybe water did seep into the concrete, not to rot it but to keep it alive. His children would learn the system, how the system worked, how it didn't. They would have to learn it because they would be of it.

In Budapest in 1985 Andris told me of a childhood friend of his, someone he referred to as 'a witness to his life', who betrayed him. The betrayal came when his friend accepted a position as a Party council representative without telling Andris or anyone else before it happened. Becoming a representative was one thing; keeping it secret from 'us' was another. It was the secrecy, the rupturing of trust, that did the damage. As Andris put it, his friend had 'sold his soul'. He had neglected the line between things. Andris had a much better idea from an early age. Years before, the two halves of the family had arranged a holiday together in north-west Italy. In Carrara, we picked up souvenir pieces of the marble for which the town was famous. Andris, then 12 or 13 years old, also took pieces as gifts for the youth Party representative.

The 'happiest barracks' of the Eastern bloc had its relative freedoms. There were pavement black markets with Poles, Romanians, Roma, Chinese and Algerians selling watches, cameras and anything else, such as the one I remember on Garay Street near Keleti Railway station. There was also an uneasy relationship with the Soviet Union.

In the mid 1980s, I saw an angry clash in a Budapest street between taxi drivers and police. The taxi drivers were flying black flags on their cars to mark the shooting dead of a colleague. The perpetrator had already been caught. He was one of two teenaged Soviet soldiers who had attempted to defect to the West. The police had forbidden the black flags so that the incident could be kept quiet and wouldn't have political repercussions. Meanwhile, the arrested soldiers had been taken away by the Soviets and executed.

A year and a half later, I was returning from long, looping, overland travels across Asia. For the final part of the return journey, I took a train from Moscow to Budapest. The whole train, compartments and corridors, was full of Soviet soldiers on leave from Afghanistan. Or, rather, having done long combat tours, they were redeploying to softer, semi-invisible garrison duties in Hungary. The new posting meant that their spirits were high. They laughed. They drank. They slapped each other's backs. Many were even younger than me, late teenagers, with thick bones and bruised faces, probably like the faces of those who had tried to defect. They had the weariness of veterans fighting a losing war.

We spoke in signs and tongues, fragmented German, English, Hungarian, even French. One told me of his long days as a borderman in Mongolia. He drew a map with his knuckle in the condensation on the window. It was somewhere far north of Ulan Bator. I'd come through there and had glimpsed the long days and endless vistas. When the soldiers grumbled, they grumbled about everything: the food, the war, the guns, the prospects in the Soviet Union. Later I asked a colonel, who spoke a mixture of English and German, about Afghanistan. 'They called for our help,' he told me. 'It was our duty to go.' Then I asked him if he thought the same of Hungary in 1956. First he said, cryptically, 'Thatcher is just a junior officer in the army of Reagan.' I said half of Britain thought the same thing. Then he added, prophetically, 'This is not forever.'

The collapse of a balcony preceded the collapse of the Soviet empire. But not by much. The cracks had appeared in that, too. In late 1989, I had been in Berlin, and had held in my hand a special piece of masonry. In fact, it was a lump of concrete handed to me by a so-called *Mauerspechte*, a 'wall woodpecker', one of the Germans, and others, who chipped away relentlessly until the Wall was gone. In Hungary, by the time Tomi was readmitted to hospital in 1990, black plastic had been used to cover the statues of the communist era, if they hadn't already been knocked down or destroyed. Walking through Budapest in early 1990, I saw even the most innocuous communist bust on an unassuming plinth in a quiet public garden effaced by black plastic, symbolizing an irreversible process, an impending extinction, a failure to last forever.

Later, in April of that year, the first free elections were held. Some citizens voted proudly, others went with a certain trepidation. Either way, just as the former regime seemed genuinely to be over and the prospect of a national democracy was being realized, Tomi's condition worsened. And continued to worsen throughout the year.

My mother remembers visiting him in early 1991. He told her he was anxious about the family, about the children leaving him, leaving Hungary. His daughter, Nóra, already had half a life in Italy. He was anxious about the cracks in the family, and about the family falling apart. That's what he told my mother. He also told her how his own extinction would come. He said that his kidneys would give up. He said that the sign of this would be peeling layers of skin. Weeks later, in exactly the way that he had predicted, he died.

The article about his accident, written three years before his death, was entitled, 'The Doctor's Tragedy'. Sure, it was singular and personal, not plural and general. But it could have been. It could have happened to anyone. Still, there is a certain irony in someone surviving the big historical picture only to be undone by twenty square feet of loose historical detail. Perhaps the greater tragedy was not leaving in 1956, and the subsequent regret that found its way into every available crack.

Andris once showed me another place, near Heroes' Square. Here, as a schoolboy, he had had to participate in an official parade. He told me how, wearing their red scarves, the boys had to line up on one side of the road. On a signal, they had to run across the road to greet various ministers, including Hungary's Communist leader, János Kádár. 'I happened to run straight to him,' says Andris. 'He asked if I was a good student. Then he kissed me.' In spite of this, we joke, Andris became a successful doctor. There is more of Tomi in him, down to his glasses, hands, smile, mannerisms, than of the system.

211

Tomi is still there, of course, in the flat where Zsuzsi lives. The brown pipe he periodically smoked is still there in a bowl among pens. There are photographs on the wall. There's his mother, Panci, blonde and bright-eyed, who helped to hide him in a cellar in 1944 and who wouldn't let him go in 1956. There's his father, Imre, who also smoked a pipe and who disappeared on forced labour with my grandfather, Nándor. There are pictures of his grandparents, the slim Aladár in a First World War cavalry officer's uniform, and the generously proportioned Berta. Also still there, behind bookcase glass, are Tomi's volumes on psychiatry and psychology. More than anything else, these remind me of him, of the scattered conversations I had with him, of the territory he inhabited.

His territory was also the pavement on Damjanich Street in the seventh district. Can all this be read in the concrete? Family history is as much about what remains as what is erased. Up above my head, 20 or more years on, there are still loose details, and crumbling balconies. People still walk their dogs around the same block, and the sky is still a greyscale open to interpretation.

A Postcard from a Fascist

I FIRST MET BLONDIE, Bunkó and Béla on account of Béla's watch. It was early 1990. I'd just come back from Berlin and was planning to go to Hungary for the first free elections. I needed some recording equipment and was meeting a relevant man in a pub in Hammersmith. Across a table I saw a watch on a wrist. It was an old Swiss mechanical wristwatch, a DOXA Anti-Magnetic from the late 1930s or early 1940s. Its original large white face was faded and its gold hands dulled. Not having been serviced for decades, the watch ran either slow or fast, and sometimes stopped when it felt like stopping. At least when it stopped it still told the right time twice a day. I knew all this at a glance because the watch was exactly the same as mine. Only the serial numbers were different.

Like a clairsentient picking up a strange object, I knew straight away that there had to be further coincidences. There were. The wearer of the watch was called Béla and, of course, he was from Hungary. Inevitably, we asked each other how we had come by our watches. Béla had got his as a hand-me-down from his father, who had told him an ever-changing story about two Armenians on a truck or a Romanian and his mother in a forest or a Serb and a Croat on a bus, and a series

213

of events involving smuggling, pawning and reclaiming. My watch was also a hand-me-down from my father, who told an ever-changing story about two Russians on a train, highly unusual circumstances and a complex trade involving too many incidental objects to recall. Béla and I realized that, while the origins of the watches would never be pinned down, at least between the two of them we could very closely estimate the right time.

For Béla, the right time was right then. He was part of the first wave of the post-Communism generation whose intention was to head west to make money. He had the appearance of a failed 1970s rock star, all feathercut and beard and John Lennon spectacles. He was travelling with his second cousin, the monolithic, silent, moustachioed Bunkó. That was not his name but my secret nickname for him. In Hungarian, *bunkó* means 'moron'. This was a little unfair because Bunkó was a pleasant and smiling individual capable of limitless physical labour.

Blondie, the third of the group, was much older, pushing 70, and rougher. He was the long-lost uncle, the brother of Béla's dead father. He had fled Hungary for Britain immediately after the war, marrying an English woman. His nickname was his own. Rather, as Blondie told me, it was the mechanics at the garage in west London where he used to work who gave it to him in recognition of his brilliantined, windproof, blond quiff. Blondie, as I soon found out but could have guessed, was a former fascist. All kinds of people had left Hungary immediately after the war but usually the ones in the biggest hurry were the ones who feared retribution. Without realizing my origins, Blondie managed to pepper pretty much any conversation with his enduring and deeply held racist convictions, mostly that the Jews were responsible for the state of things in Hungary, in Britain and any other country you cared to mention. And he made a point of mentioning a number of the other countries. 'So where can you go?' he asked rhetorically. 'Nowhere,' he answered. 'That's where.'

Béla thought he had an alternative: Milton Keynes. It was a name he had to torture himself to pronounce, and it was a town that didn't normally inspire dreams, lying 60 miles north-west of London and still clinging to its bland 1960s 'new town' atmosphere. The big idea was to sell in Milton Keynes what Béla and Bunkó had brought with them from Hungary in the van, Béla having done the driving and

Bunkó the loading. But there was a problem. Although there was a 'contact' in Milton Keynes, neither Béla nor Bunkó spoke English. Blondie did speak English. It was just that he was a mechanic, not a smooth-talker. I could see where this was heading. First I had to see what they had in the van.

The van was a partially disintegrated, Romanian-built Dacia. Its axle practically scraped the road under the weight of its cargo. Bunkó removed the padlock and opened the rear doors. '*Greepe vawter!*' Béla pronounced proudly. At first I wasn't sure what language he was speaking. Closer inspection of the cargo revealed cases of bottles. They contained *gripe water*. I knew gripe water. It was a traditional remedy for infant flatulence. It was slightly alcoholic and could be made from various regional ingredients, including the one my mother remembered: caraway seed. Apparently, as an infant, I had loved the stuff. Béla's version looked like it had been bottled by drunks and labelled by the illiterate. It had some sinister sediment suspended in it. Béla claimed the sediment would disappear with a good shake. I could see us in court, trying to explain that we hadn't meant to harm anyone, especially not the babies.

Nevertheless, a day or two later, I negotiated with the middleman in Milton Keynes. Milton Keynes went for the product. From then on, the consignments of gripe water came once a season for the next couple of years, with Béla doing the driving and Bunkó the loading. Each time Béla came, he brought me something that was as common to us as our watches: a tray of his mother's *meggyes rétes*. Cherry strudel.

But the gripe water runs soon ran into some heavyweight German firm and some nasty European legislation. The liquid was declared to be an unapproved drug. The business faltered badly. Béla and Bunkó did not return. Blondie, meanwhile, continued to live with his long-suffering English wife in London.

I didn't hear from any of them for a while until, one winter night, there was a knock at the door of the big, old, crooked squat in north London where I was living at the time. It was Blondie. His quiff was war-torn. He was desperate. His legs, he told me, were bad. That's why he hadn't been able to brake. Clearly, he'd crashed something. Then, he went on, he'd run away from all of it, 'the scene', he said, waving an arm. Most of all, he'd left his long-suffering English wife.

That was why he'd turned up. He needed help, money, anything at all, but £150 would do just to get him to Austria. From there he knew the way to his home town of Kecskemét in central Hungary. After 50 years, he was going back.

He made his usual points about Jews and blacks especially vigorously. His main hope was that he wouldn't go back simply to find that things were the same as when he left, and run by 'the same people'. Half a century ago, on a Budapest street, on an equally wintery night, would he have been in an Arrow Cross uniform, gun in hand? Would he have found himself in a dark doorway looking down at the hairs on the back of a kneeling man's neck? Would he have fired his gun?

From a nearby cash machine, I got him the £150. Then I told him I was a Jew. 'Ha!' he exclaimed. Then he added, with a laugh, 'They're not all the same.' He pocketed the money, promising never to forget it, always to remember it and, of course, much more than that, above all, it went without saying, that he would return it in full. He never did. Instead, a couple of months later, from somewhere near Kecskemét in central Hungary, I got a postcard:

Dear Niki [as he called me] *thanks for helping me. I am sorry I could not make it back but there is a lot of snow all over and no transport through Austria at all, but the snow did not help me at all my legs got bad and now I am having treatment, but as soon as I can I will come and I will phone you before I do. Béla is OK and quite fit and sends his regards. I asked him to phone you I hope he did. I got your cherry strudel on order for the time your coming so I see you soon and thank you again and again all the best Blondie.*

Whatever Blondie did or did not do, whatever he was like or not like, his was a fading world. In its lengthening shadow you might still make out the all-but-disappeared world of Hungarian Jews or Jewish Hungarians. What was he going back for? Perhaps he was escaping back. Perhaps he actually wanted to be trapped by snow with no way out across the mountains. Perhaps he would find peace somewhere in the world, after all. I don't know where they are now, Béla, Bunkó and Blondie, but I can't help thinking of them, of all the possible connections their story has to mine.

If Blondie had any feel for Yiddish, he would have understood an old saying: '*In vayte Vegen tsu vayte Tsiln.*' On distant paths to distant goals. Was Tomi right to worry about the family falling apart? In some ways. Taken together, its members came from Budapest, Arad, Vienna, Ukraine, Székesfehérvár, Hódmezővásárhely and Kassa. They ended up in Budapest, London, Florence, Paris, Essen, Toronto and Malmö. They could have ended up in Argentina or Australia. As Arthur Koestler once wrote, if there had been life on Mars it would have greeted you in Hungarian. Distant paths, distant goals.

The story of Béla, Bunkó and Blondie goes deeper. Sure, there is cherry strudel and a second generation. But the connection has to do with something else that is as hard to pin down as the origins of a watch. It has to do with the slenderness of possibilities and hopes, the fragility of families, the coming together of odd family members. It has to do with the criss-crossing of paths, the scattering of people, the common hand-me-down object in divergent lives. It has to do with the old world and the new, looking back and looking ahead, the leaving and the returning, the setting out and the 'going home'. It has to do with the tiny junctions where tiny things happen and change lives forever. It has to do with what is erased and what remains. It has to do with a knock at the door in the middle of the night, and what you do when it happens.

A Disappearing World

'WHERE AM I?' said my brother. 'I was there, too, that night. You've airbrushed me out.' I can't argue with him. He's right. It's true. He was there that bitter night on Castle Hill 50 years after the revolution. It wasn't just me and my father, the cherry strudel and the ghosts of people we resembled. Strange things happen when you tell stories. People appear and disappear. The writer becomes a totalitarian carrying out Stalinist purges, deciding who should be in the picture and who should not. Was I simplifying something to make a point? Or was I lying? A family story creaks under the weight of the unwritten stories, the ones that will never be told.

Bandi, my mother's cousin, who dined in disguise surrounded by SS officers, whose mother disappeared from a Budapest street, who became a foreign correspondent, who at first fell foul of the authorities, who almost escaped in 1956 but who stayed and won international journalism prizes, and who saw the ancestral resemblances in me and my brother, never wanted to tell his own story. Andris and I visited him in 2007, shortly before he died. He was 85 and very ill, bent double, but still working, surrounded by books and papers, writing an article. He told us that he 'forgave everyone from that period'. The phrase seemed to refer to all 'periods', the war, the revolution, post-revolutionary Hungary. And the forgiveness seemed to be dispensed generally and without prejudice. Was he lying?

Maybe he did forgive everyone. To forgive can be hard but forgiveness allows closure, and closure means an end to questions, an end to missing facts or disappeared people. But Bandi's voice returns, as if from beyond the grave, with the very questions that forgiveness silences. The questions come in the form of some short, autobiographical pieces, 'scenes' as he called them, that he wrote but never published. His widow, Klári, gave them to me. They deal with personal and defining moments. The context for these moments is a single and enduring question: What would he say, what should he say, to his child, his daughter, about all of it, about all that had happened, and especially about her identity? When one day, at some arbitrary point, she looks up from some unrelated activity and asks, 'Who am I?', what should he say? What should he say about Jews, Hungarians, Hungarian Jews, Jewish Hungarians? Was a midfielder a Jew or a footballer? Did Miklós Radnóti die a Jew or a great poet? Why should a daughter need to know these things? Why should she have to deal with them?

Bandi's answers were clear: a midfielder is a midfielder, and a poet is a poet, and that's that. But he knew that things are rarely that simple. '*Ne piszkáld ezt a dolgot. Reménytelen,*' he wrote. Don't disturb this thing. Leave it alone. It's hopeless.

If he could have answered the questions for his child, he could have answered them generally, universally. But what was the point, he wondered, because who would understand? While I was visiting Klári in her care home, in the silence of her room an alarm clock suddenly went off. 'Bandi set it,' she told me. Since then, she hasn't changed it or silenced it. The alarm goes off every day at the same time. It is the sound of a ghost, a constant reminder of a presence. It is perhaps a reminder of something else: a world might be disappearing but the questions remain, even if they remain without answer.

Who keeps asking them? 'At the swimming pool,' Zsuzsi told me one day in Budapest, 'a woman called over to me...' The woman told her that if she applied 'as soon as possible' there could be some compensation from Germany. The application had to be made to the *Bundesamt für zentrale Dienste und offene Vermögensfragen,* the Federal Office for Central Services and Unresolved Property Issues. Apparently, this was specifically '*für Arbeite in einem Ghetto*', for work in a ghetto. In 2002, having heard not from a woman in a swimming pool but from a friend of a friend in London who had heard from a friend in Australia about the Conference On Jewish Material Claims Against Germany, comprising the Fund for Former Slave and Forced Laborers, my mother and father completed the relevant paperwork. They had to submit the documentation to show or to prove this or that. Two years later, they each received £1,669.62 in compensation.

A friend of a friend; a woman at a swimming pool: six decades on, there is still paperwork, lengthy paperwork to be submitted to places with lengthy names as if to symbolize the long years and the complexity of the issues. The paperwork and the complexity will, presumably, end when the claims end. The claims will end when there are no more claimants.

Zsuzsi told me of someone she knows whose survival story has changed a hundred times. She renews it for the paperwork. She alters its detail, its emphasis and its meaning every time there is the possibility of money. Zsuzsi says, ironically, with distaste, that she's a *macher*, Yiddish for a wheeler-dealer or a fixer, literally a 'maker'. But the woman is a claimant, nevertheless, a survivor in some shape or form, someone who went and came back, and there are fewer and fewer of them to make the point.

Some have never told their story, let alone made a claim, like Éva Barabás, the childhood friend of Zsuzsi and my mother who might easily have been Zsuzsi or my mother. She told me her story one afternoon in her small, bright flat, memory and dust suspended in a shaft of sunlight. After not telling it for 65 years, her story began abruptly with her arrest. 'That's how it begins,' she said, as if there was nothing before.

I can hear Bandi. Leave this thing alone.

But Éva had already started. She was arrested in Budapest by local detectives. In a city that became notorious for its informants, she was denounced by someone at a left-wing cafe she frequented. She was tortured by the SS, taken to Auschwitz, then on to a women's forced labour camp, Parschnitz in Sudetenland, finally labouring for a German phonograph company. It took her 65 years to tell anyone that for a month in a villa on Csillag Hill in Buda, shortly after the German invasion of Hungary in March 1944, the SS put her on her stomach on the floor and beat the soles of her feet. It took her all those years to mention that in Auschwitz she was greeted by 'beautiful sunshine', that the Polish prisoner who cut her hair didn't cut it too short because she had 'such nice eyes', that she was among 25 women selected for work, that after stripping and showering, the women went to the clothes warehouse known as 'Kanada', that 'Kanada' had nothing to do with a wealthy country but originated from the German *keine da*, 'nobody there'. There was nobody there, just the clothes of ghosts.

It took her 65 years to say that she pitied the poor German girls at the phonograph company since they had it worse than the prisoners, that in early May 1945 she saw the Germans fleeing in all directions 'like spiders on a wall', that a few days later two big Russian officers arrived and told them in German: *'Kinder, Sie sind frei.'* Children, you are free.

Some people disappeared. Some, like Éva, came back and disappeared. She waited this long to tell her story, with its detail, a detail being the raising of a sleeve to show a number on an arm, a detail being the dryness of her mouth or her swollen feet or sweet and salty biscuits on a plate or her sense of humour. She told her story as if she'd been ready to tell it all along. Why did she wait this long? Because nobody had ever asked and she had never volunteered. 'I'm telling you for the last time,' Bandi wrote. 'Stop it. Leave this thing alone.' Should I? Should we? Éva's story began abruptly, and ended with her wondering where she'd left her glasses: 'In the refrigerator, I expect. As usual.'

We can't disappear people before their time. At least not until then. A second-generation friend, Judy, the daughter of Gizi Hilvert who lived on my mother's street in Budapest, called it 'a disappearing world'. Like me, she had started to research a family tree. Like me, she began with a mother tongue learned entirely from sound rather than sight. Like me, she still cannot help thinking certain thoughts in Hungarian. Certain things cannot be airbrushed. Every family suggests another, and every family is a fool stumbling on the crime scene of life. In our fragmented languages, we are guardians of our stories.

One stormy afternoon in Székesfehérvár, looking for signs of my great-grandmother's life, I wandered into the grounds of a Russian war memorial and cemetery near the train station. I wandered in really to get out of the rain under a big tree. There was a solitary man in there by the grey obelisk. He was looking at the plaque on a mass grave on which births and deaths were inscribed. Attached to one or two names were rusted oval metal photographs of hatted, red-starred, soldiers. I got talking to the man, who spoke some English. His name was Yevgeny. He was a Russian searching for his grandfather who'd been killed, aged 25, in March 1945, fighting Nazis and fascists as the warfront passed more than once through the town. He had old maps, scraps of evidence, possibilities to pursue. I told him of my great-grandmother Mária and her family who had been taken from here by train a year earlier. We had both taken trains, rattling trains with compartments full of the swirling dust of generations and corridors lined with ghosts, to get to this place. We are guardians not just of our own stories but of each other's, too.

One hot afternoon in Budapest, I found myself in a distant part of the Kozma Street Jewish cemetery. I was pulling vines and scraping earth from submerged graves to try to find familiar names, to give them an overdue, perhaps final, airing. As I brushed dust from the grave of Adolf Bruckner, my great-great-grandfather, born in 1839, died in 1917, one of the cemetery caretakers appeared from bushes behind me. Bare-chested, wearing camouflage combat trousers and armed with a shovel, he asked if I needed help, if I didn't want the graves 'cleaned up a bit'. A moment later his little blonde daughter appeared. She jumped up on the grave and started to skip. 'Angelika!' he told her, 'Don't play on the graves.' And he shooed her off. Let her live a little, I thought, and leave an ordinary grave to disappear in an ordinary way. Living memory is what counts.

So how does a family history end? With commemoration? With nostalgia? With a birth or a death or a marriage? Is the writer of such a story supposed to hang around and wait for one? Or make one happen? Or does a family history end with something else? A knock, perhaps.

We're still in touch, them and us. In fact, they're coming soon, the relatives. They're coming with their papers and their baggage, their resemblances, their jokes, their living memories and some cherry strudel. Whatever time they get here, no doubt they will knock at the door. And whatever time it is, no doubt we will open it.

Acknowledgements

THE STORY OF A FAMILY, whatever form it ultimately takes, cannot be told without a family. So my first and greatest debt is to family members who contributed, and all of them did contribute incalculably. My father, Stephen, who died in 2010, read much of what I have written here, and we discussed on many occasions all that I discovered. Some of it was new to him, such as his genealogical roots, and some of it was painful, such as reliving the loss of his father. But it was our habit to share. He wrote all his working life, and the rest of us would read what he wrote. Before I even knew it, I was following his footsteps. A family history, in which the writer writes about the living as well as the dead, carries with it particular questions: What does it mean to be true to someone's story? Does the writer of a family history appropriate everyone else's stories to make of them something greater than the sum of their parts? Or should the writer merely attempt to transmit the parts? In a way, my father began this book, and it ends with him.

In the flow of memories, and memories of memories, there is living history. My mother, apart from her many other attributes, contributed two very special things: a headful of poems, songs, ditties and anecdotes, and the magical ability to decipher the most faded and inscrutable of handwriting on the thinnest and most fragile of documents. She, like my father, has been both narrator and reader.

To Zsuzsi, my mother's sister in Budapest, with whom I talked at length on each and every visit and who was a fount of knowledge, I owe a great deal.

Likewise, I thank my cousins, first Andris Fenyvesi, with whom I shared the minutiae of our common memories, thoughts, research and investigations, and who was touchstone, sounding-board and inspiration throughout, and also Nóra Fenyvesi for our simultaneously distinguishable and indistinguishable viewpoints on our parallel lives.

An especial thanks goes to my brother, Robin, for his support, his contradictions and his protestations, all of which helped me not to lose my bearings, although he might contradict that.

For the wonderful illumination of the lives of two ballerinas, and for her memories of family, I would like to thank Mari Bassa, my mother's cousin, who is a guardian of stories we never knew.

After more than two decades, to be able to reconnect with my father's cousins, András and Ferenc Rákosi, pianist and lawyer respectively, was extraordinary, and extraordinarily helpful. There was so much to exchange about our common heritage.

I am very happy to have met Ádám Bíró, writer, editor, collector and teller of jokes, first in his home in Leányfalu on the Danube and then in Paris. His perch on a (from my point of view) distant branch of the family tree contributed greatly to my sense of the big picture.

I am also happy to have met Mari's daughter, Ági Bassa, who like Judy Hilvert, the daughter of a family friend, helped to put in context our second-generation experience.

There are also those I knew who have long gone, including my cousins' father, Tomi, and my grandmothers, Bözsi and Lili, whose memory and mystery set in train so much of my thinking.

For her memories of her late husband, my mother's cousin, Endre 'Bandi' Gömöri, and for sharing his unpublished series of 'life scenes', thanks to Klári Gömöri. Thanks also to Kati Mácsai, who knew Bandi well, and to Bandi himself, whom I was lucky enough to know.

A very special thanks to family friends László and Mari Solymár, who read early drafts of the book and whose comments and corrections were invaluable.

Thanks also to another valued family friend, János 'Jancsi' Reeves, for his recollections of Hungary during the Second World War and the revolution.

I was delighted to have met István 'Pista' Kállai, playwright and humorist, one of the triumvirate of friends that included my father and Imre Kertész. The friendship has spanned seven decades and is inseparable from the territory of my family history. I have never met Imre Kertész, perhaps I could have, but he has been a presence anyway. I have come to know him through his literature, and by knowing something of the telephone calls that passed between the three of them, one in London, one in Budapest, one in Berlin.

I would also particularly like to thank Gyuri Badacsonyi, Tomi Bárkány, Anni Frankl, Jutka Goodman, Mari Gordon, George Pick, and Ibi and Gábor Temes, whose lives crossed the lives of family members and who provided important detail, especially to do with the events of October 1944. Similarly, many thanks to Péter Kutas for sharing his experiences and his memoirs.

A profound thanks to Éva Barabás for telling me her story after all these years.

For putting me up in Kosice, my thanks go to Zsuzsa Berger, sister of my old friend, the drummer Ernest 'Bilbo' Berger, who happens to be one of the finest makers of *kőrözött* and *gulyás* outside of Hungary.

I would like to thank Georgina Stafford for shedding light on the war years and life of my godfather, Peter Simpson.

The research for this book took me to several countries, and I am indebted to archives and archivists all over Hungary, and in Romania, Slovenia, Slovakia and Austria. In particular, I would like to thank the following: National Archives of Romania (Arad); Csongrad County Archives (Hódmezővásárhely); Szabolcs-Szatmár-Bereg County Archives (Nyíregyháza); Fejér County Archives (Székesfehérvár); Budapest Holocaust Museum and Memorial Centre; the Dohány Street Synagogue Archives; the Kresz Géza Ambulance Museum and archives; the Széchenyi Library; Hungarian State Security Archives (Állambiztonsági Szolgálatok); Budapest Central Archives (Fővárosi Levéltár); the Museum of Military History Budapest; the Museum of Military History Vienna; the Museum of Stalin Town (Dunaújváros); the archives of Képes Sport; the Ferenc Liszt Academy Archives;

Auschwitz–Birkenau Memorial and Museum; the British Library; the Wiener Library.

For helping to elucidate the finer points of the Austro-Hungarian Army and its uniforms, I would like to thank author and expert P.N.R. Thomas. For additional help, thanks to Peter Enne at the Museum of Military History, Vienna.

Thanks to the many people I met who contributed unwittingly to the micro-history, including Russian soldiers, a Polish guide, a Slovenian mountaineer, a man called Dezső on a platform at Sopron station, a man called Yevgeny at a Russian war memorial, an American missionary on a train to Arad, taxi drivers foul-mouthed and wise, numerous cemetery gardeners and gravediggers, and residents of, in particular, Budapest, who leaned out of their windows to relate some story or other.

Thanks to my agent, Sarah Such, whose input helped to shape the book in its early stages.

Finally, I am grateful for the award that I received from Arts Council England, which allowed me to do the necessary research and gave me the space to discover the form the book would take.

Glossary

AVH *(Államvédelmi Hatóság)*	State Protection Authority, the Hungarian secret police up to 1956, established in 1950 as a successor to AVO
Batyu	bundle
Bevonulási központ	draft centre
Cseresznye	cherry
Csillagos Házak	yellow star houses. A yellow star had to be affixed to the entrance of residential blocks in which Jews lived from shortly after the German invasion in March 1944 to show the racial identity of those living there or forced to live there
Csiriz	a substitute for glue made from a paste of flour and water, used in postwar classrooms in Hungary to stick together the pages of text books
Dög	corpse
Eltünt	disappeared
Főhadnagy	the rank of lieutenant
Gang	the internal corridor around each floor of a block of flats, from the German verb *gehen*, 'to go'
Gyilkos	murderer, murderous

Harc   battle, struggle

Házparancsnok   house commander, non-Jewish, appointed to oversee yellow star houses during the Second World War

Hurcolkodás   literally the carrying or moving of personal possessions great and small

Kerület   district

Kibbitzer   Yiddish, from the German for a type of noisy bird, meaning someone who does not participate in a game or event but will nevertheless provide a stream of commentary and advice on the best moves or plays or decisions to make. A *kibbitzer* can generally be found standing behind card or chess players, although the same positioning applies to any other situation

Konfekció   literally a 'confection', usually referring to a particular range of goods from brassieres to knickers, gloves and scarves

Kőrözött   a spiced cream-cheese spread, usually orange in colour because of paprika

Kukucskálni   to peep out

Lichthof   a vertical shaft in the centre of a building for ventilation and light

Macher   Yiddish, from German. Literally, 'maker', someone who can make things happen, a fixer with connections

Magázni   to use the formal 'you'

Maradni   to stay

Meggy   sour or morello cherry

Megszentségtelenithetet-lenségeskedéseitekért   the longest word in Hungarian, which the *Guinness Book of Records* courageously tried to define as 'for your unprofanable actions'

Menni	to go
Mishpocheh	from Hebrew, usually taken to mean 'family clan'
Munkaszolgálat	literally 'work service', the ambiguous term used for forced labour during the Second World War in Hungary
Nemzetvezető	the nation's leader, similar to 'Führer'; the Hungarian Fascist leader Ferenc Szálasi, adopted the title when he came to power in October 1944
Nyakleves	literally 'necksoup', a type of slap delivered to the back of the neck, mostly by grandmothers
Nyilas	a member of the Arrow Cross, the Hungarian Fascist party and movement
Összeköltöztetés	literally the 'moving together', referring to the forced moving together of Jews in Hungary during the Second World War
Pálinka	Hungarian brandy usually made from fruit
Polgár	commoner, citizen, petit bourgeois
Próbapakolás	literally 'trial packing', as in the trial packing of large and unwieldy suitcases before long and difficult journeys
Puszta	the Great Hungarian Plain which accounts for over half of Hungary's territory
Razzia	originally Arabic, meaning robbery, seizure, pillage; although, more specifically, it refers to the raids carried out by Nazi or Fascist forces on Jewish homes
Rétes	a Hungarian pastry, similar to strudel, with layers usually filled with cherries, apples or cream cheese
Shtetl	Yiddish, from German, literally small town but encompassing villages, communities and settlements

Svéd torna	Swedish exercise or gymnastics, popular in Hungary before the war
Százados	the rank of captain
Szilva	plum
Szomoru Vasárnap	'Gloomy Sunday', the famous Hungarian song originally written by Rezső Seress in 1933 and still known as the 'suicide anthem'
Tegezni	to use the informal 'you'
Turul	the mythical bird of prey that guided the ancient tribes of Hungary to their present homeland
Tüzérség	artillery
Udvari	a flat in a block that faces inwards to the courtyard, as opposed to out into the street, and therefore much less desirable
Vagonírozni	to entrain, literally to put into a wagon
Védett ház	protected house, usually referring to a building in Budapest that had a Jewish or mixed population but was at least in principle protected by some authority such as a foreign legation
Zsidózni	literally 'to Jew', as in to abuse or racially slur, to act in an anti-Semitic way
Zsindely van a háztetőn	literally 'there is a tile on the roof', meaning someone can overhear our conversation

Illustrations

p. 15 At my father's typewriter: me, the author, taken by my mother in 1966.

p. 28 The last photograph: my grandfather, Nándor (right), with my cousins' grandfather, Imre, on forced labour, Ukraine, late 1942. The picture was probably taken by a bribed guard. Both men would be dead within weeks.

p. 31 Between wars: my recently born father, held in my grandmother Lili's arms, at a family gathering in Székesfehérvár in 1930.

p. 37 A funny little war: Ukraine, spring 1916, my great-grandfather, Pay Sergeant Móric Rehovitz, stands behind the pay table at a safe distance from the front line.

p. 43 Great-Great-Uncle Józsi, 1915, posing in his lieutenant's uniform while serving in the Austro-Hungarian Army on the Isonzo Front during the First World War.

p. 54 István Bokor, my father, aged seven in 1937, on the 'gang' outside the top floor flat, 59 Népszínház Street. The courtyard below would be the site of a massacre.

p. 62 Two boys, two destinies: my father (left) and my cousins' father, Tomi, in Budapest, 1940. They would marry two sisters.

231

Select Bibliography

Appelfeld, Aharon, *The Story of a Life*, translated by Aloma Halter (Penguin, London, 2006)

Barlay, Stephen and Sasdy, Peter, *Four Black Cars*, translated by Paul Tábori (Putnam, London, 1957)

Barlay, Stephen, *Menekülés és Megérkezés* ('Refugees and their Refuge'), translated by Anikó Kocsis, with a foreword by Imre Kertész (K.u.K, Budapest, 2006)

Bíró, Ádám, *Two Jews on a Train*, translated by Catherine Tihanyi (University of Chicago, Chicago and London, 2001)

———*Les Ancêtres d'Ulysse* ('The Ancestors of Ulysses') (Presses Universitaires de France, Paris, 2002)

Braham, Randolph L., *The Politics of Genocide: The Holocaust in Hungary* (Rosenthal Institute, New York, 1994)

———*Hungarian Labor Service System 1939–45* (East European Quarterly, New York, 1977)

———(ed.), *The Nazis' Last Victims: The Holocaust in Hungary* (Wayne State University Press, Detroit, 1998)

Cartledge, Bryan, *The Will to Survive: A History of Hungary* (Timewell Press, Tiverton, 2006)

Déak, István, *Jewish Soldiers in Austro-Hungarian Society* (Leo Baeck Memorial Institute Lecture 34, New York, 1994)

Eby, Cecil D., *Hungary at War: Civilians and Soldiers in World War II* (Pennsylvania State University Press, Pennsylvania, 1998)

Farkas, József, *A Zsidók Mátészalka Társadalmásban* ('Jews in Mátészalka Society') (Studia Folkloristica et Ethnographica No. 25, Debrecen, 1989)

Fekete, Márton, (ed.), *Prominent Hungarians: The Hungarian Who's Who* (Fehér Holló, London, 2000)

Földi, Pál, *Különleges Alakulatok A Magyar Hadszervezetben* ('Unique Units in the Hungarian Military') (Anno, Budapest, 2003)

Gergely, Anna, *A Székesfehérvári és Fejér Megyei Zsidóság Tragédiája* ('The Tragedy of the Jews of Székesfehérvár and Fejér Counties') (Vince, Budapest, 2003)

Gerlach, Christian and Aly, Götz, *Az Utolsó Fejezet – A Magyar Zsidók Legyilkolása* ('The Last Chapter – The Murder of the Hungarian Jews') (Noran, Budapest, 2005)

Györkei, Jenő and Horváth, Miklós (ed.), *Soviet Military Intervention in Hungary, 1956*, translated by Emma Roper Evans (Central European University Press, Budapest, 1999)

Hašek, Jaroslav, *The Good Soldier Švejk*, translated by Cecil Parrott (Penguin, London, 1973)

Hegedűs, Márton, (ed.), *A Magyar Hadviselt Zsidók Arányalbuma Az 1914–1918-as Világháboru Emlékére* ('Remembrance Album for Jews in the Hungarian Military 1914–1918') (Budapest, 1940)

Hemingway, Ernest, *A Farewell to Arms* (Cape, London, 1929)

Kaiser, Ottó, *Határtalan Iradalom* ('Borderless Literature') (Alexandra, Pécs, 2000)

Karsai, Elek, (ed.), *Fegyvertelen Álltak az Aknamezőkön* ('Weaponless They Stood in the Minefields') (Budapest, 1962)

Kertész, Imre, *Sorstalanság*, first published 1975, translated by Tim Wilkinson as *Fatelessness* (Harvill, London, 2005)

Koestler, Arthur, 'The Ubiquitous Presence', in Aczél, Tamás, (ed.), *Ten Years After* (MacGibbon and Kee, London, 1966)

Komoróczy, Géza, (ed.), *Jewish Budapest*, translated by Vera Szabó (Central European University Press, Budapest, 1999)

Konrád, George, *The Case Worker*, translated by Paul Aston (Noran Books, Budapest, 1998)

———*Elutazás és hazatérés* (Noran, Budapest, 2002), translated by Jim Tucker as *A Guest in my Own Country* (Other Press, New York, 2007)

———*The Invisible Voice*, translated by Peter Reich (Harvest, New York and London, 2000)

Kutas, Péter, *Amikor vért könnyeztek a fellegek* ('When Clouds Wept Blood') (Lauder Books, Budapest, 2008)

Lévai, Jenő, *Black Book on the Martyrdom of Hungarian Jewry* (Central European Times, Zurich, 1948)

———*Raoul Wallenberg* (Magyar Téka, Budapest, 1948)

Lukacs, John, *Budapest 1900: A Historical Portrait of a City and its Culture* (Weidenfeld, New York, 1988)

Magyar Rádió, *Az Ötven Éves Rádió* ('Fifty Years of the Hungarian Radio') (Magyar Rádió, Budapest, 1975)

Márai, Sándor, *Memoir of Hungary 1944–1948*, translated by Albert Tezla (Corvina, Budapest, 1996)

———*Napló 1943–1944* ('Diaries 1943–1944') (Akadémia and Helikon, Budapest, 1945)

May, Karl, *Winnetou*, translated by Michael Shaw (Continuum, New York and London, 2005)

Michener, James A., *The Bridge at Andau* (Transworld, London, 1958)

Mikes, George, *How to Be an Alien* (Allan Wingate, London, 1946)

Molnár, Ferenc, *The Paul Street Boys*, translated by Louis Rittenberg (Corvina, Budapest, 2008)

Müller, Rolf and Sümegi, György, (ed.), *Fényképek 1956* ('Photographs 1956') (Állambiztonsági Szolgálatok, Budapest, 2006)

Orbán, Ferenc, *Guide to Jewish Hungary*, translated by Magdaléna Seleanu (Makkabi, Budapest, 2004)

Page, Martin, *Crimefighters of London* (Inner London Probation Service Benevolent and Educational Trust, London, 1992)

Pálóczi-Horváth, George, *The Undefeated* (Secker and Warburg, London, 1959)

Pór, Dezső, (ed.), *Te Vagy a Tanu!* ('You Are the Witness!') (Kossuth, Budapest, 1947)

Pressac, Jean-Claude, *Auschwitz: Technique and Operation of the Gas Chambers* (Beate Klarsfeld Foundation, New York, 1989)

Pressburger, Georgio and Nicola, *Homage to the Eighth District*, translated by Gerald Moore (Readers International, London, 1990)

Radnóti, Miklós, *Válogatott Versei* ('Selected Poems') (Móra Ferenc, Budapest, 1962)

Roth, Joseph, *Job: The Story of a Simple Man*, translated by Dorothy Thompson (Granta, London, 2000)

——*The Radetzky March*, translated by Michael Hoffman (Granta, London, 2003)

Sárközi, Mátyás, *Hungaro-Brits – The Hungarian Contribution to British Civilisation* (Ministry of National Cultural Heritage, London, 2000)

Schindler, John R., *Isonzo – The Forgotten Sacrifice of the Great War* (Praeger, London, 2001)

Sebestyén, Viktor, *Twelve Days: The Story of the 1956 Hungarian Revolution* (Pantheon, New York, 2006)

Staud, Géza, (ed.), *A Budapesti Operaház 100 Éve* ('A Hundred Years of the Budapest Opera House') (Zeneműkiadó, Budapest, 1984)

Szép, Ernő, *Emberszag*, first published 1945, translated by John Bátki as *The Smell of Humans* (Corvina, Budapest, 1994)

Szerb, Antal, *Utas és Holdvilág*, first published 1937, translated by Len Rix as *Journey by Moonlight* (Pushkin Press, London, 2001)

Szigethy, Gábor (ed.), *Mindennapok: A Feltámadás Hite* ('Every Day: The Belief in Resurrection', Newspaper extracts from 23 October to 4 November 1956) (Holnap, Budapest, 2006)

Ungváry, Kristián, *Battle for Budapest – 100 Days in World War II*, translated by Ladislaus Löb (I.B.Tauris, London, 2003)

Vályi, Rózsi, *A Magyar Balett Történetéből* ('The History of Hungarian Ballet') (Művelt Nép, Budapest, 1956)

Zsolt, Béla, *Nine Suitcases*, translated by Ladislaus Löb (Pimlico, London, 2005)

Select Websites

www.degob.hu
The Hungarian Jewish relief organization, the National Committee for Attending Deportees (DEGOB)

www.iremember.hu
Remembrance, education and archives relating to the Holocaust in Hungary

www.iremember.hu/personal_stories/holocaust/laszlo_kiss_auschwitz_diary.html
László Kiss, Auschwitz Diary 1944–45

www.jewishgen.org
Jewish ancestry and genealogical database including the Yizkor memorial books project

www.neveklarsfeld.org and www.klarsfeldfoundation.org
The Beate Klarsfeld Foundation's website and database relating to the fate of Hungary's Jews

www.oroklet.hu
Hungarian cemetery and burial database

www.remeny.org
Hungarian Jewish faith, cultural and historical organization

www.remeny.org/node/36
Szita Szabolcs 'A Budapesti Csillagos Házak 1944–45' ('Budapest's Yellow Star Houses 1944–1945')

www.yadvashem.org
The world centre for the documentation of the Holocaust

yizkor.nypl.org
New York Public Library database of Yizkor books

Index